Hen
Pla

A Doll's House, An Enemy of the People, Hedda Gabler

This is the second of a six-volume collection presenting all sixteen of Ibsen's major plays written in the thirty-four years from 1865 to 1899. Each volume offers a cross-section of these plays so as to illustrate the different phases of his dramatic genius.

This volume contains Ibsen's two most famous plays about women: *A Doll's House* (1879), which was his first international success, and *Hedda Gabler* (1890), now one of his most popular plays, but greeted at first with bewilderment and outrage. Between them came *An Enemy of the People*, written rapidly in 1882, largely in response to the hostile reception of *Ghosts* the year before.

Michael Meyer's translations have won praise for their accuracy and liveliness on both stage and page. They have been performed extensively in the theatre and on radio and television. 'Where previous translators have adopted either a stiffly Victorian style, or one so modern as to destroy the illusion that we were seeing a period play, Mr Meyer has found a form of speech common both to the period in which the plays were written and to the present.' (*The Times*.) 'Meyer's translations of Ibsen are a major fact in one's general sense of post-war drama. Their vital pace, their unforced insistence on the poetic centre of Ibsen's genius, have beaten academic versions from the field.' (George Steiner, *The New Statesman*.)

Michael Meyer is also Ibsen's biographer and a leading authority on his work. This edition includes Meyer's illuminating introductions to each play, as well as a chronology of Ibsen's life and writings.

The front cover shows a detail from Interiør med figurer *(1886) by Harriet Backer, reproduced by kind permission of Nils Backer-Grøndahl.*

HENRIK IBSEN

Plays: Two

A Doll's House

An Enemy of the People

Hedda Gabler

translated from the Norwegian and introduced by
Michael Meyer

Methuen Drama

METHUEN WORLD CLASSICS

This collection first published in Great Britain in paperback in 1980
by Eyre Methuen Ltd. Reprinted 1982
Reprinted 1984, 1985, 1988 by Methuen London Ltd
Reprinted 1989 by Methuen Drama
an imprint of Reed International Books Ltd
Michelin House, 81 Fulham Road, London SW3 6RB
and Auckland, Melbourne, Singapore and Toronto
This corrected edition reprinted 1990. Reprinted 1991 (twice), 1992
Reissued with a new cover in 1993
Reprinted 1993, 1994 (twice), 1995

Published in the United States of America by Heinemann
a division of Reed Elsevier Inc
361 Hanover Street, Portsmouth, New Hampshire 03801 3959

A Doll's House was first published in this translation in 1965 by
Rupert Hart-Davis Ltd, and subsequently by Eyre Methuen Ltd,
in 1974. Copyright © Michael Meyer 1965. Introduction copyright
© Michael Meyer 1965, 1974. Corrected edition, 1980. Corrected
edition, 1990.

An Enemy of the People was first published in this translation in 1963 by
Rupert Hart-Davis Ltd, and subsequently by Eyre Methuen
Ltd, in 1974. Copyright © Michael Meyer 1963. Introduction copyright
© Michael Meyer 1963. Corrected for this edition, 1980.

Hedda Gabler was first published in this translation in 1962 by
Rupert Hart-Davis Ltd, and subsequently by Methuen & Co Ltd, in
1967 and in a revised edition by Eyre Methuen Ltd, in 1974.
Copyright © Michael Meyer 1962, 1974. Introduction copyright
© Michael Meyer 1962, 1974. Corrected for this edition, 1980.

ISBN 0 413 46340 0

Printed and bound in Great Britain by
Cox & Wyman Ltd, Reading, Berkshire

Contents

Henrik Johan Ibsen: A Chronology

1828   Born at Skien in south-east Norway on 20 March, the second child of Knud Ibsen, a merchant, and his wife Marichen, *née* Altenburg.

1834–5   Father becomes ruined. The family moves to Venstoep, a few miles outside Skien.

1844   Ibsen (aged fifteen) becomes assistant to an apothecary at Grimstad, a tiny seaport further down the coast. Stays there for six years in great poverty.

1846   Has an illegitimate son with a servant-girl, Else Sofie Jensdatter.

1849   Writes his first play, *Catiline* (in verse).

1850   Leaves Grimstad to become a student in Christiania (now Oslo). Writes second play, *The Warrior's Barrow*.

1851   Is invited to join Ole Bull's newly formed National Theatre at Bergen. Does so, and stays six years, writing, directing, designing costumes and keeping the accounts.

1852   Visits Copenhagen and Dresden to learn about the theatre. Writes *St John's Eve*, a romantic comedy in verse and prose.

1853   *St John's Eve* acted at Bergen. Failure.

1854   Writes *Lady Inger of Oestraat*, an historical tragedy in prose.

1855   *Lady Inger of Oestraat* acted at Bergen. Failure. Writes *The Feast at Solhaug*, another romantic verse-and-prose comedy.

1856   *The Feast at Solhaug* acted at Bergen. Small success. Meets Suzannah Thoresen. Writes *Olaf Liljekrans*, a third verse-and-prose comedy.

1857   *Olaf Liljekrans* acted at Bergen. Failure. Leaves Bergen to become artistic manager of the Christiania Norwegian Theatre. Writes *The Vikings at Helgeland*, an historical prose tragedy.

1858   Marries Suzannah Thoresen. *The Vikings at Helgeland* staged. Small success.

1859   His only child, Sigurd, born.

1860–1   Years of poverty and despair. Unable to write.

1862   Writes *Love's Comedy*, a modern verse satire, his first play for five years. It is rejected by his own theatre, which goes bankrupt.

1863   Ibsen gets part-time job as literary adviser to the Danish-controlled Christiania Theatre. Extremely poor. Applies unsuccessfully to Government for financial support. Resorts to moneylenders. Writes *The Pretenders*, another historical prose tragedy. Is granted a travel stipend by the Government; this is augmented by a collection raised by Bjoernson and other friends

1864   *The Pretenders* staged in Christiania. A success. He leaves Norway and settles in Rome. Remains resident abroad for the next twenty-seven years. Begins *Emperor and Galilean*.

1865   Writes *Brand*, in verse (as a play for reading, not acting), in Rome and Ariccia.

1866   *Brand* published. Immense success; Ibsen becomes famous throughout Scandinavia (but it is not acted for nineteen years).

1867   Writes *Peer Gynt*, in verse (also to be read, not acted), in Rome, Ischia and Sorrento. It, too, is a great success; but is not staged for seven years.

1868   Moves from Rome and settles in Dresden.

1869   Attends opening of Suez Canal as Norwegian delegate. Completes *The League of Youth*, a modern prose comedy.

1871   Revises his shorter poems and issues them in a volume. His farewell to verse; for the rest of his life he publishes exclusively in prose.

1873   Completes (after nine years) *Emperor and Galilean*, his last historical play. Begins to be known in Germany and England.

1874   Returns briefly to Norway for first time in ten years. The students hold a torchlight procession in his honour.

1875   Leaves Dresden after seven years and settles in Munich. Begins *The Pillars of Society*, the first of his twelve great modern prose dramas.

1876   *Peer Gynt* staged for first time. *The Vikings at Helgeland* is performed in Munich, the first of his plays to be staged outside Scandinavia.

1877   Completes *The Pillars of Society*. This makes him famous in Germany, where it is widely acted.

1878   Returns to Italy for a year.

1879   Writes *A Doll's House* in Rome and Amalfi. It causes an
         immediate sensation, though a decade elapses before it
         makes Ibsen internationally famous. Returns for a year to
         Munich.

1880   Resettles in Italy for a further five years. First performance
         of an Ibsen play in England (*The Pillars of Society* for a
         single matineé in London).

1881   Writes *Ghosts* in Rome and Sorrento. Violently attacked;
         all theatres reject it, and bookshops return it to the pub-
         lisher.

1882   Writes *An Enemy of the People* in Rome. Cordially received.
         Ghosts receives its first performance (in Chicago).

1884   Writes *The Wild Duck* in Rome and Gossensass. It, and
         all his subsequent plays, were regarded as obscure and were
         greeted with varying degrees of bewilderment.

1885   Revisits Norway again, for the first time since 1874. Leaves
         Rome and resettles in Munich.

1886   Writes *Rosmersholm* in Munich.

1888   Writes *The Lady from the Sea* in Munich.

1889   Meets and becomes infatuated with the eighteen-year-old
         Emilie Bardach in Gossensass. Does not see her again, but
         the experience shadows the remainder of his writing. Janet
         Achurch acts Nora in London, the first major English-
         speaking production of Ibsen.

1890   Writes *Hedda Gabler* in Munich.

1891   Returns to settle permanently in Norway.

1892   Writes *The Master Builder* in Christiania.

1894   Writes *Little Eyolf* in Christiania.

1896   Writes *John Gabriel Borkman* in Christiania.

1899   Writes *When We Dead Awaken* in Christiania.

1901   First stroke. Partly paralysed.

1903   Second stroke. Left largely helpless.

1906   Dies in Christiania on 23 May, aged seventy-eight.

A Doll's House

Introduction

Ibsen wrote *A Doll's House* in Rome and Amalfi during the summer of 1879, at the age of fifty-one. It was his first international success. *Brand* (1865) and *Peer Gynt* (1867) had been written to be read, not acted, and had established him only in Scandinavia. *The Pillars of Society* (1877) had spread his fame to Germany. But *A Doll's House* was – after a lapse of a decade, due to the assumption that nothing of universal interest could be written in so obscure a language as Norwegian – to become a subject of world-wide discussion. Books and pamphlets were written about it, public meetings were held to dissect it, sermons were preached on it, sequels were penned to it. It aroused extraordinary controversy wherever it was staged or read; and by the end of the century, there was scarcely a civilized country where it had not been performed.

The problem of women's rights was particularly topical at that time in Norway. Many books had been published on the subject since John Stuart Mill's *On the Subjection of Women* had been translated in 1869. Ibsen had returned briefly to Norway in 1874, after ten years of self-imposed exile in Italy and Germany, and had noted the unrest. His wife, Suzannah, was an outspoken champion of the feminine cause; so was the Norwegian novelist Camilla Collett, who had seen a good deal of Ibsen in Dresden in 1871 and had been scandalized at what she regarded as the old-fashionedness of his ideas about woman's place in society. His previous heroines, such as Svanhild in *Love's Comedy*, Agnes in *Brand* and Solveig in *Peer Gynt*, had accepted their position with the placidity of Dickensian maidens. Selma Bratsberg, however, a minor character in Ibsen's comedy *The League of Youth* (1869), had complained to her husband: 'You dressed me up like a doll; you played with me as one plays with a child.' The Danish critic Georg Brandes then suggested to Ibsen that she, or a character like her, might make a good central theme for a later play; and in his next work, *The Pillars of Society*, Ibsen created two more women, Lona Hessel and Dina Dorf, who rebelled violently against the subordinate position

to which a man-dominated society was trying to degrade them.
Thus, women's rights were the starting-point, though not (Ibsen
was to protest) the theme, of *A Doll's House*.

Eight years before he wrote *A Doll's House*, in 1871, Ibsen had
become acquainted with a young Norwegian girl named Laura
Petersen, who had written, and sent him, a sequel to *Brand*. He
took a great fancy to her, and called her his 'skylark'. In 1872 she
married a Danish schoolmaster named Victor Kieler. He contracted
tuberculosis, and the doctor said he must go to a warmer climate.
Since they were poor, and her husband became neurotically
hysterical at any mention of money, she secretly arranged a loan,
for which a friend stood security. The trip (to Italy, in 1876)
proved successful. But in 1878 repayment of the loan was demanded; she did not have the money, dared not tell her husband,
and the friend who had stood security had himself fallen into
straits and told her he would be ruined if pressed for payment.
Having no means of earning money but her pen, she wrote a novel
and asked Ibsen to recommend it to his publisher. He thought it
bad and told her in stern but kindly terms that he could not
recommend it.

On receipt of his letter, she burned the manuscript and forged a
cheque. The forgery was discovered and the bank refused payment;
whereupon she told her husband the full story. He, regardless of the
fact that she had done it purely for his sake, treated her like a
criminal, told her she was unworthy to have charge of their children
and, when she in consequence suffered a nervous breakdown, had
her committed to a public asylum (where she lived in a ward
among lunatics), and demanded a separation so that the children
could be removed from her care. After a month she was discharged
from the asylum and, for the children's sake, begged her husband
to take her back, which he very grudgingly agreed to do. The
incident must have seemed to Ibsen to crystallize not merely
woman's, but mankind's fight against conventional morality and
prejudice.

At the end of September 1878, a couple of months after hearing
of Laura's committal to the asylum, Ibsen returned to Rome for
the first time in ten years. Within three weeks of his arrival, on
19 October, he jotted down the following 'Notes for a Modern
Tragedy':

There are two kinds of moral laws, two kinds of conscience,
one for men and one, quite different, for women. They don't

understand each other; but in practical life, woman is judged by masculine law, as though she weren't a woman but a man.

The wife in the play ends by having no idea what is right and what is wrong; natural feelings on the one hand and belief in authority on the other lead her to utter distraction.

A woman cannot be herself in modern society. It is an exclusively male society, with laws made by men and with prosecutors and judges who assess female conduct from a male standpoint.

She has committed forgery, which is her pride; for she has done it out of love for her husband, to save his life. But this husband of hers takes his standpoint, conventionally honourable, on the side of the law, and sees the situation with male eyes.

Moral conflict. Weighted down and confused by her trust in authority, she loses faith in her own morality, and in her fitness to bring up her children. Bitterness. A mother in modern society, like certain insects, retires and dies once she has done her duty by propagating the race. Love of life, of home, of husband and children and family. Now and then, as women do, she shrugs off her thoughts. Suddenly anguish and fear return. Everything must be borne alone. The catastrophe approaches, mercilessly, inevitably. Despair, conflict and defeat.

On the concluding sheet of these notes, Ibsen, possibly somewhat later, added a cast list. This corresponds precisely with his final list of characters, apart from the names; Helmer is 'Stenborg, a civil servant', Mrs Linde is 'Miss Lind' (corrected to 'Mrs . . . , widow'), Dr Rank is, unattractively to English ears, Dr Hank, and the Nurse is 'Karen' instead of Anne-Marie. There is also a detailed scenario of each act; the only substantial difference from the play as we know it is the absence of the tarantella scene.*

It was, though, to be another six months before he actually sat down to write the dialogue; it was his method to ponder a theme at length and then write the play swiftly in a matter of weeks. He was touchy and nervous that winter in Rome, keeping more to himself and mixing much less with other Scandinavians than had been his practice during his previous stay there in 1864-8. 'We live, in

---

* But William Archer may have been right in surmising that Ibsen originally schemed a 'happy ending', to be achieved by Krogstad's return of the forged document, the rest to be 'a more or less conventional winding-up'. (How otherwise, asks Archer, explain 'the invention, to that end alone, of Mrs Linde's relation to, and influence over, Krogstad?') As Professor Didrik Arup Seip has shown, Ibsen only wrote the scenario for each act after he had *finished* the draft of the previous act.

general, pretty quietly', he wrote on 22 January 1879 to the painter, Marcus Grønvold. 'Lunch is brought in to us, and our landlady prepares our breakfast and supper. Everything is much cheaper here than in Munich, and wine especially is to be had for practically nothing this winter . . . 3 soldi [less than a penny] a litre!'

Six days later he emerged from his shell to place two proposals before the Scandinavian Club of Rome: that the post of paid librarian should be thrown open to women, and that women should have the right to vote on all Club matters. When these proposals came to be debated, on 27 February, he delivered a lengthy and impassioned speech. 'Youth', he declared, 'has an instinctive genius which unconsciously hits upon the right answer. And it is precisely this instinct which women share with youth, and with the true artist. That is why I want us to allow women to vote at our annual general meeting. I fear women, youth and inexperience as little as I fear the true artist. What I do fear is the wordly wisdom of the old; what I fear is men with little ambitions and little thoughts, little scruples and little fears.'

His first motion, concerning the librarianship, was accepted; but the second failed by a single vote to get the necessary two-thirds majority. Ibsen was furious. He left the Club immediately and sat alone in a café, refusing to speak to anyone who had voted against him. Some days later, however, to the general amazement, he attended a gala evening at the Club, and the playwright and director Gunnar Heiberg, who was present, has left a picturesque account of what happened:

No one would have guessed it – but Ibsen came. He looked magnificent, in full panoply, with medals to boot. He ran his hand ceaselessly through his rich, grizzled hair, greeting no one in particular but everyone in general. There was a deep peace in his face, but his eyes were watchful, so watchful. He sat alone. We all thought he had forgiven his fellow mortals, and some even supposed him penitent. This helped the atmosphere to be unusually gay and euphoric. Then, suddenly, he rose and stepped forward to a big table, so that he was facing the whole ballroom with its dancing couples.

'Ladies and gentlemen!' It was a tense and dramatic moment. What was going to happen? Was he about to admit the error of his ways? Surely he was not going to propose a toast? . . . He stroked his hair calmly. Then he began, softly, but with a terrifying earnestness. He had recently wished to do the Club a service, he might almost say a great favour, by bringing its members abreast with contemporary ideas. No one could escape these mighty developments. Not even here – in this community – in this duckpond! He did not actually use the word duckpond, but the contempt around his mouth proclaimed it loudly. And how had his offer been received? As a criminal attempt! Rejected by a paltry couple of votes. And how had the women reacted – the women for whom his gift had been intended? They had intrigued and agitated against him. They had thrown his gift into the mud. What kind of women are these? They are worse – worse than the dregs, worse than scum –

Now he was no longer speaking calmly, no longer thoughtfully stroking his hair. He shook his head with its grey mane. He folded his arms across his breast. His eyes shone. His voice shook, his mouth trembled, and he thrust out his underlip. He resembled a lion, nay, more – he resembled that future enemy of the people, Dr Stockmann. He repeated and repeated; what kind of women are these, what kind of a sex, ignorant, in the truest sense ill-bred, immoral, dregs, contemptible –

Thump! A lady, Countess B., fell to the floor. She, like the rest of us, flinched from the unspeakable. So she took time by the forelock and swooned. She was carried out. Ibsen continued. Perhaps slightly more calmly. But eloquently and lucidly, never searching for a word. He intoxicated himself with his rhetoric against the ignorant, contemptible and rigid resistance that mankind, and especially women, was attempting to offer to these new ideas, whose purpose was to make people bigger, richer and better. He looked remote, ecstatic. As his voice thundered it was as though he were clarifying his own secret thoughts, as his tongue chastised it was as though his spirit were scouring the darkness in search of his immediate spiritual goal, his play – as though he were personally living out his theories, incarnating his characters. And when he was done, he went out into the hall, took his overcoat and walked home. Calm and silent.

'My new dramatic work occupies all my thoughts and all my interest', he had written to his publisher Frederik Hegel on 18 February; but still he had not written a line of dialogue. It was not until 2 May that he began his first draft; but then, as usual once he had started, the work went quickly. Act One occupied him from 2–24 May, and on 25 May he wrote optimistically to the novelist Jonas Lie that he hoped to have the play ready in a month. In the event Act Two took him, even in draft, nearly six weeks; he began it on 4 June and did not complete it until 14 July. However, he had a good excuse. 'For reasons of health', he explained to Hegel on 19 June, 'we have decided to change our original plan for our summer holiday. We had at first thought to go to one of the mountain villages around Rome; but the sanitary conditions there leave much to be desired, so we have decided to retire to Amalfi, on the coast south of Naples, where there are facilities for sea-bathing. This will in some measure delay the completion of my play; in addition to which I have, in order to perfect as far as possible the language and the dialogue, decided to rewrite it once again, making various improvements and alterations, before sending you the final fair copy. It is therefore highly probable that you will receive nothing from me before August; but this will be soon enough. Once I start sending you the manuscript, the rest will follow very quickly.'

In Amalfi Ibsen with his wife and son took 'two small rooms with three plain iron bedsteads' in the Albergo della Luna, an old monastery converted into a hotel, which still stands on a cliff overlooking a sheer drop into the sea, and where the desk at which one of the most influential of all plays came to be written may still be seen. Here he was able to bathe and take long walks in the hills. He always worked well in the heat; he began Act Three on 18 July, four days after finishing Act Two, and completed it in less than three weeks, on 3 August. 'I cannot recall any work of mine', he informed Hegel on 15 September, enclosing the fair copy, 'that has given me more satisfaction in the solving of specific problems.' And indeed, the technical advance on The Pillars of Society is enormous; no one could complain of A Doll's House, as of its predecessor, that it was let down by the final act.

A Doll's House was published on 4 December 1879 in an edition of 8,000 copies, the largest printing to that date of any of Ibsen's plays. Its success was immediate and sensational. Despite its size, the first edition sold out within a month; a second edition of 3,000 copies appeared on 4 January, and a third of 2,500 copies on 8 March. Such sales (proportionately equivalent to something around 150,000 in the United Kingdom today) were without precedent for a play in Scandinavia, and certainly no play, in Norway or anywhere else, had had quite such an effect. 'A Doll's House', recalled Halvdan Koht, who was a child when it appeared, 'exploded like a bomb into contemporary life . . . The Pillars of Society, though it attacked reigning social conventions, still retained the traditional theatrical happy ending, so that it bit less sharply. But A Doll's

House knew no mercy; ending not in reconciliation, but in inexorable calamity, it pronounced a death sentence on accepted social ethics ... Ibsen was hailed, not only as the revolutionary champion of intellectual liberty, but as the especial champion of women, and those who were against revolution, against social and moral upheaval, against female emancipation, came to see in Ibsen their greatest and most dangerous enemy.'

Several times during that famous last act Ibsen seems about to settle for a happy ending – when Krogstad promises Mrs Linde to take back his letter, when he returns Helmer's I.O.U., and when, in the closing moments of the play, Helmer remembers and echoes Nora's words: 'The miracle of miracles – ?' But the terrible offstage slamming of that front door which brings down the curtain resounded through more apartments than Torvald Helmer's. No play had ever before contributed so momentously to the social debate, nor been so widely and furiously discussed among people who were not normally interested in theatrical or even artistic matters. Even Strindberg, who disapproved of it as being calculated to encourage just the kind of woman he dreaded most (and was infallibly drawn to), and attacked it in his volume of stories, *Getting Married* (1884), admitted in his preface that, thanks to *A Doll's House*, 'marriage was revealed as being a far from divine institution, people stopped regarding it as an automatic provider of absolute bliss, and divorce between incompatible parties came at last to be accepted as conceivably justifiable'. What other play has achieved as much?

So explosive was the message of *A Doll's House* – that a marriage was not sacrosanct, that a man's authority in his home should not go unchallenged, and that the prime duty of anyone was to find out who he or she really was and to become that person – that the technical originality of the play is often forgotten. It achieved the most powerful and moving effect by the highly untraditional methods of extreme simplicity and economy of language – a kind of literary Cubism. The Danish playwright and critic Erik Bøgh perceptively noted this when *A Doll's House* received its world premiere at the Royal Theatre in Copenhagen on 21 December 1879. 'It is long', he wrote, 'since any new play was awaited with such excitement, and even longer since a new play brought so much that is original to the stage, but it is beyond memory since a play so simple in its action and so everyday in its dress made such an impression of artistic mastery ... Not a single declamatory phrase, no high dramatics, no drop of blood, not even a tear; never for a

moment was the dagger of tragedy raised . . . Every needless line
is cut, every exchange carries the action a step forward, there is not
a superfluous effect in the whole play . . . The mere fact that the
author succeeded with the help of only these five characters in
keeping our interest sustained through a whole evening is sufficient
proof of Ibsen's technical mastery.' *The Pillars of Society* had used
nineteen characters. And there are other ways in which *A Doll's
House* marks a considerable technical advance over *The Pillars of
Society*. The characters do not (as occasionally happens in the
earlier play) tell each other what the listener already knows for the
benefit of the audience; points once made are not drummed home
in the manner beloved by politicians; the final curtain is not
tediously delayed after the climax has been reached (an elementary
fault which every playwright learns reluctantly to avoid, the more
reluctantly if he has ever written a novel, in which such rapid wind-
ups seem melodramatic). Only in the sub-plot of Krogstad does a
trace of the old melodramatic machinery remain.

The Copenhagen premiere was followed in January by productions in Stockholm, Christiania and Bergen. In all three cities the
play was a triumph; and March saw the first German production,
at Flensburg, under curious circumstances. Frau Hedwig Niemann-
Raabe, who was to play Nora, refused to perform the final scene as
written, on the grounds that '*I* would never leave my children!' In
the absence of copyright protection, Ibsen's hands were tied; and
he decided that, as the lesser of two evils, a 'happy' ending written
by himself would be preferable to one by another hand which
could be published and performed at other German theatres. 'To
forestall any such possibility', he explained in an open letter (17
February 1880) to the Danish newspaper *Nationaltidende*, 'I sent
my translator and agent for use in an emergency a drafted emendation in which Nora does not leave the house but is forced by Helmer
to the doorway of the children's bedroom; here a few lines are
exchanged, Nora sinks down by the floor and the curtain falls. This
emendation I have myself described to my translator as a "barbaric
outrage" on the play . . . But if any such outrage is threatened, I
prefer, on the basis of previous experience, to commit it myself
rather than submit my work to the treatment and "adaptation" of
less tender and competent hands.'

Frau Niemann-Raabe accepted this distorted version and acted
it in February at Flensburg and later in Hamburg, Dresden,
Hanover, and Berlin. In the last-named city there was a public
protest at the perversion (though when, subsequently, the original

ending was used, there were further protests on the ground that the play had obviously been shorn of its fourth act!). The 'happy ending' was never a success, and eventually even Frau Niemann-Raabe returned to the original text.

Meanwhile, on 3 March, the first unbowdlerized German production had taken place in Munich, with Ibsen himself among the audience. The Norwegian novelist John Paulsen accompanied him and recorded his reactions. Ibsen had attended several rehearsals; the play was, to Paulsen's mind, well acted, and went down excellently with the public. After the premiere, Ibsen thanked everyone who had taken part in the production warmly. But afterwards, at home, he was full of criticisms, not merely of the interpretation of the play and the various roles, but of details such as that Nora had the wrong-sized hands (whether too big or too small Paulsen could not remember), and that the colour of the wallpaper in the Helmers' apartment was wrong and conveyed a false atmosphere. Paulsen wondered that Ibsen had not mentioned at any rate this last point during rehearsals; but the actors later told Paulsen that Ibsen had 'neither praised nor blamed, but just remained silent', and that when they asked him if they had fulfilled his intentions, he merely complimented them, which frustrated rather than pleased them, 'since they knew they were far from perfect'. Even now that he was famous, and anything he had said would have been obeyed, Ibsen was as reluctant to offer advice as in the old days in Norway. Paulsen recalled that the Norwegian actress Lucie Wolf told him that, when a director in Christiania, Ibsen had 'always seemed happy with what we had done, though this was often moderate'.

As stated earlier, although *A Doll's House* was to make Ibsen internationally famous, that fame did not come to him at once, or even quickly. It was to be two years before the play was performed outside Scandinavia and Germany, and ten years before a recognizably faithful version was seen in England or America, although perverted adaptations were to make brief and unsuccessful appearances.* France, even further behind the times, did not see the play until 1894. By the time it took its place in the general European repertoire, Ibsen was over sixty and had moved on to a very different kind of writing.

A Doll's House has been professionally performed more often in both England and the United States than any other of Ibsen's

---

*It is significant that even Bernard Shaw does not mention Ibsen in his letters until 1889, ten years after the publication of *A Doll's House*.

plays, followed, in each country, by *Ghosts*. In the early days, especially, these two were automatically thought of when Ibsen's name was mentioned. William Archer, in his introduction to the play (1906), noted the consequence. 'The fact that for many years he was known to thousands of people solely as the author of *A Doll's House*, and its successor *Ghosts*, was largely responsible for the extravagant misconceptions of his genius and character which prevailed during the last decade of the nineteenth century, and are not yet entirely extinct. In these plays he seemed to be delivering a direct assault on marriage, from the standpoint of feminine individualism; wherefore he was taken to be a preacher and a pamphleteer rather than a poet. In these plays, and in these only, he made physical disease a considerable factor in the action; whence it was concluded that he had a morbid predilection for "nauseous" subjects. In these plays he laid special and perhaps disproportionate stress on the influence of heredity; whence he was believed to be possessed by a monomania on the point. In these plays, finally, he was trying to act the essentially incongenial part of the prosaic realist. The effort broke down at many points, and the poet reasserted himself; but these flaws in the prosaic texture were regarded as mere bewildering errors and eccentricities. In short, he was introduced to the world at large through two plays which showed his power, indeed, almost in perfection, but left the higher and subtler qualities of his genius for the most part unrepresented. Hence the grotesquely distorted vision of him which for so long haunted the minds even of intelligent people. Hence, for example, the amazing opinion, given forth as a truism by more than one critic of great ability, that the author of *Peer Gynt* was devoid of humour.'

Ibsen himself repeatedly protested against *any* of his plays being regarded as social or moral tracts. Nineteen years after he wrote *A Doll's House*, he was invited to address the Norwegian Association for Women's Rights in Christiania. He accepted; but his speech must sadly have disappointed that militant audience. 'I am not a member of the Association for Women's Rights', he stated (26 May 1898). 'I have never written any play to further a social purpose. I have been more of a poet and less of a social philosopher than most people seem inclined to believe. I thank you for your good wishes, but I must decline the honour of being said to have worked for the Women's Rights movement. I am not even very sure what Women's Rights really are' (i.e. as differentiated from human rights in general). *A Doll's House*, in other words, was not about female emancipation any more than *Ghosts* was about syphilis or *An Enemy of the People* about bad hygiene. Its theme, like theirs, was the need of every individual to find out the kind of person he or she really is, and to strive to *become* that person. He knew what Freud and Jung were later to assert, that liberation can only come from within; which was why he expressed to George Brandes his lack of interest in 'special revolutions, revolutions in externals, in the political sphere . . . What is really wanted', he declared, 'is a revolution of the spirit of man.'

MICHAEL MEYER

This translation of A Doll's House *was first performed on 16 October 1964 at the Playhouse, Oxford. The cast was:*

TORVALD HELMER, *a lawyer*	Richard Gale
NORA, *his wife*	Barbara Young
DR RANK	James Cairncross
MRS LINDE	Pamela Lane
NILS KROGSTAD, *also a lawyer*	John Warner
NURSE, ANNE-MARIE	Gabrielle Hamilton
MAID, HELEN	Yvette Byrne
(THE HELMERS' THREE SMALL CHILDREN)	
(A PORTER)	

Directed by Robert Chetwyn

This translation was performed by the Royal Shakespeare Company at The Other Place, Stratford-upon-Avon on 9 July 1981, and transferred to the Barbican Theatre, London on 17 June 1982. The cast was:

TORVALD HELMER	Stephen Moore
NORA	Cheryl Campbell
DR RANK	John Franklyn-Robbins
MRS LINDE	Marjorie Bland
NILS KROGSTAD	Bernard Lloyd
ANNE-MARIE	Charlotte Mitchell
HELEN	Diana Hardcastle
EMMY	Lucy Holland
BOB	Richard Parry
IVAR	Daniel Grimley

Directed by Adrian Noble

ACT ONE

A comfortably and tastefully, but not expensively furnished room. Backstage right a door leads to the hall; backstage left, another door to HELMER's *study. Between these two doors stands a piano. In the middle of the left-hand wall is a door, with a window downstage of it. Near the window, a round table with armchairs and a small sofa. In the right-hand wall, slightly upstage, is a door; downstage of this, against the same wall, a stove lined with porcelain tiles, with a couple of armchairs and a rocking-chair in front of it. Between the stove and the side door is a small table. Engravings on the wall. A what-not with china and other bric-à-brac; a small bookcase with leather-bound books. A carpet on the floor; a fire in the stove. A winter day.*

> *A bell rings in the hall outside. After a moment we hear the front door being opened.* NORA *enters the room, humming contentedly to herself. She is wearing outdoor clothes and carrying a lot of parcels, which she puts down on the table right. She leaves the door to the hall open; through it, we can see a* PORTER *carrying a Christmas tree and a basket. He gives these to the* MAID, *who has opened the door for them.*

NORA. Hide that Christmas tree away, Helen. The children mustn't see it before I've decorated it this evening. (*To the* PORTER, *taking out her purse*) How much – ?

PORTER. A shilling.

NORA. Here's a pound. No, keep it.

> *The* PORTER *touches his cap and goes.* NORA *closes the door. She continues to laugh happily to herself as she removes her coat, etc.* [*She takes from her pocket a bag containing macaroons and eats a couple. Then she tiptoes across and listens at her husband's door*]

NORA. Yes, he's here. (*Starts humming again as she goes over to the table, right.*)

HELMER (*from his room*). Is that my skylark twittering out there?

NORA (*opening some of the parcels*). It is!

HELMER. Is that my squirrel rustling?

NORA. Yes!

HELMER. When did my squirrel come home?

NORA. Just now. (*Pops the bag of macaroons in her pocket and wipes her mouth.*) Come out here, Torvald, and see what I've bought.

HELMER. You mustn't disturb me!

Short pause; then he opens the door and looks in, his pen in his hand.

HELMER. Bought, did you say? All that? Has my little squander-bird been overspending again?

NORA. Oh, Torvald, surely we can let ourselves go a little this year! It's the first Christmas we don't have to scrape.

HELMER. Well, you know, we can't afford to be extravagant.

NORA. Oh yes, Torvald, we can be a little extravagant now. Can't we? Just a tiny bit? You've got a big salary now, and you're going to make lots and lots of money.

HELMER. Next year, yes. But my new salary doesn't start till April.

NORA. Pooh; we can borrow till then.

HELMER. Nora! (*Goes over to her and takes her playfully by the ear.*) What a little spendthrift you are! Suppose I were to borrow fifty pounds today, and you spent it all over Christmas, and then on New Year's Eve a tile fell off a roof on to my head –

NORA (*puts her hand over his mouth*). Oh, Torvald! Don't say such dreadful things!

HELMER. Yes, but suppose something like that did happen? What then?

NORA. If anything as frightful as that happened, it wouldn't make much difference whether I was in debt or not.

HELMER. But what about the people I'd borrowed from?

NORA. Them? Who cares about them? They're strangers.

HELMER. Oh, Nora, Nora, how like a woman! No, but seriously, Nora, you know how I feel about this. No debts! Never borrow! A home that is founded on debts and borrowing can never be a place of freedom and beauty. We two have stuck it out bravely up to now; and we shall continue to do so for the few weeks that remain.

NORA (*goes over towards the stove*). Very well, Torvald. As you say.

HELMER (*follows her*). Now, now! My little songbird mustn't droop her wings. What's this? Is little squirrel sulking? (*Takes out his purse.*) Nora; guess what I've got here!

NORA (*turns quickly*). Money!

HELMER. Look. (*Hands her some banknotes.*) I know how these small expenses crop up at Christmas.

NORA (*counts them*). One – two – three – four. Oh, thank you, Torvald, thank you! I should be able to manage with this.

HELMER. You'll have to.

NORA. Yes, yes, of course I will. But come over here, I want to show you everything I've bought. And so cheap! Look, here are new clothes for Ivar – and a sword. And a horse and a trumpet for Bob. And a doll and a cradle for Emmy – they're nothing much, but she'll pull them apart in a few days. And some bits of material and handkerchiefs for the maids. Old Anne-Marie ought to have had something better, really.

HELMER. And what's in that parcel?

NORA (*cries*). No, Torvald, you mustn't see that before this evening!

HELMER. Very well. But now, tell me, my little spendthrift, what do you want for Christmas?

NORA. Me? Oh, pooh, I don't want anything.

HELMER. Oh yes, you do. Now tell me, what within reason would you most like?

NORA. No, I really don't know. Oh, yes – Torvald – !

HELMER. Well?

NORA (*plays with his coat-buttons; not looking at him*). If you really want to give me something, you could – you could –

HELMER. Come on, out with it.

NORA (*quickly*). You could give me money, Torvald. Only as much as you feel you can afford; then later I'll buy something with it.

HELMER. But, Nora –

NORA. Oh yes, Torvald dear, please! Please! Then I'll wrap up the notes in pretty gold paper and hang them on the Christmas tree. Wouldn't that be fun?

HELMER. What's the name of that little bird that can never keep any money?

NORA. Yes, yes, squanderbird; I know. But let's do as I say, Torvald; then I'll have time to think about what I need most. Isn't that the best way? Mm?

HELMER (*smiles*). To be sure it would be, if you could keep what I give you and really buy yourself something with it. But you'll spend it on all sorts of useless things for the house, and then I'll have to put my hand in my pocket again.

NORA. Oh, but Torvald –

HELMER. You can't deny it, Nora dear. (*Puts his arm around her waist.*) The squanderbird's a pretty little creature, but she gets through an awful lot of money. It's incredible what an expensive pet she is for a man to keep.

NORA. For shame! How can you say such a thing? I save every penny I can.

HELMER (*laughs*). That's quite true. Every penny you can. But you can't.

NORA (*hums and smiles, quietly gleeful*). Hm. If you only knew how many expenses we larks and squirrels have, Torvald.

HELMER. You're a funny little creature. Just like your father used to be. Always on the look-out for some way to get money, but as soon as you have any it just runs through your fingers and you never know where it's gone. Well, I suppose I must

take you as you are. It's in your blood. Yes, yes, yes, these
things are hereditary, Nora.

NORA. Oh, I wish I'd inherited more of papa's qualities.

HELMER. And I wouldn't wish my darling little songbird to be
any different from what she is. By the way, that reminds
me. You look awfully – how shall I put it? – awfully guilty
today.

NORA. Do I?

HELMER. Yes, you do. Look me in the eyes.

NORA (*looks at him*). Well?

HELMER (*wags his finger*). Has my little sweet-tooth been indulg-
ing herself in town today, by any chance?

NORA. No, how can you think such a thing?

HELMER. Not a tiny little digression into a pastry shop?

NORA. No, Torvald, I promise –

HELMER. Not just a wee jam tart?

NORA. Certainly not.

HELMER. Not a little nibble at a macaroon?

NORA. No, Toryald – I promise you, honestly – !

HELMER. There, there. I was only joking.

NORA (*goes over to the table, right*). You know I could never act
against your wishes.

HELMER. Of course not. And you've given me your word – (*Goes
over to her.*) Well, my beloved Nora, you keep your little Christmas secrets to yourself. They'll be revealed this evening, I've
no doubt, once the Christmas tree has been lit.

NORA. Have you remembered to invite Dr Rank?

HELMER. No. But there's no need; he knows he'll be dining
with us. Anyway, I'll ask him when he comes this morning.
I've ordered some good wine. Oh, Nora, you can't imagine
how I'm looking forward to this evening.

NORA. So am I. And, Torvald, how the children will love it!

HELMER. Yes, it's a wonderful thing to know that one's position
is assured and that one has an ample income. Don't you agree?
It's good to know that, isn't it?

NORA. Yes, it's almost like a miracle.

HELMER. Do you remember last Christmas? For three whole weeks you shut yourself away every evening to make flowers for the Christmas tree, and all those other things you were going to surprise us with. Ugh, it was the most boring time I've ever had in my life.

NORA. I didn't find it boring.

HELMER (*smiles*). But it all came to nothing in the end, didn't it?

NORA. Oh, are you going to bring that up again? How could I help the cat getting in and tearing everything to bits?

HELMER. No, my poor little Nora, of course you couldn't. You simply wanted to make us happy, and that's all that matters. But it's good that those hard times are past.

NORA. Yes, it's wonderful.

HELMER. I don't have to sit by myself and be bored. And you don't have to tire your pretty eyes and your delicate little hands –

NORA (*claps her hands*). No, Torvald, that's true, isn't it? I don't have to any longer! Oh, it's really all just like a miracle. (*Takes his arm.*) Now I'm going to tell you what I thought we might do, Torvald. As soon as Christmas is over –

   A bell rings in the hall.

Oh, there's the doorbell. (*Tidies up one or two things in the room.*) Someone's coming. What a bore.

HELMER. I'm not at home to any visitors. Remember!

MAID (*in the doorway*). A lady's called, madam. A stranger.

NORA. Well, ask her to come in.

MAID. And the doctor's here too, sir.

HELMER. Has he gone to my room?

MAID. Yes, sir.

   HELMER *goes into his room. The* MAID *shows in* MRS LINDE, *who is dressed in travelling clothes; then closes the door.*

MRS LINDE (*shyly and a little hesitantly*). Good morning, Nora.

NORA. (*uncertainly*). Good morning –

MRS LINDE. I don't suppose you recognize me.

NORA. No, I'm afraid I – Yes, wait a minute – surely – !
(*Exclaims.*) Why, Christine! Is it really you?

MRS LINDE. Yes, it's me.

NORA. Christine! And I didn't recognize you! But how could I – ?
(*More quietly.*) How you've changed, Christine!

MRS LINDE. Yes, I know. It's been nine years – nearly ten –

NORA. Is it so long? Yes, it must be. Oh, these last eight years
have been such a happy time for me! So you've come to town?
All that way in winter! How brave of you!

MRS LINDE. I arrived by the steamer this morning.

NORA. Yes, of course, to enjoy yourself over Christmas. Oh, how
splendid! We'll have to celebrate! But take off your coat. You're
not cold, are you? (*Helps her off with it.*) There! Now let's sit
down here by the stove and be comfortable. No, you take the
armchair. I'll sit here in the rocking-chair. (*Clasps* MRS LINDE's
hands.) Yes, now you look like your old self. Just at first I –
you've got a little paler, though, Christine. And perhaps a bit
thinner.

MRS LINDE. And older, Nora. Much, much older.

NORA. Yes, perhaps a little older. Just a tiny bit. Not much.
(*Checks herself suddenly and says earnestly.*) Oh, but how
thoughtless of me to sit here and chatter away like this! Dear,
sweet Christine, can you forgive me?

MRS LINDE. What do you mean, Nora?

NORA (*quietly*). Poor Christine, you've become a widow.

MRS LINDE. Yes. Three years ago.

NORA. I know, I know — I read it in the papers. Oh, Christine,
I meant to write to you so often, honestly. But I always put it
off, and something else always cropped up.

MRS LINDE. I understand, Nora dear.

NORA. No, Christine, it was beastly of me. Oh, my poor darling,
what you've gone through! And he didn't leave you anything?

MRS LINDE. No.

NORA. No children, either?

MRS LINDE. No.

NORA. Nothing at all, then?

MRS LINDE. Not even a feeling of loss or sorrow.

NORA (*looks incredulously at her.*) But, Christine, how is that possible?

MRS LINDE (*smiles sadly and strokes* NORA'*s hair*). Oh, these things happen, Nora.

NORA. All alone. How dreadful that must be for you. I've three lovely children. I'm afraid you can't see them now, because they're out with Nanny. But you must tell me everything –

MRS LINDE. No, no, no. I want to hear about you.

NORA. No, you start. I'm not going to be selfish today, I'm just going to think about you. Oh, but there's one thing I *must* tell you. Have you heard of the wonderful luck we've just had?

MRS LINDE. No. What?

NORA. Would you believe it – my husband's just been made vice-president of the bank!

MRS LINDE. Your husband? Oh, how lucky – !

NORA. Yes, isn't it? Being a lawyer is so uncertain, you know, especially if one isn't prepared to touch any case that isn't – well – quite nice. And of course Torvald's been very firm about that – and I'm absolutely with him. Oh, you can imagine how happy we are! He's joining the bank in the New Year, and he'll be getting a big salary, and lots of percentages too. From now on we'll be able to live quite differently – we'll be able to do whatever we want. Oh, Christine, it's such a relief! I feel so happy! Well, I mean, it's lovely to have heaps of money and not to have to worry about anything. Don't you think?

MRS LINDE. It must be lovely to have enough to cover one's needs, anyway.

NORA. Not just our needs! We're going to have heaps and heaps of money!

MRS LINDE (*smiles*). Nora, Nora, haven't you grown up yet? When we were at school you were a terrible little spendthrift.

NORA (*laughs quietly*). Yes, Torvald still says that. (*Wags her finger.*) But 'Nora, Nora' isn't as silly as you think. Oh, we've been in no position for me to waste money. We've both had to work.

MRS LINDE. You too?

NORA. Yes, little things – fancy work, crocheting, embroidery and so forth. (*Casually.*) And other things too. I suppose you know Torvald left the Ministry when we got married? There were no prospects of promotion in his department, and of course he needed more money. But the first year he over-worked himself dreadfully. He had to take on all sorts of extra jobs, and worked day and night. But it was too much for him, and he became frightfully ill. The doctors said he'd have to go to a warmer climate.

MRS LINDE. Yes, you spent a whole year in Italy, didn't you?

NORA. Yes. It wasn't easy for me to get away, you know. I'd just had Ivar. But, of course, we had to do it. Oh, it was a marvellous trip! And it saved Torvald's life. But it cost an awful lot of money, Christine.

MRS LINDE. I can imagine.

NORA. Two hundred and fifty pounds. That's a lot of money, you know.

MRS LINDE. How lucky you had it.

NORA. Well, actually, we got it from my father.

MRS LINDE. Oh, I see. Didn't he die just about that time?

NORA. Yes, Christine, just about then. Wasn't it dreadful, I couldn't go and look after him. I was expecting little Ivar any day. And then I had my poor Torvald to care for – we really didn't think he'd live. Dear, kind papa! I never saw him again, Christine. Oh, it's the saddest thing that's happened to me since I got married.

MRS LINDE. I know you were very fond of him. But you went to Italy – ?

NORA. Yes. Well, we had the money, you see, and the doctors said we mustn't delay. So we went the month after papa died.

MRS LINDE. And your husband came back completely cured?

NORA. Fit as a fiddle!

MRS LINDE. But – the doctor?

NORA. How do you mean?

MRS LINDE. I thought the maid said that the gentleman who arrived with me was the doctor.

NORA. Oh yes, that's Dr Rank, but he doesn't come because anyone's ill. He's our best friend, and he looks us up at least once every day. No, Torvald hasn't had a moment's illness since we went away. And the children are fit and healthy and so am I. (*Jumps up and claps her hands.*) Oh, God, oh God, Christine, isn't it a wonderful thing to be alive and happy! Oh, but how beastly of me! I'm only talking about myself. (*Sits on a footstool and rests her arms on* MRS LINDE's *knee.*) Oh, please don't be angry with me! Tell me, is it really true you didn't love your husband? Why did you marry him, then?

MRS LINDE. Well, my mother was still alive; and she was helpless and bedridden. And I had my two little brothers to take care of. I didn't feel I could say no.

NORA. Yes, well, perhaps you're right. He was rich then, was he?

MRS LINDE. Quite comfortably off, I believe. But his business was unsound, you see, Nora. When he died it went bankrupt and there was nothing left.

NORA. What did you do?

MRS LINDE. Well, I had to try to make ends meet somehow, so I started a little shop, and a little school, and anything else I could turn my hand to. These last three years have been just one endless slog for me, without a moment's rest. But now it's over, Nora. My poor dead mother doesn't need me any more; she's passed away. And the boys don't need me either; they've got jobs now and can look after themselves.

NORA. How relieved you must feel –

MRS LINDE. No, Nora. Just unspeakably empty. No one to live for any more. (*Gets up restlessly.*) That's why I couldn't bear to stay out there any longer, cut off from the world. I thought it'd be easier to find some work here that will exercise and occupy my mind. If only I could get a regular job – office work of some kind –

NORA. Oh but, Christine, that's dreadfully exhausting; and you look practically finished already. It'd be much better for you if you could go away somewhere.

MRS LINDE (*goes over to the window*). I have no pappa to pay for my holidays, Nora.

NORA (*gets up*). Oh, please don't be angry with me.

MRS LINDE. My dear Nora, it's I who should ask you not to be angry. That's the worst thing about this kind of situation – it makes one so bitter. One has no one to work for; and yet one has to be continually sponging for jobs. One has to live; and so one becomes completely egocentric. When you told me about this luck you've just had with Torvald's new job – can you imagine? – I was happy not so much on your account, as on my own.

NORA. How do you mean? Oh, I understand. You mean Torvald might be able to do something for you?

MRS LINDE. Yes, I was thinking that.

NORA. He will too, Christine. Just you leave it to me. I'll lead up to it so delicately, so delicately; I'll get him in the right mood. Oh, Christine, I do so want to help you.

MRS LINDE. It's sweet of you to bother so much about me, Nora. Especially since you know so little of the worries and hardships of life.

NORA. I? You say *I* know little of – ?

MRS LINDE (*smiles*). Well, good heavens – those bits of fancy-work of yours – well, really! You're a child, Nora.

NORA (*tosses her head and walks across the room*). You shouldn't say that so patronizingly.

MRS LINDE. Oh?

NORA. You're like the rest. You all think I'm incapable of getting down to anything serious –

MRS LINDE. My dear –

NORA. You think I've never had any worries like the rest of you.

MRS LINDE. Nora dear, you've just told me about all your difficulties –

NORA. Pooh – that! (*Quietly.*) I haven't told you about the big thing.

MRS LINDE. What big thing? What do you mean?

NORA. You patronize me, Christine; but you shouldn't. You're proud that you've worked so long and so hard for your mother.

MRS LINDE. I don't patronize anyone, Nora. But you're right – I am both proud and happy that I was able to make my mother's last months on earth comparatively easy.

NORA. And you're also proud at what you've done for your brothers.

MRS LINDE. I think I have a right to be.

NORA. I think so too. But let me tell you something, Christine. I too have done something to be proud and happy about.

MRS LINDE. I don't doubt it. But – how do you mean?

NORA. Speak quietly! Suppose Torvald should hear! He mustn't, at any price – no one must know, Christine – no one but you.

MRS LINDE. But what is this?

NORA. Come over here. (*Pulls her down on to the sofa beside her.*) Yes, Christine – I too have done something to be happy and proud about. It was I who saved Torvald's life.

MRS LINDE. Saved his – ? How did you save it?

NORA. I told you about our trip to Italy. Torvald couldn't have lived if he hadn't managed to get down there –

MRS LINDE. Yes, well – your father provided the money –

NORA (*smiles*). So Torvald and everyone else thinks. But –

MRS LINDE. Yes?

NORA. Papa didn't give us a penny. It was I who found the money.

MRS LINDE. You? All of it?

NORA. Two hundred and fifty pounds. What do you say to that?

MRS LINDE. But, Nora, how could you? Did you win a lottery or something?

NORA (*scornfully*). Lottery? (*Sniffs.*) What would there be to be proud of in that?

MRS LINDE. But where did you get it from, then?

NORA (*hums and smiles secretively*). Hm; tra-la-la-la!

MRS LINDE. You couldn't have borrowed it.

NORA. Oh? Why not?

MRS LINDE. Well, a wife can't borrow money without her husband's consent.

NORA (*tosses her head*). Ah, but when a wife has a little business sense, and knows how to be clever –

MRS LINDE. But Nora, I simply don't understand –

NORA. You don't have to. No one has said I borrowed the money. I could have got it in some other way. (*Throws herself back on the sofa.*) I could have got it from an admirer. When a girl's as pretty as I am –

MRS LINDE. Nora, you're crazy!

NORA. You're dying of curiosity now, aren't you, Christine?

MRS LINDE. Nora dear, you haven't done anything foolish?

NORA (*sits up again*). Is it foolish to save one's husband's life?

MRS LINDE. I think it's foolish if without his knowledge you –

NORA. But the whole point was that he mustn't know! Great heavens, don't you see? He hadn't to know how dangerously ill he was. It was me they told that his life was in danger and that only going to a warm climate could save him. Do you suppose I didn't try to think of other ways of getting him down there? I told him how wonderful it would be for me to go abroad like other young wives; I cried and prayed; I asked him to remember my condition, and said he ought to be nice and tender to me; and then I suggested he might quite easily borrow the money. But then he got almost angry with me, Christine. He said I was frivolous, and that it was his duty as a husband not to pander to my moods and caprices – I think that's what he called them. Well, well, I thought, you've got to be saved somehow. And then I thought of a way –

MRS LINDE. But didn't your husband find out from your father that the money hadn't come from him?

NORA. No, never. Papa died just then. I'd thought of letting him into the plot and asking him not to tell. But since he was so ill – ! And as things turned out, it didn't become necessary.

MRS LINDE. And you've never told your husband about this?

NORA. For heaven's sake, no! What an idea! He's frightfully strict about such matters. And besides – he's so proud of being a man – it'd be so painful and humiliating for him to know that he owed anything to me. It'd completely wreck our relationship. This life we have built together would no longer exist.

MRS LINDE. Will you never tell him?

NORA (*thoughtfully, half-smiling*). Yes – some time, perhaps. Years from now, when I'm no longer pretty. You mustn't laugh! I mean, of course, when Torvald no longer loves me as he does now; when it no longer amuses him to see me dance and dress up and play the fool for him. Then it might be useful to have something up my sleeve. (*Breaks off.*) Stupid, stupid, stupid! That time will never come. Well, what do you think of my big secret, Christine? I'm not completely useless, am I? Mind you, all this has caused me a frightful lot of worry. It hasn't been easy for me to meet my obligations punctually. In case you don't know, in the world of business there are things called quarterly instalments and interest, and they're a terrible problem to cope with. So I've had to scrape a little here and save a little there, as best I can. I haven't been able to save much on the housekeeping money, because Torvald likes to live well; and I couldn't let the children go short of clothes – I couldn't take anything out of what he gives me for them. The poor little angels!

MRS LINDE. So you've had to stint yourself, my poor Nora?

NORA. Of course. Well, after all, it was my problem. Whenever Torvald gave me money to buy myself new clothes, I never used more than half of it; and I always bought what was cheapest and plainest. Thank heaven anything suits me, so that Torvald's never noticed. But it made me a bit sad sometimes, because it's lovely to wear pretty clothes. Don't you think?

MRS LINDE. Indeed it is.

NORA. And then I've found one or two other sources of income. Last winter I managed to get a lot of copying to do. So I shut myself away and wrote every evening, late into the night. Oh, I often got so tired, so tired. But it was great fun, though, sitting there working and earning money. It was almost like being a man.

MRS LINDE. But how much have you managed to pay off like this?

NORA. Well, I can't say exactly. It's awfully difficult to keep an exact check on these kind of transactions. I only know I've paid everything I've managed to scrape together. Sometimes I really didn't know where to turn. (*Smiles.*) Then I'd sit here and imagine some rich old gentleman had fallen in love with me –

MRS LINDE. What! What gentleman?

NORA. Silly! And that now he'd died and when they opened his will it said in big letters: 'Everything I possess is to be paid forthwith to my beloved Mrs Nora Helmer in cash.'

MRS LINDE. But, Nora dear, who was this gentleman?

NORA. Great heavens, don't you understand? There wasn't any old gentleman; he was just something I used to dream up as I sat here evening after evening wondering how on earth I could raise some money. But what does it matter? The old bore can stay imaginary as far as I'm concerned, because now I don't have to worry any longer! (*Jumps up.*) Oh, Christine, isn't it wonderful? I don't have to worry any more! No more troubles! I can play all day with the children, I can fill the house with pretty things, just the way Torvald likes. And, Christine, it'll soon be spring, and the air'll be fresh and the skies blue – and then perhaps we'll be able to take a little trip somewhere. I shall

be able to see the sea again. Oh, yes, yes, it's a wonderful thing
to be alive and happy!

The bell rings in the hall.

MRS LINDE (*gets up*). You've a visitor. Perhaps I'd better go.

NORA. No, stay. It won't be for me. It's someone for Torvald –

MAID (*in the doorway*). Excuse me, madam, a gentleman's called
who says he wants to speak to the master. But I didn't know –
seeing as the doctor's with him –

NORA. Who is this gentleman?

KROGSTAD (*in the doorway*). It's me, Mrs Helmer.

MRS LINDE *starts, composes herself and turns away to the
window.*

NORA (*takes a step towards him and whispers tensely*). You? What
is it? What do you want to talk to my husband about?

KROGSTAD. Business – you might call it. I hold a minor post in
the bank, and I hear your husband is to become our new chief –

NORA. Oh – then it isn't – ?

KROGSTAD. Pure business, Mrs Helmer. Nothing more.

NORA. Well, you'll find him in his study.

*Nods indifferently as she closes the hall door behind him. Then
she walks across the room and sees to the stove.*

MRS LINDE. Nora, who was that man?

NORA. A lawyer called Krogstad.

MRS LINDE. It was him, then.

NORA. Do you know that man?

MRS LINDE. I used to know him – some years ago. He was a
solicitor's clerk in our town, for a while.

NORA. Yes, of course, so he was.

MRS LINDE. How he's changed!

NORA. He was very unhappily married, I believe.

MRS LINDE. Is he a widower now?

NORA. Yes, with a lot of children. Ah, now it's alight.

*She closes the door of the stove and moves the rocking-chair a
little to one side.*

MRS LINDE. He does – various things now, I hear?

NORA. Does he? It's quite possible – I really don't know. But don't let's talk about business. It's so boring.

    DR RANK enters from HELMER's study.

DR RANK (*still in the doorway*). No, no, my dear chap, don't see me out. I'll go and have a word with your wife. (*Closes the door and notices MRS LINDE.*) Oh, I beg your pardon. I seem to be *de trop* here too.

NORA. Not in the least. (*Introduces them.*) Dr Rank. Mrs Linde.

RANK. Ah! A name I have often heard in this house. I believe I passed you on the stairs as I came up.

MRS LINDE. Yes. Stairs tire me. I have to take them slowly.

RANK. Oh, have you hurt yourself?

MRS LINDE. No, I'm just a little run down.

RANK. Ah, is that all? Then I take it you've come to town to cure yourself by a round of parties?

MRS LINDE. I have come here to find work.

RANK. Is that an approved remedy for being run down?

MRS LINDE. One has to live, Doctor.

RANK. Yes, people do seem to regard it as a necessity.

NORA. Oh, really, Dr Rank. I bet you want to stay alive.

RANK. You bet I do. However wretched I sometimes feel, I still want to go on being tortured for as long as possible. It's the same with all my patients; and with people who are morally sick, too. There's a moral cripple in with Helmer at this very moment –

MRS LINDE (*softly*). Oh!

NORA. Whom do you mean?

RANK. Oh, a lawyer fellow called Krogstad – you wouldn't know him. He's crippled all right; morally twisted. But even he started off by announcing, as though it were a matter of enormous importance, that he had to live.

NORA. Oh? What did he want to talk to Torvald about?

RANK. I haven't the faintest idea. All I heard was something about the bank.

NORA. I didn't know that Krog – that this man Krogstad had any connection with the bank.

RANK. Yes, he's got some kind of job down there. (*To* MRS LINDE.) I wonder if in your part of the world you too have a species of creature that spends its time fussing around trying to smell out moral corruption? And when they find a case they give him some nice, comfortable position so that they can keep a good watch on him. The healthy ones just have to lump it.

MRS LINDE. But surely it's the sick who need care most?

RANK (*shrugs his shoulders*). Well, there we have it. It's that attitude that's turning human society into a hospital.

　　NORA, *lost in her own thoughts, laughs half to herself and claps her hands.*

RANK. Why are you laughing? Do you really know what society is?

NORA. What do I care about society? I think it's a bore. I was laughing at something else – something frightfully funny. Tell me, Dr Rank – will everyone who works at the bank come under Torvald now?

RANK. Do you find that particularly funny?

NORA (*smiles and hums*). Never you mind! Never you mind! (*Walks around the room.*) Yes, I find it very amusing to think that we – I mean, Torvald – has obtained so much influence over so many people. (*Takes the paper bag from her pocket.*) Dr Rank, would you like a small macaroon?

RANK. Macaroons! I say! I thought they were forbidden here.

NORA. Yes, well, these are some Christine gave me.

MRS LINDE. What? I – ?

NORA. All right, all right, don't get frightened. You weren't to know Torvald had forbidden them. He's afraid they'll ruin my teeth. But, dash it – for once – ! Don't you agree, Dr Rank? Here! (*Pops a macaroon into his mouth.*) You too, Christine. And I'll have one too. Just a little one. Two at the most (*Begins to walk round again.*) Yes, now I feel really, really happy. Now there's just one thing in the world I'd really love to do.

RANK. Oh? And what is that?

NORA. Just something I'd love to say to Torvald.

RANK. Well, why don't you say it?

NORA. No, I daren't. It's too dreadful.

MRS LINDE. Dreadful?

RANK. Well then, you'd better not. But you can say it to us. What is it you'd so love to say to Torvald?

NORA. I've the most extraordinary longing to say: 'Bloody hell!'

RANK. Are you mad?

MRS LINDE. My dear Nora – !

RANK. Say it. Here he is.

NORA (*hiding the bag of macaroons*). Ssh! Ssh!

HELMER, *with his overcoat on his arm and his hat in his hand, enters from his study.*

NORA (*goes to meet him*). Well, Torvald dear, did you get rid of him?

HELMER. Yes, he's just gone.

NORA. May I introduce you – ? This is Christine. She's just arrived in town.

HELMER. Christine – ? Forgive me, but I don't think –

NORA. Mrs Linde, Torvald dear. Christine Linde.

HELMER. Ah. A childhood friend of my wife's, I presume?

MRS LINDE. Yes, we knew each other in earlier days.

NORA. And imagine, now she's travelled all this way to talk to you.

HELMER. Oh?

MRS LINDE. Well, I didn't really –

NORA. You see, Christine's frightfully good at office work, and she's mad to come under some really clever man who can teach her even more than she knows already –

HELMER. Very sensible, madam.

NORA. So when she heard you'd become head of the bank – it was in her local paper – she came here as quickly as she could and – Torvald, you will, won't you? Do a little something to help Christine? For my sake?

HELMER. Well, that shouldn't be impossible. You are a widow, I take it, Mrs Linde?

MRS LINDE. Yes.

HELMER. And you have experience of office work?

MRS LINDE. Yes, quite a bit.

HELMER. Well then, it's quite likely I may be able to find some job for you –

NORA (*claps her hànds*). You see, you see!

HELMER. You've come at a lucky moment, Mrs Linde.

MRS LINDE. Oh, how can I ever thank you – ?

HELMER. There's absolutely no need. (*Puts on his overcoat.*) But now I'm afraid I must ask you to excuse me –

RANK. Wait. I'll come with you.

He gets his fur coat from the hall and warms it at the stove.

NORA. Don't be long, Torvald dear.

HELMER. I'll only be an hour.

NORA. Are you going too, Christine?

MRS LINDE (*puts on her outdoor clothes*). Yes, I must start to look round for a room.

HELMER. Then perhaps we can walk part of the way together.

NORA (*helps her*). It's such a nuisance we're so cramped here – I'm afraid we can't offer to –

MRS LINDE. Oh, I wouldn't dream of it. Goodbye, Nora dear, and thanks for everything.

NORA. *Au revoir.* You'll be coming back this evening, of course. And you too, Dr Rank. What? If you're well enough? Of course you'll be well enough. Wrap up warmly, though.

They go out, talking, into the hall. Children's voices are heard from the stairs.

NORA. Here they are! Here they are!

She runs out and opens the door. The NURSE, ANNE-MARIE, *enters with the children.*

NORA. Come in, come in! (*Stoops down and kisses them.*) Oh, my sweet darlings – ? Look at them, Christine! Aren't they beautiful?

RANK. Don't stand here chattering in this draught!

HELMER. Come, Mrs Linde. This is for mothers only.

DR RANK, HELMER and MRS LINDE go down the stairs. The NURSE brings the children into the room. NORA follows, and closes the door to the hall.

NORA. How well you look! What red cheeks you've got! Like apples and roses!

The CHILDREN answer her inaudibly as she talks to them.

NORA. Have you had fun? That's splendid. You gave Emmy and Bob a ride on the sledge? What, both together? I say! What a clever boy you are, Ivar! Oh, let me hold her for a moment Anne-Marie! My sweet little baby doll! (*Takes the smallest child from the NURSE and dances with her.*) Yes, yes, mummy will dance with Bob too. What? Have you been throwing snowballs? Oh, I wish I'd been there! No, don't – I'll undress them myself, Anne-Marie. No, please let me; it's such fun. Go inside and warm yourself; you look frozen. There's some hot coffee on the stove.

The NURSE goes into the room on the left. NORA takes off the children's outdoor clothes and throws them anywhere while they all chatter simultaneously.

NORA. What? A big dog ran after you? But he didn't bite you? No, dogs don't bite lovely little baby dolls. Leave those parcels alone, Ivar. What's in them? Ah, wouldn't you like to know! No, no; it's nothing nice. Come on, let's play a game. What shall we play? Hide and seek? Yes, let's play hide and seek. Bob shall hide first. You want me to? All right, let me hide first.

NORA and the CHILDREN play around the room, and in the adjacent room to the right, laughing and shouting. At length NORA hides under the table. The CHILDREN rush in, look, but cannot find her. Then they hear her half-stifled laughter, run to the table, lift up the cloth and see her. Great excitement. She crawls out as though to frighten them. Further excitement. Mean-

while, there has been a knock on the door leading from the hall, but no one has noticed it. Now the door is half opened and KROG- STAD *enters. He waits for a moment; the game continues.*

KROGSTAD. Excuse me, Mrs Helmer –

NORA (*turns with a stifled cry and half jumps up*). Oh! What do you want?

KROGSTAD. I beg your pardon – the front door was ajar. Some- one must have forgotten to close it.

NORA (*gets up*). My husband is not at home, Mr Krogstad.

KROGSTAD. I know.

NORA. Well, what do you want here, then?

KROGSTAD. A word with you.

NORA. With – ? (*To the* CHILDREN, *quietly*.) Go inside to Anne- Marie. What? No, the strange gentleman won't do anything to hurt mummy. When he's gone we'll start playing again.

She takes the children into the room on the left and closes the door behind them.

NORA (*uneasy, tense*). You want to speak to me?

KROGSTAD. Yes.

NORA. Today? But it's not the first of the month yet.

KROGSTAD. No, it is Christmas Eve. Whether or not you have a merry Christmas depends on you.

NORA. What do you want? I can't give you anything today –

KROGSTAD. We won't talk about that for the present. There's something else. You have a moment to spare?

NORA. Oh, yes. Yes, I suppose so – though –

KROGSTAD. Good, I was sitting in the café down below and I saw your husband cross the street –

NORA. Yes.

KROGSTAD. With a lady.

NORA. Well?

KROGSTAD. Might I be so bold as to ask; was not that lady a Mrs Linde?

NORA. Yes.

KROGSTAD. Recently arrived in town?

NORA. Yes, today.

KROGSTAD. She is a good friend of yours, is she not?

NORA. Yes, she is. But I don't see –

KROGSTAD. I used to know her, too, once.

NORA. I know.

KROGSTAD. Oh? You've discovered that. Yes, I thought you
would. Well then, may I ask you a straight question: is Mrs
Linde to be employed at the bank?

NORA. How dare you presume to cross-examine me, Mr Krogstad? You, one of my husband's employees? But since you ask,
you shall have an answer. Yes, Mrs Linde is to be employed
by the bank. And I arranged it, Mr Krogstad. Now you know.

KROGSTAD. I guessed right, then.

NORA (*walks up and down the room*). Oh, one has a little influence,
you know. Just because one's a woman it doesn't necessarily
mean that – When one is in a humble position, Mr Krogstad,
one should think twice before offending someone who – hm – !

KROGSTAD. – who has influence?

NORA. Precisely.

KROGSTAD (*changes his tone*). Mrs Helmer, will you have the
kindness to use your influence on my behalf?

NORA. What? What do you mean?

KROGSTAD. Will you be so good as to see that I keep my humble
position at the bank?

NORA. What do you mean? Who is thinking of removing you
from your position?

KROGSTAD. Oh, you don't need to play the innocent with me. I
realize it can't be very pleasant for your friend to risk bumping
into me. And now I also realize whom I have to thank for being
hounded out like this.

NORA. But I assure you –

KROGSTAD. Look, let's not beat about the bush. There's still
time, and I'd advise you to use your influence to stop it.

NORA. But, Mr Krogstad, I have no influence!

KROGSTAD. Oh? I thought you just said –

NORA. But I didn't mean it like that! I? How on earth could you imagine that I would have any influence over my husband?

KROGSTAD. Oh, I've known your husband since we were students together. I imagine he has his weaknesses like other married men.

NORA. If you speak impertinently of my husband, I shall show you the door.

KROGSTAD. You're a bold woman, Mrs Helmer.

NORA. I'm not afraid of you any longer. Once the New Year is in, I'll soon be rid of you.

KROGSTAD (*more controlled*). Now listen to me, Mrs Helmer. If I'm forced to, I shall fight for my little job at the bank as I would fight for my life.

NORA. So it sounds.

KROGSTAD. It isn't just the money – that's the last thing I care about. There's something else. Well, you might as well know. It's like this, you see. You know of course, as everyone else does, that some years ago I committed an indiscretion.

NORA. I think I did hear something –

KROGSTAD. It never came into court; but from that day, every opening was barred to me. So I turned my hand to the kind of business you know about. I had to do something; and I don't think I was one of the worst. But now I want to give up all that. My sons are growing up: for their sake, I must try to regain what respectability I can. This job in the bank was the first step on the ladder. And now your husband wants to kick me off that ladder back into the dirt.

NORA. But, my dear Mr Krogstad, it simply isn't in my power to help you.

KROGSTAD. You say that because you don't want to help me. But I have the means to make you.

NORA. You don't mean you'd tell my husband that I owe you money?

KROGSTAD. And if I did?

NORA. That'd be a filthy trick! (*Almost in tears.*) This secret that

is my pride and my joy – that he should hear about it in such a
filthy, beastly way – hear about it from you! It'd involve me in
the most dreadful unpleasantness –

KROGSTAD. Only – unpleasantness?

NORA (*vehemently*). All right, do it! You'll be the one who'll suffer.
It'll show my husband the kind of man you are, and then you'll
never keep your job.

KROGSTAD. I asked you whether it was merely domestic unpleasantness you were afraid of.

NORA. If my husband hears about it, he will of course immediately pay you whatever is owing. And then we shall have nothing
more to do with you.

KROGSTAD (*takes a step closer*). Listen, Mrs Helmer. Either
you've a bad memory or else you know very little about financial
transactions. I had better enlighten you.

NORA. What do you mean?

KROGSTAD. When your husband was ill, you came to me to
borrow two hundred and fifty pounds.

NORA. I didn't know anyone else.

KROGSTAD. I promised to find that sum for you –

NORA. And you did find it.

KROGSTAD. I promised to find that sum for you on certain
conditions. You were so worried about your husband's illness
and so keen to get the money to take him abroad that I don't
think you bothered much about the details. So it won't be out of
place if I refresh your memory. Well – I promised to get you the
money in exchange for an I.O.U., which I drew up.

NORA. Yes, and which I signed.

KROGSTAD. Exactly. But then I added a few lines naming your
father as security for the debt. This paragraph was to be signed
by your father.

NORA. Was to be? He did sign it.

KROGSTAD. I left the date blank for your father to fill in when he
signed this paper. You remember, Mrs Helmer?

NORA. Yes, I think so –

KROGSTAD. Then I gave you back this I.O.U. for you to post to your father. Is that not correct?

NORA. Yes.

KROGSTAD. And of course you posted it at once; for within five or six days you brought it along to me with your father's signature on it. Whereupon I handed you the money.

NORA. Yes, well. Haven't I repaid the instalments as agreed?

KROGSTAD. Mm – yes, more or less. But to return to what we were speaking about – that was a difficult time for you just then, wasn't it, Mrs Helmer?

NORA. Yes, it was.

KROGSTAD. Your father was very ill, if I am not mistaken.

NORA. He was dying.

KROGSTAD. He did in fact die shortly afterwards?

NORA. Yes.

KROGSTAD. Tell me, Mrs Helmer, do you by any chance remember the date of your father's death? The day of the month, I mean.

NORA. Pappa died on the twenty-ninth of September.

KROGSTAD. Quite correct; I took the trouble to confirm it. And that leaves me with a curious little problem – (*Takes out a paper.*) – which I simply cannot solve.

NORA. Problem? I don't see –

KROGSTAD. The problem, Mrs Helmer, is that your father signed this paper three days after his death.

NORA. What? I don't understand –

KROGSTAD. Your father died on the twenty-ninth of September. But look at this. Here your father has dated his signature the second of October. Isn't that a curious little problem, Mrs Helmer?

    NORA *is silent.*

KROGSTAD. Can you suggest any explanation?

    She remains silent.

KROGSTAD. And there's another curious thing. The words 'second of October' and the year are written in a hand which is not your father's, but which I seem to know. Well, there's a simple explanation to that. Your father could have forgotten to write in the date when he signed, and someone else could have added it before the news came of his death. There's nothing criminal about that. It's the signature itself I'm wondering about. It *is* genuine, I suppose, Mrs Helmer? It was your father who wrote his name here?

NORA (*after a short silence, throws back her head and looks defiantly at him*). No, it was not. It was I who wrote pappa's name there.

KROGSTAD. Look, Mrs Helmer, do you realize this is a dangerous admission?

NORA. Why? You'll get your money.

KROGSTAD. May I ask you a question? Why didn't you send this paper to your father?

NORA. I couldn't. Pappa was very ill. If I'd asked him to sign this, I'd have had to tell him what the money was for. But I couldn't have told him in his condition that my husband's life was in danger. I couldn't have done that!

KROGSTAD. Then you would have been wiser to have given up your idea of a holiday.

NORA. But I couldn't! It was to save my husband's life. I couldn't put it off.

KROGSTAD. But didn't it occur to you that you were being dishonest towards me?

NORA. I couldn't bother about that. I didn't care about you. I hated you because of all the beastly difficulties you'd put in my way when you knew how dangerously ill my husband was.

KROGSTAD. Mrs Helmer, you evidently don't appreciate exactly what you have done. But I can assure you that it is no bigger nor worse a crime than the one I once committed and thereby ruined my whole social position.

NORA. You? Do you expect me to believe that you would have taken a risk like that to save your wife's life?

KROGSTAD. The law does not concern itself with motives.

NORA. Then the law must be very stupid.

KROGSTAD. Stupid or not, if I show this paper to the police, you will be judged according to it.

NORA. I don't believe that. Hasn't a daughter the right to shield her father from worry and anxiety when he's old and dying? Hasn't a wife the right to save her husband's life? I don't know much about the law, but there must be something somewhere that says that such things are allowed. You ought to know that, you're meant to be a lawyer, aren't you? You can't be a very good lawyer, Mr Krogstad.

KROGSTAD. Possibly not. But business, the kind of business we two have been transacting – I think you'll admit I understand something about that? Good. Do as you please. But I tell you this. If I get thrown into the gutter for a second time, I shall take you with me.

He bows and goes out through the hall.

NORA (*stands for a moment in thought, then tosses her head*). What nonsense! He's trying to frighten me! I'm not that stupid. (*Busies herself gathering together the children's clothes; then she suddenly stops.*) But – ? No, it's impossible. I did it for love, didn't I?

CHILDREN (*in the doorway, left*). Mummy, the strange gentleman has gone out into the street.

NORA. Yes, yes, I know. But don't talk to anyone about the strange gentleman. You hear? Not even to Daddy.

CHILDREN. No, Mummy. Will you play with us again now?

NORA. No, no. Not now.

CHILREN. Oh but, Mummy, you promised!

NORA. I know, but I can't just now. Go back to the nursery. I've a lot to do. Go away, my darlings, go away.

She pushes them gently into the other room, and closes the door behind them. She sits on the sofa, takes up her embroidery, stitches for a few moments, but soon stops.

NORA. No! (*Throws the embroidery aside, gets up, goes to the door leading to the hall and calls.*) Helen! Bring in the Christmas tree! (*She goes to the table on the left and opens the drawer in it; then pauses again.*) No, but it's utterly impossible!

MAID (*enters with the tree*). Where shall I put it, madam?

NORA. There, in the middle of the room.

MAID. Will you be wanting anything else?

NORA. No, thank you. I have everything I need.

The MAID *puts down the tree and goes out.*

NORA (*busy decorating the tree*). Now – candles here – and flowers here. That loathsome man! Nonsense, nonsense, there's nothing to be frightened about. The Christmas tree must be beautiful. I'll do everything that you like, Torvald. I'll sing for you, dance for you –

HELMER, *with a bundle of papers under his arm, enters.*

NORA. Oh – are you back already?

HELMER. Yes. Has anyone been here?

NORA. Here? No.

HELMER. That's strange. I saw Krogstad come out of the front door.

NORA. Did you? Oh yes, that's quite right – Krogstad was here for a few minutes.

HELMER. Nora, I can tell from your face, he has been here and asked you to put in a good word for him.

NORA. Yes.

HELMER. And you were to pretend you were doing it of your own accord? You weren't going to tell me he'd been here? He asked you to do that too, didn't he?

NORA. Yes, Torvald. But –

HELMER. Nora, Nora! And you were ready to enter into such a conspiracy? Talking to a man like that, and making him promises – and then, on top of it all, to tell me an untruth!

NORA. An untruth?

HELMER. Didn't you say no one had been here? (*Wags his finger.*) My little songbird must never do that again. A songbird must have a clean beak to sing with. Otherwise she'll start twittering out of tune. (*Puts his arm round her waist.*) Isn't that the way we want things? Yes, of course it is. (*Lets go of her.*) So let's hear no more about that. (*Sits down in front of the stove.*) Ah, how cosy and peaceful it is here! (*Glances for a few moments at his papers.*)

NORA (*busy with the tree; after a short silence*). Torvald.

HELMER. Yes.

NORA. I'm terribly looking forward to that fancy-dress ball at the Stenborgs on Boxing Day.

HELMER. And I'm terribly curious to see what you're going to surprise me with.

NORA. Oh, it's so maddening.

HELMER. What is?

NORA. I can't think of anything to wear. It all seems so stupid and meaningless.

HELMER. So my little Nora has come to that conclusion, has she?

NORA (*behind his chair, resting her arms on its back*). Are you very busy, Torvald?

HELMER. Oh –

NORA. What are those papers?

HELMER. Just something to do with the bank.

NORA. Already?

HELMER. I persuaded the trustees to give me authority to make certain immediate changes in the staff and organization. I want to have everything straight by the New Year.

NORA. Then that's why this poor man Krogstad –

HELMER. Hm.

NORA (*still leaning over his chair, slowly strokes the back of his head*). If you hadn't been so busy, I was going to ask you an enormous favour, Torvald.

HELMER. Well, tell me. What was it to be?

NORA. You know I trust your taste more than anyone's. I'm so anxious to look really beautiful at the fancy-dress ball. Torvald, couldn't you help me to decide what I shall go as, and what kind of costume I ought to wear?

HELMER. Aha! So little Miss Independent's in trouble and needs a man to rescue her, does she?

NORA. Yes, Torvald. I can't get anywhere without your help.

HELMER. Well, well, I'll give the matter thought. We'll find something.

NORA. Oh, how kind of you! (*Goes back to the tree. Pause.*) How pretty these red flowers look! But, tell me, is it so dreadful, this thing that Krogstad's done?

HELMER. He forged someone else's name. Have you any idea what that means?

NORA. Mightn't he have been forced to do it by some emergency?

HELMER. He probably just didn't think – that's what usually happens. I'm not so heartless as to condemn a man for an isolated action.

NORA. No, Torvald, of course not!

HELMER. Men often succeed in re-establishing themselves if they admit their crime and take their punishment.

NORA. Punishment?

HELMER. But Krogstad didn't do that. He chose to try and trick his way out of it. And that's what has morally destroyed him.

NORA. You think that would – ?

HELMER. Just think how a man with that load on his conscience must always be lying and cheating and dissembling – how he must wear a mask even in the presence of those who are dearest to him, even his own wife and children! Yes, the children. That's the worst danger, Nora.

NORA. Why?

HELMER. Because an atmosphere of lies contaminates and poisons every corner of the home. Every breath that the children draw in such a house contains the germs of evil.

NORA (*comes closer behind him*). Do you really believe that?

HELMER. Oh, my dear, I've come across it so often in my work at the bar. Nearly all young criminals are the children of mothers who are constitutional liars.

NORA. Why do you say mothers?

HELMER. It's usually the mother – though of course the father can have the same influence. Every lawyer knows that only too well. And yet this fellow Krogstad has been sitting at home all these years poisoning his children with his lies and pretences. That's why I say that, morally speaking, he is dead. (*Stretches out his hand towards her*.) So my pretty little Nora must promise me not to plead his case. Your hand on it. Come, come, what's this? Give me your hand. There. That's settled, now. I assure you it'd be quite impossible for me to work in the same building as him. I literally feel physically ill in the presence of a man like that.

NORA (*draws her hand from his and goes over to the other side of the Christmas tree*). How hot it is in here! And I've so much to do.

HELMER (*gets up and gathers his papers*). Yes, and I must try to get some of this read before dinner. I'll think about your costume too. And I may even have something up my sleeve to hang in gold paper on the Christmas tree. (*Lays his hand on her head*.) My precious little songbird!

He goes into his study and closes the door.

NORA (*softly, after a pause*). It's nonsense. It must be. It's impossible. It *must* be impossible!

NURSE (*in the doorway, left*). The children are asking if they can come in to Mummy.

NORA. No, no, no – don't let them in. You stay with them, Anne-Marie.

NURSE. Very good, madam. (*Closes the door.*)

NORA (*pale with fear*). Corrupt my little children – ! Poison my home! (*Short pause. She throws back her head.*) It isn't true! It *couldn't* be true!

ACT TWO

The same room. In the corner by the piano the Christmas tree stands,
stripped and dishevelled, its candles burned to their sockets. NORA's
outdoor clothes lie on the sofa. She is alone in the room, walking
restlessly to and fro. At length she stops by the sofa and picks up her
coat.

NORA (*drops the coat again*). There's someone coming! (*Goes to*
the door and listens.) No, it's no one. Of course – no one'll come
today, it's Christmas Day. Nor tomorrow. But perhaps – !
(*Opens the door and looks out.*) No. Nothing in the letter-box.
Quite empty. (*Walks across the room.*) Silly, silly. Of course he
won't do anything. It couldn't happen. It isn't possible. Why,
I've three small children.

    The NURSE, *carrying a large cardboard box, enters from the*
room on the left.

NURSE. I found those fancy dress clothes at last, madam.

NORA. Thank you. Put them on the table.

NURSE (*does so*). They're all rumpled up.

NORA. Oh, I wish I could tear them into a million pieces!

NURSE. Why, madam! They'll be all right. Just a little patience.

NORA. Yes, of course. I'll go and get Mrs Linde to help me.

NURSE. What, out again? In this dreadful weather? You'll catch
a chill, madam.

NORA. Well, that wouldn't be the worst. How are the children?

NURSE. Playing with their Christmas presents, poor little dears.
But –

NORA. Are they still asking to see me?

NURSE. They're so used to having their mummy with them.

NORA. Yes, but, Anne-Marie, from now on I shan't be able to
spend so much time with them.

NURSE. Well, children get used to anything in time.

NORA. Do you think so? Do you think they'd forget their mother if she went away from them – for ever?

NURSE. Mercy's sake, madam! For ever!

NORA. Tell me, Anne-Marie – I've so often wondered. How could you bear to give your child away – to strangers?

NURSE. But I had to when I came to nurse my little Miss Nora.

NORA. Do you mean you wanted to?

NURSE. When I had the chance of such a good job? A poor girl what's got into trouble can't afford to pick and choose. That good-for-nothing didn't lift a finger.

NORA. But your daughter must have completely forgotten you.

NURSE. Oh no, indeed she hasn't. She's written to me twice, once when she got confirmed and then again when she got married.

NORA (*hugs her*). Dear old Anne-Marie, you were a good mother to me.

NURSE. Poor little Miss Nora, you never had any mother but me.

NORA. And if my little ones had no one else, I know you would – no, silly, silly, silly! (*Opens the cardboard box.*) Go back to them, Anne-Marie. Now I must – ! Tomorrow you'll see how pretty I shall look.

NURSE. Why, there'll be no one at the ball as beautiful as my Miss Nora.

She goes into the room, left.

NORA (*begins to unpack the clothes from the box, but soon throws them down again*). Oh, if only I dared go out! If I could be sure no one would come and nothing would happen while I was away! Stupid, stupid! No one will come. I just mustn't think about it. Brush this muff. Pretty gloves, pretty gloves! Don't think about it, don't think about it! One, two, three, four, five, six – (*Cries.*) Ah – they're coming – !

She begins to run towards the door, but stops uncertainly. MRS LINDE *enters from the hall, where she has been taking off her outdoor clothes.*

NORA. Oh, it's you, Christine. There's no one else outside, is there? Oh, I'm so glad you've come.

MRS LINDE. I hear you were at my room asking for me.

NORA. Yes, I just happened to be passing. I want to ask you to help me with something. Let's sit down here on the sofa. Look at this. There's going to be a fancy-dress ball tomorrow night upstairs at Consul Stenborg's, and Torvald wants me to go as a Neapolitan fisher-girl and dance the tarantella. I learned it in Capri.

MRS LINDE. I say, are you going to give a performance?

NORA. Yes, Torvald says I should. Look, here's the dress. Torvald had it made for me in Italy – but now it's all so torn, I don't know –

MRS LINDE. Oh, we'll soon put that right – the stitching's just come away. Needle and thread? Ah, here we are.

NORA. You're being awfully sweet.

MRS LINDE (*sews*). So you're going to dress up tomorrow, Nora? I must pop over for a moment to see how you look. Oh, but I've completely forgotten to thank you for that nice evening yesterday.

NORA (*gets up and walks across the room*). Oh, I didn't think it was as nice as usual. You ought to have come to town a little earlier, Christine. . . . Yes, Torvald understands how to make a home look attractive.

MRS LINDE. I'm sure you do, too. You're not your father's daughter for nothing. But, tell me – is Dr Rank always in such low spirits as he was yesterday?

NORA. No, last night it was very noticeable. But he's got a terrible disease – he's got spinal tuberculosis, poor man. His father was a frightful creature who kept mistresses and so on. As a result Dr Rank has been sickly ever since he was a child – you understand –

MRS LINDE (*puts down her sewing*). But, my dear Nora, how on earth did you get to know about such things?

NORA (*walks about the room*). Oh, don't be silly, Christine – when one has three children, one comes into contact with women who – well, who know about medical matters, and they tell one a thing or two.

MRS LINDE (*sews again; a short silence*). Does Dr Rank visit you every day?

NORA. Yes, every day. He's Torvald's oldest friend, and a good friend to me too. Dr Rank's almost one of the family.

MRS LINDE. But, tell me – is he quite sincere? I mean, doesn't he rather say the sort of thing he thinks people want to hear?

NORA. No, quite the contrary. What gave you that idea?

MRS LINDE. When you introduced me to him yesterday, he said he'd often heard my name mentioned here. But later I noticed your husband had no idea who I was. So how could Dr Rank –

NORA. Yes, that's quite right, Christine. You see, Torvald's so hopelessly in love with me that he wants to have me all to himself – those were his very words. When we were first married, he got quite jealous if I as much as mentioned any of my old friends back home. So naturally, I stopped talking about them. But I often chat with Dr Rank about that kind of thing. He enjoys it, you see.

MRS LINDE. Now listen, Nora. In many ways you're still a child; I'm a bit older than you and have a little more experience of the world. There's something I want to say to you. You ought to give up this business with Dr Rank.

NORA. What business?

MRS LINDE. Well, everything. Last night you were speaking about this rich admirer of yours who was going to give you money –

NORA. Yes, and who doesn't exist – unfortunately. But what's that got to do with – ?

MRS LINDE. Is Dr Rank rich?

NORA. Yes.

MRS LINDE. And he has no dependants?

NORA. No, no one. But –

MRS LINDE. And he comes here to see you every day?

NORA. Yes, I've told you.

MRS LINDE. But how dare a man of his education be so forward?

NORA. What on earth are you talking about?

MRS LINDE. Oh, stop pretending, Nora. Do you think I haven't guessed who it was who lent you that two hundred pounds?

NORA. Are you out of your mind? How could you imagine such a thing? A friend, someone who comes here every day! Why, that'd be an impossible situation!

MRS LINDE. Then it really wasn't him?

NORA. No, of course not. I've never for a moment dreamed of – anyway, he hadn't any money to lend then. He didn't come into that till later.

MRS LINDE. Well, I think that was a lucky thing for you, Nora dear.

NORA. No, I could never have dreamed of asking Dr Rank – Though I'm sure that if ever I did ask him –

MRS LINDE. But of course you won't.

NORA. Of course not. I can't imagine that it should ever become necessary. But I'm perfectly sure that if I did speak to Dr Rank –

MRS LINDE. Behind your husband's back?

NORA. I've got to get out of this other business – and *that's* been going on behind his back. I've *got* to get out of it.

MRS LINDE. Yes, well, that's what I told you yesterday. But –

NORA (*walking up and down*). It's much easier for a man to arrange these things than a woman –

MRS LINDE. One's own husband, yes.

NORA. Oh, bosh. (*Stops walking.*) When you've completely repaid a debt, you get your I.O.U. back, don't you?

MRS LINDE. Yes, of course.

NORA. And you can tear it into a thousand pieces and burn the filthy, beastly thing!

MRS LINDE (*looks hard at her, puts down her sewing and gets up slowly*). Nora, you're hiding something from me.

NORA. Can you see that?

MRS LINDE. Something has happened since yesterday morning. Nora, what is it?

NORA (*goes towards her*). Christine! (*Listens.*) Ssh! There's Torvald. Would you mind going into the nursery for a few minutes? Torvald can't bear to see sewing around. Anne-Marie'll help you.

MRS LINDE (*gathers some of her things together*). Very well. But I shan't leave this house until we've talked this matter out.

She goes into the nursery, left. As she does so, HELMER *enters from the hall.*

NORA (*runs to meet him*). Oh, Torvald dear, I've been so longing for you to come back!

HELMER. Was that the dressmaker?

NORA. No, it was Christine. She's helping me mend my costume. I'm going to look rather splendid in that.

HELMER. Yes, that was quite a bright idea of mine, wasn't it?

NORA. Wonderful! But wasn't it nice of me to give in to you?

HELMER (*takes her chin in his hand*). Nice – to give in to your husband? All right, little silly, I know you didn't mean it like that. But I won't disturb you. I expect you'll be wanting to try it on.

NORA. Are you going to work now?

HELMER. Yes. (*Shows her a bundle of papers.*) Look at these. I've been down to the bank – (*Turns to go into his study.*)

NORA. Torvald.

HELMER (*stops*). Yes.

NORA. If little squirrel asked you really prettily to grant her a wish –

HELMER. Well?

NORA. Would you grant it to her?

HELMER. First I should naturally have to know what it was.

NORA. Squirrel would do lots of pretty tricks for you if you granted her wish.

HELMER. Out with it, then.

NORA. Your little skylark would sing in every room –

HELMER. My little skylark does that already.

NORA. I'd turn myself into a little fairy and dance for you in the moonlight, Torvald.

HELMER. Nora, it isn't that business you were talking about this morning?

NORA (*comes closer*). Yes, Torvald – oh, please! I beg of you!

HELMER. Have you really the nerve to bring that up again?

NORA. Yes, Torvald, yes, you must do as I ask! You must let Krogstad keep his place at the bank!

HELMER. My dear Nora, his is the job I'm giving to Mrs Linde.

NORA. Yes, that's terribly sweet of you. But you can get rid of one of the other clerks instead of Krogstad.

HELMER. Really, you're being incredibly obstinate. Just because you thoughtlessly promised to put in a word for him, you expect me to –

NORA. No, it isn't that, Helmer. It's for your own sake. That man writes for the most beastly newspapers – you said so yourself. He could do you tremendous harm. I'm so dreadfully frightened of him –

HELMER. Oh, I understand. Memories of the past. That's what's frightening you.

NORA. What do you mean?

HELMER. You're thinking of your father, aren't you?

NORA. Yes, yes. Of course. Just think what those dreadful men wrote in the papers about papa! The most frightful slanders. I really believe it would have lost him his job if the Ministry hadn't sent you down to investigate, and you hadn't been so kind and helpful to him.

HELMER. But, my dear little Nora, there's a considerable difference between your father and me. Your father was not a man of unassailable reputation. But I am. And I hope to remain so all my life.

NORA. But no one knows what spiteful people may not dig up. We could be so peaceful and happy now, Torvald – we could be free from every worry – you and I and the children. Oh, please, Torvald, please – !

HELMER. The very fact of your pleading his cause makes it impossible for me to keep him. Everyone at the bank already knows that I intend to dismiss Krogstad. If the rumour got about that the new vice-president had allowed his wife to persuade him to change his mind –

NORA. Well, what then?

HELMER. Oh, nothing, nothing. As long as my little Miss Obstinate gets her way – ! Do you expect me to make a laughing-stock of myself before my entire staff – give people the idea that I am open to outside influence? Believe me, I'd soon feel the consequences! Besides – there's something else that makes it impossible for Krogstad to remain in the bank while I am its manager.

NORA. What is that?

HELMER. I might conceivably have allowed myself to ignore his moral obloquies –

NORA. Yes, Torvald, surely?

HELMER. And I hear he's quite efficient at his job. But we – well, we were school friends. It was one of those friendships that one enters into over-hastily and so often comes to regret later in life. I might as well confess the truth. We – well, we're on Christian name terms. And the tactless idiot makes no attempt to conceal it when other people are present. On the contrary, he thinks it gives him the right to be familiar with me. He shows off the whole time, with 'Torvald this', and 'Torvald that'. I can tell you, I find it damned annoying. If he stayed, he'd make my position intolerable.

NORA. Torvald, you can't mean this seriously.

HELMER. Oh? And why not?

NORA. But it's so petty.

HELMER. What did you say? Petty? You think I am petty?

NORA. No, Torvald dear, of course you're not. That's just why –

HELMER. Don't quibble! You call my motives petty. Then I

must be petty too. Petty! I see. Well, I've had enough of this. (*Goes to the door and calls into the hall.*) Helen!

NORA. What are you going to do?

HELMER (*searching among his papers*). I'm going to settle this matter once and for all.

The MAID *enters.*

HELMER. Take this letter downstairs at once. Find a messenger and see that he delivers it. Immediately! The address is on the envelope. Here's the money.

MAID. Very good, sir. (*Goes out with the letter.*)

HELMER (*putting his papers in order*). There now, little Miss Obstinate.

NORA (*tensely*). Torvald – what was in that letter?

HELMER. Krogstad's dismissal.

NORA. Call her back, Torvald! There's still time. Oh, Torvald, call her back! Do it for my sake – for your own sake – for the children! Do you hear me, Torvald? Please do it! You don't realize what this may do to us all!

HELMER. Too late.

NORA. Yes. Too late.

HELMER. My dear Nora, I forgive you this anxiety. Though it is a bit of an insult to me. Oh, but it is! Isn't it an insult to imply that I should be frightened by the vindictiveness of a depraved hack journalist? But I forgive you, because it so charmingly testifies to the love you bear me. (*Takes her in his arms.*) Which is as it should be, my own dearest Nora. Let what will happen, happen. When the real crisis comes, you will not find me lacking in strength or courage. I am man enough to bear the burden for us both.

NORA (*fearfully*). What do you mean?

HELMER. The whole burden, I say –

NORA (*calmly*). I shall never let you do that.

HELMER. Very well. We shall share it, Nora – as man and wife. And that's as it should be. (*Caresses her.*) Are you happy now? There, there, there; don't look at me with those frightened little eyes. You're simply imagining things. You go ahead now and do your tarantella, and get some practice on that tambourine. I'll sit in my study and close the door. Then I won't hear anything, and you can make all the noise you want. (*Turns in the doorway.*) When Dr Rank comes, tell him where to find me. (*He nods to her, goes into his room with his papers and closes the door.*)

NORA (*desperate with anxiety, stands as though transfixed, and whispers*). He said he'd do it. He will do it. He will do it, and nothing'll stop him. No, never that. I'd rather anything. There must be some escape – Some way out – !

The bell rings in the hall.

NORA. Dr Rank – ! Anything but that! Anything, I don't care – !
She passes her hand across her face, composes herself, walks across and opens the door to the hall. DR RANK is standing there, hanging up his fur coat. During the following scene it begins to grow dark.

NORA. Good evening, Dr Rank. I recognized your ring. But you mustn't go in to Torvald yet. I think he's busy.

RANK. And – you?

NORA (*as he enters the room and she closes the door behind him*). Oh, you know very well I've always time to talk to you.

RANK. Thank you. I shall avail myself of that privilege as long as I can.

NORA. What do you mean by that? As long as you *can*?

RANK. Yes. Does that frighten you?

NORA. Well, it's rather a curious expression. Is something going to happen?

RANK. Something I've been expecting to happen for a long time. But I didn't think it would happen quite so soon.

NORA (*seizes his arm*). What is it? Dr Rank, you must tell me!

RANK (*sits down by the stove*). I'm on the way out. And there's nothing to be done about it.

NORA (*sighs with relief*). Oh, it's you – ?

RANK. Who else? No, it's no good lying to oneself. I am the

most wretched of all my patients, Mrs Helmer. These last few days I've been going through the books of this poor body of mine, and I find I am bankrupt. Within a month I may be rotting up there in the churchyard.

NORA. Ugh, what a nasty way to talk!

RANK. The facts aren't exactly nice. But the worst is that there's so much else that's nasty that's got to come first. I've only one more test to make. When that's done I'll have a pretty accurate idea of when the final disintegration is likely to begin. I want to ask you a favour. Helmer's a sensitive chap, and I know how he hates anything ugly. I don't want him to visit me when I'm in hospital –

NORA. Oh but, Dr Rank –

RANK. I don't want him there. On any pretext. I shan't have him allowed in. As soon as I know the worst, I'll send you my visiting card with a black cross on it, and then you'll know that the final filthy process has begun.

NORA. Really, you're being quite impossible this evening. And I did hope you'd be in a good mood.

RANK. With death on my hands? And all this to atone for someone else's sin? Is there justice in that? And in every single family, in one way or another, the same merciless law of retribution is at work –

NORA (*holds her hands to her ears*). Nonsense! Cheer up! Laugh!

RANK. Yes, you're right. Laughter's all the damned thing's fit for. My poor innocent spine must pay for the fun my father had as a gay young lieutenant.

NORA (*at the table, left*). You mean he was too fond of asparagus and *foie gras*?

RANK. Yes; and truffles too.

NORA. Yes, of course, truffles, yes. And oysters too, I suppose?

RANK. Yes, oysters, oysters. Of course.

NORA. And all that port and champagne to wash them down. It's too sad that all those lovely things should affect one's spine.

RANK. Especially a poor spine that never got any pleasure out of them.

NORA. Oh yes, that's the saddest thing of all.

RANK (*looks searchingly at her*). Hm –

NORA (*after a moment*). Why did you smile?

RANK. No, it was you who laughed.

NORA. No, it was you who smiled, Dr Rank!

RANK (*gets up*). You're a worse little rogue than I thought.

NORA. Oh, I'm full of stupid tricks today.

RANK. So it seems.

NORA. (*puts both her hands on his shoulders*). Dear, dear Dr Rank, you mustn't die and leave Torvald and me.

RANK. Oh, you'll soon get over it. Once one is gone, one is soon forgotten.

NORA (*looks at him anxiously*). Do you believe that?

RANK. One finds replacements, and then –

NORA. Who will find a replacement?

RANK. You and Helmer both will, when I am gone. You seem to have made a start already, haven't you? What was this Mrs Linde doing here yesterday evening?

NORA. Aha! But surely you can't be jealous of poor Christine?

RANK. Indeed I am. She will be my successor in this house. When I have moved on, this lady will –

NORA. Ssh – don't speak so loud! She's in there!

RANK. Today again? You see!

NORA. She's only come to mend my dress. Good heavens, how unreasonable you are! (*Sits on the sofa.*) Be nice now, Dr Rank. Tomorrow you'll see how beautifully I shall dance; and you must imagine I'm doing it just for you. And for Torvald, of course – obviously. (*Takes some things out of the box.*) Dr Rank, sit down here and I'll show you something.

RANK (*sits*). What's this?

NORA. Look here! Look!

RANK. Silk stockings!

NORA. Flesh-coloured. Aren't they beautiful? It's very dark in here now, of course, but tomorrow – ! No, no, no – only the soles. Oh well, I suppose you can look a bit higher if you want to.

RANK. Hm –

NORA. Why are you looking so critical? Don't you think they'll fit me?

RANK. I can't really give you a qualified opinion on that.

NORA (*looks at him for a moment*). Shame on you! (*Flicks him on the ear with the stockings.*) Take that. (*Puts them back in the box.*)

RANK. What other wonders are to be revealed to me?

NORA. I shan't show you anything else. You're being naughty.

She hums a little and looks among the things in the box.

RANK (*after a short silence*). When I sit here like this being so intimate with you, I can't think – I cannot imagine what would have become of me if I had never entered this house.

NORA (*smiles*). Yes, I think you enjoy being with us, don't you?

RANK (*more quietly, looking into the middle distance*). And now to have to leave it all –

NORA. Nonsense. You're not leaving us.

RANK (*as before*). And not to be able to leave even the most wretched token of gratitude behind; hardly even a passing sense of loss; only an empty space, to be filled by the next comer.

NORA. Suppose I were to ask you to – ? No –

RANK. To do what?

NORA. To give me proof of your friendship –

RANK. Yes, yes?

NORA. No, I mean – to do me a very great service –

RANK. Would you really for once grant me that happiness?

NORA. But you've no idea what it is.

RANK. Very well, tell me, then.

NORA. No, but, Dr Rank, I can't. It's far too much – I want your help and advice, and I want you to do something for me.

RANK. The more the better. I've no idea what it can be. But tell me. You do trust me, don't you?

NORA. Oh, yes, more than anyone. You're my best and truest friend. Otherwise I couldn't tell you. Well then, Dr Rank, there's something you must help me to prevent. You know how much Torvald loves me - he'd never hesitate for an instant to lay down his life for me -

RANK (*leans over towards her*). Nora - do you think he is the only one - ?

NORA (*with a slight start*). What do you mean?

RANK. Who would gladly lay down his life for you?

NORA (*sadly*). Oh, I see.

RANK. I swore to myself I would let you know that before I go. I shall never have a better opportunity. . . . Well, Nora, now you know that. And now you also know that you can trust me as you can trust nobody else.

NORA (*rises ; calmly and quietly*). Let me pass, please

RANK (*makes room for her but remains seated*). Nora -

NORA (*in the doorway to the hall*). Helen, bring the lamp. (*Goes over to the stove.*) Oh, dear, Dr Rank, this was really horrid of you.

RANK (*gets up*). That I have loved you as deeply as anyone else has? Was that horrid of me?

NORA. No - but that you should go and tell me. That was quite unnecessary -

RANK. What do you mean? Did you know, then - ?

The MAID *enters with the lamp, puts it on the table and goes out.*

RANK. Nora - Mrs Helmer! I am asking you, did you know this?

NORA. Oh, what do I know, what did I know, what didn't I know - ? I really can't say. How could you be so stupid, Dr Rank? Everything was so nice.

RANK. Well, at any rate, now you know that I am ready to serve you, body and soul. So - please continue.

NORA (*looks at him*). After this?

RANK. Please tell me what it is.

NORA. I can't possibly tell you now.

RANK. Yes, yes! You mustn't punish me like this. Let me be allowed to do what I can for you.

NORA. You can't do anything for me now. Anyway, I don't need any help. It was only my imagination – you'll see. Yes, really. Honestly. (*Sits in the rocking-chair, looks at him and smiles.*) Well, upon my word you *are* a fine gentleman, Dr Rank. Aren't you ashamed of yourself, now that the lamp's been lit?

RANK. Frankly, no. But perhaps I ought to say – *adieu?*

NORA. Of course not. You will naturally continue to visit us as before. You know quite well how Torvald depends on your company.

RANK. Yes, but you?

NORA. Oh, I always think it's enormous fun having you here.

RANK. That was what misled me. You're a riddle to me, you know. I'd often felt you'd just as soon be with me as with Helmer.

NORA. Well, you see, there are some people whom one loves, and others whom it's almost more fun to be with.

RANK. Oh, yes, there's some truth in that.

NORA. When I was at home, of course, I loved papa best. But I always used to think it was terribly amusing to go down and talk to the servants; because they never told me what I ought to do; and they were such fun to listen to.

RANK. I see. So I've taken their place?

NORA (*jumps up and runs over to him*). Oh, dear, sweet Dr Rank, I didn't mean that at all. But I'm sure you understand – I feel the same about Torvald as I did about papa.

MAID (*enters from the hall*). Excuse me, madam. (*Whispers to her and hands her a visiting card.*)

NORA (*glances at the card*). Oh! (*Puts it quickly in her pocket.*)

RANK. Anything wrong?

NORA. No, no, nothing at all. It's just something that – it's my new dress.

RANK. What? But your costume is lying over there.

NORA. Oh – that, yes – but there's another – I ordered it specially – Torvald mustn't know –

RANK. Ah, so that's your big secret?

NORA. Yes, yes. Go in and talk to him – he's in his study – keep him talking for a bit –

RANK. Don't worry. He won't get away from me. (*Goes into* HELMER's *study*.)

NORA (*to the* MAID). Is he waiting in the kitchen?

MAID. Yes, madam, he came up the back way –

NORA. But didn't you tell him I had a visitor?

MAID. Yes, but he wouldn't go.

NORA. Wouldn't go?

MAID. No, madam, not until he's spoken with you.

NORA. Very well, show him in. But quietly. Helen, you mustn't tell anyone about this. It's a surprise for my husband.

MAID. Very good, madam. I understand. (*Goes*.)

NORA. It's happening. It's happening after all. No, no, no, it can't happen, it mustn't happen.

> *She walks across and bolts the door of* HELMER's *study. The* MAID *opens the door from the hall to admit* KROGSTAD, *and closes it behind him. He is wearing an overcoat, heavy boots and a fur cap.*

NORA (*goes towards him*). Speak quietly. My husband's at home.

KROGSTAD. Let him hear.

NORA. What do you want from me?

KROGSTAD. Information.

NORA. Hurry up, then. What is it?

KROGSTAD. I suppose you know I've been given the sack.

NORA. I couldn't stop it, Mr Krogstad. I did my best for you, but it didn't help.

KROGSTAD. Does your husband love you so little? He knows what I can do to you, and yet he dares to –

NORA. Surely you don't imagine I told him?

KROGSTAD. No, I didn't really think you had. It wouldn't have

been like my old friend Torvald Helmer to show that much
courage —

NORA. Mr Krogstad, I'll trouble you to speak respectfully of
my husband.

KROGSTAD. Don't worry, I'll show him all the respect he
deserves. But since you're so anxious to keep this matter
hushed up, I presume you're better informed than you were
yesterday of the gravity of what you've done?

NORA. I've learned more than you could ever teach me.

KROGSTAD. Yes, a bad lawyer like me —

NORA. What do you want from me?

KROGSTAD. I just wanted to see how things were with you, Mrs
Helmer. I've been thinking about you all day. Even duns and
hack journalists have hearts, you know.

NORA. Show some heart, then. Think of my little children.

KROGSTAD. Have you and your husband thought of mine? Well,
let's forget that. I just wanted to tell you, you don't need to take
this business too seriously. I'm not going to take any action, for
the present.

NORA. Oh, no – you won't will you? I knew it.

KROGSTAD. It can all be settled quite amicably. There's no need
for it to become public. We'll keep it among the three of us.

NORA. My husband must never know about this.

KROGSTAD. How can you stop him? Can you pay the balance of
what you owe me?

NORA. Not immediately.

KROGSTAD. Have you any means of raising the money during the
next few days?

NORA. None that I would care to use.

KROGSTAD. Well, it wouldn't have helped anyway. However
much money you offered me now I wouldn't give you back
that paper.

NORA. What are you going to do with it?

KROGSTAD. Just keep it. No one else need ever hear about it.
So in case you were thinking of doing anything desperate —

NORA. I am.

KROGSTAD. Such as running away –

NORA. I am.

KROGSTAD. Or anything more desperate –

NORA. How did you know?

KROGSTAD. – just give up the idea.

NORA. How did you know?

KROGSTAD. Most of us think of that at first. I did. But I hadn't the courage –

NORA (*dully*). Neither have I.

KROGSTAD (*relieved*). It's true, isn't it? You haven't the courage, either?

NORA. No. I haven't. I haven't.

KROGSTAD. It'd be a stupid thing to do anyway. Once the first little domestic explosion is over . . . I've got a letter in my pocket here addressed to your husband –

NORA. Telling him everything?

KROGSTAD. As delicately as possible.

NORA (*quickly*). He must never see that letter. Tear it up. I'll find the money somehow –

KROGSTAD. I'm sorry, Mrs Helmer, I thought I'd explained –

NORA. Oh, I don't mean the money I owe you. Let me know how much you want from my husband, and I'll find it for you.

KROGSTAD. I'm not asking your husband for money.

NORA. What do you want, then?

KROGSTAD. I'll tell you. I want to get on my feet again, Mrs Helmer. I want to get to the top. And your husband's going to help me. For eighteen months now my record's been clean. I've been in hard straits all that time: I was content to fight my way back inch by inch. Now I've been chucked back into the mud, and I'm not going to be satisfied with just getting back my job. I'm going to get to the top, I tell you. I'm going to get back into the bank, and it's going to be higher up. Your husband's going to create a new job for me –

NORA. He'll never do that!

KROGSTAD. Oh yes, he will. I know him. He won't dare to risk a scandal. And once I'm in there with him, you'll see! Within a year I'll be his right-hand man. It'll be Nils Krogstad who'll be running that bank, not Torvald Helmer!

NORA. That will never happen.

KROGSTAD. Are you thinking of – ?

NORA. Now I *have* the courage.

KROGSTAD. Oh, you can't frighten me. A pampered little pretty like you –

NORA. You'll see! You'll see!

KROGSTAD. Under the ice? Down in the cold, black water? And then, in the spring, to float up again, ugly, unrecognizable, hairless – ?

NORA. You can't frighten me.

KROGSTAD. And you can't frighten me. People don't do such things, Mrs Helmer. And anyway, what'd be the use? I've got him in my pocket.

NORA. But afterwards? When I'm no longer – ?

KROGSTAD. Have you forgotten that then your reputation will be in my hands?

She looks at him speechlessly.

KROGSTAD. Well, I've warned you. Don't do anything silly. When Helmer's read my letter, he'll get in touch with me. And remember, it's your husband who has forced me to act like this. And for that I'll never forgive him. Goodbye, Mrs Helmer. (*He goes out through the hall.*)

NORA (*runs to the hall door, opens it a few inches and listens*). He's going. He's not going to give him the letter. Oh, no, no, it couldn't possibly happen. (*Opens the door, a little wider.*) What's he doing? Standing outside the front door. He's not going downstairs. Is he changing his mind? Yes, he – !

A letter falls into the letter-box. KROGSTAD's *footsteps die away down the stairs.*

NORA (*with a stifled cry, runs across the room towards the table by the sofa. A pause*). In the letter-box. (*Steals timidly over towards the hall door.*) There it is! Oh, Torvald, Torvald! Now we're lost!

MRS LINDE (*enters from the nursery with* NORA'*s costume*). Well, I've done the best I can. Shall we see how it looks – ?

NORA (*whispers hoarsely*). Christine, come here.

MRS LINDE (*throws the dress on the sofa*). What's wrong with you? You look as though you'd seen a ghost!

NORA. Come here. Do you see that letter? There – look – through the glass of the letter-box.

MRS LINDE. Yes, yes, I see it.

NORA. That letter's from Krogstad –

MRS LINDE. Nora! It was Krogstad who lent you the money!

NORA. Yes. And now Torvald's going to discover everything.

MRS LINDE. Oh, believe me, Nora, it'll be best for you both.

NORA. You don't know what's happened. I've committed a forgery –

MRS LINDE. But, for heaven's sake – !

NORA. Christine, all I want is for you to be my witness.

MRS LINDE. What do you mean? Witness what?

NORA. If I should go out of my mind – and it might easily happen –

MRS LINDE. Nora!

NORA. Or if anything else should happen to me – so that I wasn't here any longer –

MRS LINDE. Nora, Nora, you don't know what you're saying!

NORA. If anyone should try to take the blame, and say it was all his fault – you understand – ?

MRS LINDE. Yes, yes – but how can you think – ?

NORA. Then you must testify that it isn't true, Christine. I'm not mad – I know exactly what I'm saying – and I'm telling you, no one else knows anything about this. I did it entirely on my own. Remember that.

MRS LINDE. All right. But I simply don't understand –

NORA. Oh, how could you understand? A – miracle – is about to happen.

MRS LINDE. Miracle?

NORA. Yes. A miracle. But it's so frightening, Christine. It mustn't happen, not for anything in the world.

MRS LINDE. I'll go over and talk to Krogstad.

NORA. Don't go near him. He'll only do something to hurt you.

MRS LINDE. Once upon a time he'd have done anything for my sake.

NORA. He?

MRS LINDE. Where does he live?

NORA. Oh, how should I know – ? Oh yes, wait a moment – ! (*Feels in her pocket.*) Here's his card. But the letter, the letter – !

HELMER (*from his study, knocks on the door*). Nora!

NORA (*cries in alarm*). What is it?

HELMER. Now, now, don't get alarmed. We're not coming in – you've closed the door. Are you trying on your costume?

NORA. Yes, yes – I'm trying on my costume. I'm going to look so pretty for you, Torvald.

MRS LINDE (*who has been reading the card*). Why, he lives just round the corner.

NORA. Yes; but it's no use. There's nothing to be done now. The letter's lying there in the box.

MRS LINDE. And your husband has the key?

NORA. Yes, he always keeps it.

MRS LINDE. Krogstad must ask him to send the letter back unread. He must find some excuse –

NORA. But Torvald always opens the box at just about this time –

MRS LINDE. You must stop him. Go in and keep him talking. I'll be back as quickly as I can.

She hurries out through the hall.

NORA (*goes over to* HELMER's *door, opens it and peeps in*). Torvald!

HELMER (*offstage*). Well, may a man enter his own drawing-room again? Come on, Rank, now we'll see what – (*In the doorway.*) But what's this?

NORA. What, Torvald dear?

HELMER. Rank's been preparing me for some great transformation scene.

RANK (*in the doorway*). So I understood. But I seem to have been mistaken.

NORA. Yes, no one's to be allowed to see me before tomorrow night.

HELMER. But, my dear Nora, you look quite worn out. Have you been practising too hard?

NORA. No, I haven't practised at all yet.

HELMER. Well, you must.

NORA. Yes. Torvald. I must, I know. But I can't get anywhere without your help. I've completely forgotten everything.

HELMER. Oh. we'll soon put that to rights.

NORA. Yes, help me, Torvald. Promise me you will? Oh, I'm so nervous. All those people – ! You must forget everything except me this evening. You mustn't think of business – I won't even let you touch a pen. Promise me, Torvald?

HELMER. I promise. This evening I shall think of nothing but you – my poor, helpless little darling. Oh, there's just one thing I must see to – (*Goes towards the hall door.*)

NORA. What do you want out there?

HELMER. I'm only going to see if any letters have come.

NORA. No, Torvald, no!

HELMER. Why what's the matter?

NORA. Torvald, I beg you. There's nothing there.

HELMER. Well, I'll just make sure.

He moves towards the door. NORA *runs to the piano and plays the first bars of the* Tarantella.

HELMER (*at the door, turns*). Aha!

NORA. I can't dance tomorrow if I don't practise with you now.

HELMER (*goes over to her*). Are you really so frightened, Nora dear?

NORA. Yes. terribly frightened. Let me start practising now, at once – we've still time before dinner. Oh, do sit down and play for me, Torvald dear. Correct me, lead me, the way you always do.

HELMER. Very well, my dear, if you wish it.

He sits down at the piano. NORA *seizes the tambourine and a long multi-coloured shawl from the cardboard box, wraps the shawl hastily around her, then takes a quick leap into the centre of the room and cries.*

NORA. Play for me! I want to dance!

HELMER *plays and* NORA *dances.* DR RANK *stands behind* HELMER *at the piano and watches her.*

HELMER (*as he plays*). Slower, slower!

NORA. I can't!

HELMER. Not so violently, Nora.

NORA. I must!

HELMER (*stops playing*). No, no, this won't do at all.

NORA (*laughs and swings her tambourine*). Isn't that what I told you?

RANK. Let me play for her.

HELMER (*gets up*). Yes, would you? Then it'll be easier for me to show her.

RANK *sits down at the piano and plays.* NORA *dances more and more wildly.* HELMER *has stationed himself by the stove and tries repeatedly to correct her, but she seems not to hear him. Her hair works loose and falls over her shoulders; she ignores it and continues to dance.* MRS LINDE *enters.*

MRS LINDE (*stands in the doorway as though tongue-tied*). Ah – !

NORA (*as she dances*). Oh, Christine, we're having such fun!

HELMER. But, Nora darling, you're dancing as if your life depended on it.

NORA. It does.

HELMER. Rank, stop it! This is sheer lunacy. Stop it, I say!

RANK *ceases playing.* NORA *suddenly stops dancing.*

HELMER (*goes over to her*). I'd never have believed it. You've forgotten everything I taught you.

NORA (*throws away the tambourine*). You see!

HELMER. I'll have to show you every step.

NORA. You see how much I need you! You must show me every step of the way. Right to the end of the dance. Promise me you will, Torvald?

HELMER. Never fear. I will.

NORA. You mustn't think about anything but me – today or tomorrow. Don't open any letters – don't even open the letter-box –

HELMER. Aha, you're still worried about that fellow –

NORA. Oh, yes, yes, him too.

HELMER. Nora, I can tell from the way you're behaving, there's a letter from him already lying there.

NORA. I don't know. I think so. But you mustn't read it now. I don't want anything ugly to come between us till it's all over.

RANK (*quietly to* HELMER). Better give her her way.

HELMER (*puts his arm round her*). My child shall have her way. But tomorrow night, when your dance is over –

NORA. Then you will be free.

MAID (*appears in the doorway, right*). Dinner is served, madam.

NORA. Put out some champagne, Helen.

MAID. Very good, madam. (*Goes.*)

HELMER. I say! What's this, a banquet?

NORA. We'll drink champagne until dawn! (*Calls.*) And, Helen! Put out some macaroons! Lots of macaroons – for once!

HELMER (*takes her hands in his*). Now, now, now. Don't get so excited. Where's my little songbird, the one I know?

NORA. All right. Go and sit down – and you, too, Dr Rank. I'll be with you in a minute. Christine, you must help me put my hair up.

RANK (*quietly, as they go*). There's nothing wrong, is there? I mean, she isn't – er – expecting – ?

HELMER. Good heavens no, my dear chap. She just gets scared like a child sometimes – I told you before –

    They go out, right.

NORA. Well?

MRS LINDE. He's left town.

NORA. I saw it from your face.

MRS LINDE. He'll be back tomorrow evening. I left a note for him.

NORA. You needn't have bothered. You can't stop anything now. Anyway, it's wonderful really, in a way – sitting here and waiting for the miracle to happen.

MRS LINDE. Waiting for what?

NORA. Oh, you wouldn't understand. Go in and join them. I'll be with you in a moment.

    MRS LINDE *goes into the dining-room.*

NORA (*stands for a moment as though collecting herself. Then she looks at her watch*). Five o'clock. Seven hours till midnight. Then another twenty-four hours till midnight tomorrow. And then the tarantella will be finished. Twenty-four and seven? Thirty-one hours to live.

HELMER (*appears in the doorway, right*). What's happened to my little songbird?

NORA (*runs to him with her arms wide*). Your songbird is here!

ACT THREE

The same room. The table which was formerly by the sofa has been moved into the centre of the room; the chairs surround it as before. A lamp is burning on the table. The door to the hall stands open. Dance music can be heard from the floor above. MRS LINDE is seated at the table, absent-mindedly glancing through a book. She is trying to read, but seems unable to keep her mind on it. More than once she turns and listens anxiously towards the front door.

MRS LINDE (*looks at her watch*). Not here yet. There's not much time left. Please God he hasn't – ! (*Listens again.*) Ah, here he is.

    Goes out into the hall and cautiously opens the front door. Footsteps can be heard softly ascending the stairs.

MRS LINDE (*whispers*). Come in. There's no one here.

KROGSTAD (*in the doorway*). I found a note from you at my lodgings. What does this mean?

MRS LINDE. I must speak with you.

KROGSTAD. Oh? And must our conversation take place in this house?

MRS LINDE. We couldn't meet at my place; my room has no separate entrance. Come in. We're quite alone. The maid's asleep, and the Helmers are at the dance upstairs.

KROGSTAD (*comes into the room*). Well, well! So the Helmers are dancing this evening? Are they indeed?

MRS LINDE. Yes, why not?

KROGSTAD. True enough. Why not?

MRS LINDE. Well, Krogstad. You and I must have a talk together.

KROGSTAD. Have we two anything further to discuss?

MRS LINDE. We have a great deal to discuss.

KROGSTAD. I wasn't aware of it.

MRS LINDE. That's because you've never really understood me.

KROGSTAD. Was there anything to understand? It's the old story, isn't it – a woman chucking a man because something better turns up?

MRS LINDE. Do you really think I'm so utterly heartless? You think it was easy for me to give you up?

KROGSTAD. Wasn't it?

MRS LINDE. Oh, Nils, did you really believe that?

KROGSTAD. Then why did you write to me the way you did?

MRS LINDE. I had to. Since I had to break with you, I thought it my duty to destroy all the feelings you had for me.

KROGSTAD (*clenches his fists*). So that was it. And you did this for money!

MRS LINDE. You mustn't forget I had a helpless mother to take care of, and two little brothers. We couldn't wait for you, Nils. It would have been so long before you'd have had enough to support us.

KROGSTAD. Maybe. But you had no right to cast me off for someone else.

MRS LINDE. Perhaps not. I've often asked myself that.

KROGSTAD (*more quietly*). When I lost you, it was just as though all solid ground had been swept from under my feet. Look at me. Now I'm a shipwrecked man, clinging to a spar.

MRS LINDE. Help may be near at hand.

KROGSTAD. It was near. But then you came, and stood between it and me.

MRS LINDE. I didn't know, Nils. No one told me till today that this job I'd found was yours.

KROGSTAD. I believe you, since you say so. But now you know, won't you give it up?

MRS LINDE. No – because it wouldn't help you even if I did.

KROGSTAD. Wouldn't it? I'd do it all the same.

MRS LINDE. I've learned to look at things practically. Life and poverty have taught me that.

KROGSTAD. And life has taught me to distrust fine words.

MRS LINDE. Then it has taught you a useful lesson. But surely you still believe in actions?

KROGSTAD. What do you mean?

MRS LINDE. You said you were like a shipwrecked man clinging to a spar.

KROGSTAD. I have good reason to say it.

MRS LINDE. I'm in the same position as you. No one to care about, no one to care for.

KROGSTAD. You made your own choice.

MRS LINDE. I had no choice – then.

KROGSTAD. Well?

MRS LINDE. Nils, suppose we two shipwrecked souls could join hands?

KROGSTAD. What are you saying?

MRS LINDE. Castaways have a better chance of survival together than on their own.

KROGSTAD. Christine!

MRS LINDE. Why do you suppose I came to this town?

KROGSTAD. You mean – you came because of me?

MRS LINDE. I must work if I'm to find life worth living. I've always worked, for as long as I can remember. It's been the greatest joy of my life – my only joy. But now I'm alone in the world, and I feel so dreadfully lost and empty. There's no joy in working just for oneself. Oh, Nils, give me something – someone – to work for.

KROGSTAD. I don't believe all that. You're just being hysterical and romantic. You want to find an excuse for self-sacrifice.

MRS LINDE. Have you ever known me to be hysterical?

KROGSTAD. You mean you really – ? Is it possible? Tell me – you know all about my past?

MRS LINDE. Yes.

KROGSTAD. And you know what people think of me here?

MRS LINDE. You said just now that with me you might have become a different person.

KROGSTAD. I know I could have.

MRS LINDE. Couldn't it still happen?

KROGSTAD. Christine – do you really mean this? Yes – you do – I see it in your face. Have you really the courage – ?

MRS LINDE. I need someone to be a mother to; and your children need a mother. And you and I need each other. I believe in you, Nils. I am afraid of nothing – with you.

KROGSTAD (*clasps her hands*). Thank you, Christine – thank you! Now I shall make the world believe in me as you do! Oh – but I'd forgotten –

MRS LINDE (*listens*). Ssh! The tarantella! Go quickly, go!

KROGSTAD. Why? What is it?

MRS LINDE. You hear that dance? As soon as it's finished, they'll be coming down.

KROGSTAD. All right, I'll go. It's no good, Christine. I'd forgotten – you don't know what I've just done to the Helmers.

MRS LINDE. Yes, Nils. I know.

KROGSTAD. And yet you'd still have the courage to – ?

MRS LINDE. I know what despair can drive a man like you to.

KROGSTAD. Oh, if only I could undo this!

MRS LINDE. You can. Your letter is still lying in the box.

KROGSTAD. Are you sure?

MRS LINDE. Quite sure. But –

KROGSTAD (*looks searchingly at her*). Is that why you're doing this? You want to save your friend at any price? Tell me the truth. Is that the reason?

MRS LINDE. Nils, a woman who has sold herself once for the sake of others doesn't make the same mistake again.

KROGSTAD. I shall demand my letter back.

MRS LINDE. No, no.

KROGSTAD. Of course I shall. I shall stay here till Helmer comes down. I'll tell him he must give me back my letter – I'll say it was only to do with my dismissal, and that I don't want him to read it –

MRS LINDE. No, Nils, you mustn't ask for that letter back.

KROGSTAD. But – tell me – wasn't that the real reason you asked me to come here?

MRS LINDE. Yes – at first, when I was frightened. But a day has passed since then, and in that time I've seen incredible things happen in this house. Helmer must know the truth. This unhappy secret of Nora's must be revealed. They must come to a full understanding. There must be an end of all these shiftings and evasions.

KROGSTAD. Very well. If you're prepared to risk it. But one thing I can do – and at once –

MRS LINDE (*listens*). Hurry! Go, go! The dance is over. We aren't safe here another moment.

KROGSTAD. I'll wait for you downstairs.

MRS LINDE. Yes, do. You can see me home.

KROGSTAD. I've never been so happy in my life before!

He goes out through the front door. The door leading from the room into the hall remains open.

MRS LINDE (*tidies the room a little and gets her hat and coat*). What a change! Oh, what a change! Someone to work for – to live for! A home to bring joy into! I won't let this chance of happiness slip through my fingers. Oh, why don't they come? (*Listens.*) Ah, here they are. I must get my coat on.

She takes her hat and coat. HELMER's *and* NORA's *voices become audible outside. A key is turned in the lock and* HELMER *leads* NORA *almost forcibly into the hall. She is dressed in an Italian costume with a large black shawl. He is in evening dress, with a black coat.*

NORA (*still in the doorway, resisting him*). No, no, no – not in here! I want to go back upstairs. I don't want to leave so early.

HELMER. But my dearest Nora –

NORA. Oh, please, Torvald, please! Just another hour!

HELMER. Not another minute, Nora, my sweet. You know what we agreed. Come along, now. Into the drawing-room. You'll catch cold if you stay out here.

He leads her, despite her efforts to resist him, gently into the room.

MRS LINDE. Good evening.

NORA. Christine!

HELMER. Oh, hullo, Mrs Linde. You still here?

MRS LINDE. Please forgive me. I did so want to see Nora in her costume.

NORA. Have you been sitting here waiting for me?

MRS LINDE. Yes. I got here too late, I'm afraid. You'd already gone up. And I felt I really couldn't go home without seeing you.

HELMER (*takes off Nora's shawl*). Well, take a good look at her. She's worth looking at, don't you think? Isn't she beautiful, Mrs Linde?

MRS LINDE. Oh, yes, indeed –

HELMER. Isn't she unbelievably beautiful? Everyone at the party said so. But dreadfully stubborn she is, bless her pretty little heart. What's to be done about that? Would you believe it, I practically had to use force to get her away!

NORA. Oh, Torvald, you're going to regret not letting me stay – just half an hour longer.

HELMER. Hear that, Mrs Linde? She dances her tarantella – makes a roaring success – and very well deserved – though possibly a trifle too realistic – more so than was aesthetically necessary, strictly speaking. But never mind that. Main thing is – she had a success – roaring success. Was I going to let her stay on after that and spoil the impression? No, thank you! I took my beautiful little Capri signorina – my capricious little Capricienne, what? – under my arm – a swift round of the ballroom, a curtsy to the company, and, as they say in novels, the beautiful apparition disappeared! An exit should always be dramatic, Mrs Linde. But unfortunately that's just what I can't get Nora to realize. I say, it's hot in here. (*Throws his cloak on a chair and opens the door to his study.*) What's this? It's dark in here. Ah, yes, of course – excuse me. (*Goes in and lights a couple of candles.*)

NORA (*whispers softly, breathlessly*). Well?

MRS LINDE (*quietly*). I've spoken to him.

NORA. Yes?

MRS LINDE. Nora – you must tell your husband everything.

NORA (*dully*). I knew it.

MRS LINDE. You have nothing to fear from Krogstad. But you must tell him.

NORA. I shan't tell him anything.

MRS LINDE. Then the letter will.

NORA. Thank you, Christine. Now I know what I must do. Ssh!

HELMER (*returns*). Well, Mrs Linde, finished admiring her?

MRS LINDE. Yes. Now I must say good night.

HELMER. Oh, already? Does this knitting belong to you?

MRS LINDE (*takes it*). Thank you, yes. I nearly forgot it.

HELMER. You knit, then?

MRS LINDE. Why, yes.

HELMER. Know what? You ought to take up embroidery.

MRS LINDE. Oh? Why?

HELMER. It's much prettier. Watch me, now. You hold the embroidery in your left hand, like this, and then you take the needle in your right hand and go in and out in a slow, easy movement – like this. I am right, aren't I?

MRS LINDE. Yes, I'm sure –

HELMER. But knitting, now – that's an ugly business – can't help it. Look – arms all huddled up – great clumsy needles going up and down – makes you look like a damned Chinaman. I say that really was a magnificent champagne they served us.

MRS LINDE. Well, good night, Nora. And stop being stubborn! Remember!

HELMER. Quite right, Mrs Linde!

MRS LINDE. Good night, Mr Helmer.

HELMER (*accompanies her to the door*). Good night, good night!

I hope you'll manage to get home all right? I'd gladly – but you haven't far to go, have you? Good night, good night.

She goes. He closes the door behind her and returns.

HELMER. Well, we've got rid of her at last. Dreadful bore that woman is!

NORA. Aren't you very tired, Torvald?

HELMER. No, not in the least.

NORA. Aren't you sleepy?

HELMER. Not a bit. On the contrary, I feel extraordinary exhilarated. But what about you? Yes, you look very sleepy and tired.

NORA. Yes, I am very tired. Soon I shall sleep.

HELMER. You see, you see! How right I was not to let you stay longer!

NORA. Oh, you're always right, whatever you do.

HELMER (*kisses her on the forehead*). Now my little songbird's talking just like a real big human being. I say, did you notice how cheerful Rank was this evening?

NORA. Oh? Was he? I didn't have a chance to speak with him.

HELMER. I hardly did. But I haven't seen him in such a jolly mood for ages. (*Looks at her for a moment, then comes closer.*) I say, it's nice to get back to one's home again, and be all alone with you. Upon my word, you're a distractingly beautiful young woman.

NORA. Don't look at me like that, Torvald!

HELMER. What, not look at my most treasured possession? At all this wonderful beauty that's mine, mine alone, all mine.

NORA (*goes round to the other side of the table*). You mustn't talk to me like that tonight.

HELMER (*follows her*). You've still the tarantella in your blood, I see. And that makes you even more desirable. Listen! Now the other guests are beginning to go. (*More quietly.*) Nora – soon the whole house will be absolutely quiet.

NORA. Yes, I hope so.

HELMER. Yes, my beloved Nora, of course you do! You know – when I'm out with you among other people like we were tonight, do you know why I say so little to you, why I keep so aloof from you, and just throw you an occasional glance? Do you know why I do that? It's because I pretend to myself that you're my secret mistress, my clandestine little sweetheart, and that nobody knows there's anything at all between us.

NORA. Oh, yes, yes, yes – I know you never think of anything but me.

HELMER. And then when we're about to go, and I wrap the shawl round your lovely young shoulders, over this wonderful curve of your neck – then I pretend to myself that you are my young bride, that we've just come from the wedding, that I'm taking you to my house for the first time – that, for the first time, I am alone with you – quite alone with you, as you stand there young and trembling and beautiful. All evening I've had no eyes for anyone but you. When I saw you dance the tarantella, like a huntress, a temptress, my blood grew hot, I couldn't stand it any longer! That was why I seized you and dragged you down here with me –

NORA. Leave me, Torvald! Get away from me! I don't want all this.

HELMER. What? Now, Nora, you're joking with me. Don't want, don't want – ? Aren't I your husband?

There is a knock on the front door.

NORA (*starts*). What was that?

HELMER (*goes towards the hall*). Who is it?

DR RANK (*outside*). It's me. May I come in for a moment?

HELMER (*quietly, annoyed*). Oh, what does he want now? (*Calls.*) Wait a moment. (*Walks over and opens the door.*) Well! Nice of you not to go by without looking in.

RANK. I thought I heard your voice, so I felt I had to say goodbye. (*His eyes travel swiftly around the room.*) Ah, yes – these dear rooms, how well I know them. What a happy, peaceful home you two have.

HELMER. You seemed to be having a pretty happy time yourself upstairs.

RANK. Indeed I did. Why not? Why shouldn't one make the most of this world? As much as one can, and for as long as one can. The wine was excellent –

HELMER. Especially the champagne.

RANK. You noticed that too? It's almost incredible how much I managed to get down.

NORA. Torvald drank a lot of champagne too, this evening.

RANK. Oh?

NORA. Yes. It always makes him merry afterwards.

RANK. Well, why shouldn't a man have a merry evening after a well-spent day?

HELMER. Well-spent? Oh, I don't know that I can claim that.

RANK (*slaps him across the back*). I can, though, my dear fellow!

NORA. Yes, of course, Dr Rank – you've been carrying out a scientific experiment today, haven't you?

RANK. Exactly.

HELMER. Scientific experiment! Those are big words for my little Nora to use!

NORA. And may I congratulate you on the finding?

RANK. You may indeed.

NORA. It was good then?

RANK. The best possible finding – both for the doctor and the patient. Certainty.

NORA (*quickly*). Certainty?

RANK. Absolute certainty. So aren't I entitled to have a merry evening after that?

NORA. Yes, Dr Rank. You were quite right to.

HELMER. I agree. Provided you don't have to regret it tomorrow.

RANK. Well, you never get anything in this life without paying for it.

NORA. Dr Rank – you like masquerades, don't you?

RANK. Yes, if the disguises are sufficiently amusing.

NORA. Tell me. What shall we two wear at the next masquerade?

HELMER. You little gadabout! Are you thinking about the next one already?

RANK. We two? Yes, I'll tell you. You must go as the Spirit of
  Happiness –

HELMER. You try to think of a costume that'll convey that.

RANK. Your wife need only appear as her normal, everyday self –

HELMER. Quite right! Well said! But what are you going to be?
  Have you decided that?

RANK. Yes, my dear friend. I have decided that.

HELMER. Well?

RANK. At the next masquerade, I shall be invisible.

HELMER. Well, that's a funny idea.

RANK. There's a big, black hat – haven't you heard of the
  invisible hat? Once it's over your head, no one can see you any
  more.

HELMER (*represses a smile*). Ah yes, of course.

RANK. But I'm forgetting what I came for. Helmer, give me a
  cigar. One of your black Havanas.

HELMER. With the greatest pleasure. (*Offers him the box.*)

RANK (*takes one and cuts off the tip*). Thank you.

NORA (*strikes a match*). Let me give you a light.

RANK. Thank you. (*She holds out the match for him. He lights his
  cigar.*) And now – goodbye.

HELMER. Goodbye, my dear chap, goodbye.

NORA. Sleep well, Dr Rank.

RANK. Thank you for that kind wish.

NORA. Wish me the same.

RANK. You? Very well – since you ask. Sleep well. And thank
  you for the light. (*He nods to them both and goes.*)

HELMER (*quietly*). He's been drinking too much.

NORA (*abstractedly*). Perhaps.

  HELMER *takes his bunch of keys from his pocket and goes out
  into the hall.*

NORA. Torvald, what do you want out there?

HELMER. I must empty the letter-box. It's absolutely full.
  There'll be no room for the newspapers in the morning.

NORA. Are you going to work tonight?

HELMER. You know very well I'm not. Hullo, what's this? Someone's been at the lock.

NORA. At the lock –

HELMER. Yes, I'm sure of it. Who on earth – ? Surely not one of the maids? Here's a broken hairpin. Nora, it's yours –

NORA (*quickly*). Then it must have been the children.

HELMER. Well, you'll have to break them of that habit. Hm, hm. Ah, that's done it. (*Takes out the contents of the box and calls into the kitchen.*) Helen! Helen! Put out the light on the staircase. (*Comes back into the drawing-room and closes the door to the hall.*)

HELMER (*with the letters in his hand*). Look at this! You see how they've piled up? (*Glances through them.*) What on earth's this?

NORA (*at the window*). The letter! Oh no, Torvald, no!

HELMER. Two visiting cards – from Rank.

NORA. From Dr Rank?

HELMER (*looks at them*). Peter Rank, M.D. They were on top. He must have dropped them in as he left.

NORA. Has he written anything on them?

HELMER. There's a black cross above his name. Rather gruesome, isn't it? It looks just as thought he was announcing his death.

NORA. He is.

HELMER. What? Do you know something? Has he told you anything?

NORA. Yes. When these cards come, it means he's said goodbye to us. He wants to shut himself up in his house and die.

HELMER. Ah, poor fellow. I knew I wouldn't be seeing him for much longer. But so soon – ! And now he's going to slink away and hide like a wounded beast.

NORA. When the time comes, it's best to go silently. Don't you think so, Torvald?

HELMER (*walks up and down*). He was so much a part of our life. I can't realize that he's gone. His suffering and loneliness seemed to provide a kind of dark background to the happy sunlight of our marriage. Well, perhaps it's best this way. For him, anyway. (*Stops walking.*) And perhaps for us too, Nora.

Now we have only each other. (*Embraces her.*) Oh, my beloved wife – I feel as though I could never hold you close enough. Do you know, Nora, often I wish some terrible danger might threaten you, so that I could offer my life and my blood, everything, for your sake.

NORA (*tears herself loose and says in a clear, firm voice*). Read your letters now, Torvald.

HELMER. No, no. Not tonight. Tonight I want to be with you, my darling wife –

NORA. When your friend is about to die – ?

HELMER. You're right. This news has upset us both. An ugliness has come between us; thoughts of death and dissolution. We must try to forget them. Until then – you go to your room; I shall go to mine.

NORA (*throws her arms round his neck*). Good night, Torvald! Good night!

HELMER (*kisses her on the forehead*). Good night, my darling little songbird. Sleep well, Nora. I'll go and read my letters.

    He goes into the study with the letters in his hand, and closes the door.

NORA (*wild-eyed, fumbles around, seizes* HELMER's *cloak, throws it round herself and whispers quickly, hoarsely*). Never see him again. Never. Never. Never. (*Throws the shawl over her head.*) Never see the children again. Them, too. Never. Never. Oh – the icy black water! Oh – that bottomless – that – ! Oh, if only it were all over! Now he's got it – he's reading it. Oh no, no! Not yet! Goodbye Torvald! Goodbye my darlings!

    She turns to run into the hall. As she does so, HELMER *throws open his door and stands there with an open letter in his hand.*

HELMER. Nora!

NORA (*shrieks*). Ah – !

HELMER. What is this? Do you know what is in this letter?

NORA. Yes, I know. Let me go! Let me go!

HELMER (*holding her back*). Go? Where?

NORA (*tries to tear herself loose*). You mustn't try to save me, Torvald!

HELMER (*staggers back*). Is it true? Is it true, what he writes? Oh, my God! No, no – it's impossible, it can't be true!

NORA. It *is* true. I've loved you more than anything else in the world.

HELMER. Oh, don't try to make silly excuses.

NORA (*takes a step towards him*). Torvald –

HELMER. Wretched woman! What have you done?

NORA. Let me go! You're not going to suffer for my sake. I won't let you!

HELMER. Stop being theatrical. (*Locks the front door.*) You're going to stay here and explain yourself. Do you understand what you've done? Answer me! Do you understand?

NORA (*looks unflinchingly at him and, her expression growing colder, says*). Yes. Now I am beginning to understand.

HELMER (*walking round the room*). Oh, what a dreadful awakening! For eight whole years – she who was my joy and pride – a hypocrite, a liar – worse, worse – a criminal! Oh, the hideousness of it! Shame on you, shame!

NORA *is silent and stares unblinkingly at him.*

HELMER (*stops in front of her*). I ought to have guessed that something of this sort would happen. I should have foreseen it. All your father's recklessness and instability – be quiet! – I repeat, all your father's recklessness and instability he has handed on to you! No religion, no morals, no sense of duty! Oh, how I have been punished for closing my eyes to his faults! I did it for your sake. And now you reward me like this.

NORA. Yes. Like this.

HELMER. Now you have destroyed all my happiness. You have ruined my whole future. Oh, it's too dreadful to contemplate! I am in the power of a man who is completely without scruples. He can do what he likes with me, demand what he pleases, order me to do anything – I dare not disobey him. I am condemned to humiliation and ruin simply for the weakness of a woman.

NORA. When I am gone from this world, you will be free.

HELMER. Oh, don't be melodramatic. Your father was always ready with that kind of remark. How would it help me if you were 'gone from this world', as you put it? It wouldn't assist me in the slightest. He can still make all the facts public; and if he does, I may quite easily be suspected of having been an accomplice in your crime. People may think that I was behind it – that it was I who encouraged you! And for all this I have to thank you, you whom I have carried on my hands through all the years of our marriage! Now do you realize what you've done to me?

NORA (*coldly calm*). Yes.

HELMER. It's so unbelievable I can hardly credit it. But we must try to find some way out. Take off that shawl. Take it off, I say! I must try to buy him off somehow. This thing must be hushed up at any price. As regards our relationship – we must appear to be living together just as before. Only *appear*, of course. You will therefore continue to reside here. That is understood. But the children shall be taken out of your hands. I dare no longer entrust them to you. Oh, to have to say this to the woman I once loved so dearly – and whom I still – ! Well, all that must be finished. Henceforth there can be no question of happiness; we must merely strive to save what shreds and tatters –

The front door bell rings. HELMER *starts.*

HELMER. What can that be? At this hour? Surely not – ? He wouldn't – ? Hide yourself, Nora. Say you're ill.

NORA *does not move.* HELMER *goes to the door of the room and opens it. The* MAID *is standing half-dressed in the hall.*

MAID. A letter for madam.

HELMER. Give it me. (*Seizes the letter and shuts the door.*) Yes, it's from him. You're not having it. I'll read this myself.

NORA. Read it.

HELMER (*by the lamp*). I hardly dare to. This may mean the end for us both. No. I must know. (*Tears open the letter hastily; reads a few lines; looks at a piece of paper which is enclosed with it; utters a cry of joy.*) Nora! (*She looks at him questioningly.*) Nora! No – I must read it once more. Yes, yes, it's true! I am saved! Nora, I am saved!

NORA. What about me?

HELMER. You too, of course. We're both saved, you and I. Look! He's returning your I.O.U. He writes that he is sorry for what has happened – a happy accident has changed his life – oh, what does it matter what he writes? We are saved, Nora! No one can harm you now. Oh, Nora, Nora – no, first let me destroy this filthy thing. Let me see – ! (*Glances at the I.O.U.*) No, I don't want to look at it. I shall merely regard the whole business as a dream. (*He tears the I.O.U. and both letters into pieces, throws them into the stove and watches them burn.*) There. Now they're destroyed. He wrote that ever since Christmas Eve you've been – oh, these must have been three dreadful days for you, Nora.

NORA. Yes. It's been a hard fight.

HELMER. It must have been terrible – seeing no way out except – no, we'll forget the whole sordid business. We'll just be happy and go on telling ourselves over and over again: 'It's over! It's over!' Listen to me, Nora. You don't seem to realize. It's over! Why are you looking so pale? Ah, my poor little Nora, I understand. You can't believe that I have forgiven you. But I have, Nora. I swear it to you. I have forgiven you everything. I know that what you did you did for your love of me.

NORA. That is true.

HELMER. You have loved me as a wife should love her husband. It was simply that in your inexperience you chose the wrong means. But do you think I love you any the less because you don't know how to act on your own initiative? No, no. Just lean on me. I shall counsel you. I shall guide you. I would not be a true man if your feminine helplessness did not make you doubly attractive in my eyes. You mustn't mind the hard words I said to you in those first dreadful moments when my whole world seemed to be tumbling about my ears. I have forgiven you, Nora. I swear it to you; I have forgiven you.

NORA. Thank you for your forgiveness. (*She goes out through the door, right.*)

HELMER. No, don't go – (*Looks in.*) What are you doing there?

NORA (*offstage*). Taking off my fancy dress.

HELMER (*by the open door*). Yes, do that. Try to calm yourself and get your balance again, my frightened little songbird. Don't be afraid. I have broad wings to shield you. (*Begins to walk around near the door.*) How lovely and peaceful this little home of ours is, Nora. You are safe here; I shall watch over you like a hunted dove which I have snatched unharmed from the claws of the falcon. Your wildly beating little heart shall find peace with me. It will happen, Nora; it will take time, but it will happen, believe me. Tomorrow all this will seem quite different. Soon everything will be as it was before. I shall no longer need to remind you that I have forgiven you; your own heart will tell you that it is true. Do you really think I could ever bring myself to disown you, or even to reproach you? Ah, Nora, you don't understand what goes on in a husband's heart. There is something indescribably wonderful and satisfying for a husband in knowing that he has forgiven his wife – forgiven her unreservedly, from the bottom of his heart. It means that she has become his property in a double sense; he has, as it were, brought her into the world anew; she is now not only his wife but also his child. From now on that is what you shall be to me, my poor, helpless, bewildered little creature. Never be frightened of anything again, Nora. Just open your heart to me. I shall be both your will and your conscience. What's this? Not in bed? Have you changed?

NORA (*in her everyday dress*). Yes, Torvald. I've changed.

HELMER. But why now – so late – ?

NORA. I shall not sleep tonight.

HELMER. But, my dear Nora –

NORA (*looks at her watch*). It isn't that late. Sit down there, Torvald. You and I have a lot to talk about.

She sits down on one side of the table.

HELMER. Nora, what does this mean? You look quite drawn –

NORA. Sit down. It's going to take a long time. I've a lot to say to you.

HELMER (*sits down on the other side of the table*). You alarm me, Nora. I don't understand you.

NORA. No, that's just it. You don't understand me. And I've never understood you – until this evening. No, don't interrupt me. Just listen to what I have to say. You and I have got to face facts, Torvald.

HELMER. What do you mean by that?

NORA (*after a short silence*). Doesn't anything strike you about the way we're sitting here?

HELMER. What?

NORA. We've been married for eight years. Does it occur to you that this is the first time we two, you and I, man and wife, have ever had a serious talk together?

HELMER. Serious? What do you mean, serious?

NORA. In eight whole years – no, longer – ever since we first met – we have never exchanged a serious word on a serious subject.

HELMER. Did you expect me to drag you into all my worries – worries you couldn't possibly have helped me with?

NORA. I'm not talking about worries. I'm simply saying that we have never sat down seriously to try to get to the bottom of anything.

HELMER. But, my dear Nora, what on earth has that got to do with you?

NORA. That's just the point. You have never understood me. A great wrong has been done to me, Torvald. First by papa, and then by you.

HELMER. What? But we two have loved you more than anyone in the world!

NORA (*shakes her head*). You have never loved me. You just thought it was fun to be in love with me.

HELMER. Nora, what kind of a way is this to talk?

NORA. It's the truth, Torvald. When I lived with papa, he used to tell me what he thought about everything, so that I never had any opinions but his. And if I did have any of my own, I kept them quiet, because he wouldn't have liked them. He called me his little doll, and he played with me just the way I played with my dolls. Then I came here to live in your house –

HELMER. What kind of a way is that to describe our marriage?

NORA (*undisturbed*). I mean, then I passed from papa's hands into yours. You arranged everything the way you wanted it, so that I simply took over your taste in everything – or pretended I did – I don't really know – I think it was a little of both – first one and then the other. Now I look back on it, it's as if I've been living here like a pauper, from hand to mouth. I performed tricks for you, and you gave me food and drink. But that was how you wanted it. You and papa have done me a great wrong. It's your fault that I have done nothing with my life.

HELMER. Nora, how can you be so unreasonable and ungrateful? Haven't you been happy here?

NORA. No; never. I used to think I was. But I haven't ever been happy.

HELMER. Not – not happy?

NORA. No. I've just had fun. You've always been very kind to me. But our home has never been anything but a playroom. I've been your doll-wife, just as I used to be papa's doll-child. And the children have been my dolls. I used to think it was fun when you came in and played with me, just as they think it's fun when I go in and play games with them. That's all our marriage has been, Torvald.

HELMER. There may be a little truth in what you say, though you exaggerate and romanticize. But from now on it'll be different. Playtime is over. Now the time has come for education.

NORA. Whose education? Mine or the children's?

HELMER. Both yours and the children's, my dearest Nora.

NORA. Oh, Torvald, you're not the man to educate me into being the right wife for you.

HELMER. How can you say that?

NORA. And what about me? Am I fit to educate the children?

HELMER. Nora!

NORA. Didn't you say yourself a few minutes ago that you dare not leave them in my charge?

HELMER. In a moment of excitement. Surely you don't think I meant it seriously?

NORA. Yes. You were perfectly right. I'm not fitted to educate them. There's something else I must do first. I must educate myself. And you can't help me with that. It's something I must do by myself. That's why I'm leaving you.

HELMER (jumps up). What did you say?

NORA. I must stand on my own feet if I am to find out the truth about myself and about life. So I can't go on living here with you any longer.

HELMER. Nora, Nora!

NORA. I'm leaving you now, at once. Christine will put me up for tonight –

HELMER. You're out of your mind! You can't do this! I forbid you!

NORA. It's no use your trying to forbid me any more. I shall take with me nothing but what is mine. I don't want anything from you, now or ever.

HELMER. What kind of madness is this?

NORA. Tomorrow I shall go home – I mean, to where I was born. It'll be easiest for me to find some kind of a job there.

HELMER. But you're blind! You've no experience of the world –

NORA. I must try to get some, Torvald.

HELMER. But to leave your home, your husband, your children! Have you thought what people will say?

NORA. I can't help that. I only know that I must do this.

HELMER. But this is monstrous! Can you neglect your most sacred duties?

NORA. What do you call my most sacred duties?

HELMER. Do I have to tell you? Your duties towards your husband, and your children.

NORA. I have another duty which is equally sacred.

HELMER. You have not. What on earth could that be?

NORA. My duty towards myself.

HELMER. First and foremost you are a wife and mother.

NORA. I don't believe that any longer. I believe that I am first and foremost a human being, like you – or anyway, that I must try to become one. I know most people think as you do, Torvald, and I know there's something of the sort to be found in books. But I'm no longer prepared to accept what people say and what's written in books. I must think things out for myself, and try to find my own answer.

HELMER. Do you need to ask where your duty lies in your own home? Haven't you an infallible guide in such matters – your religion?

NORA. Oh, Torvald, I don't really know what religion means.

HELMER. What are you saying?

NORA. I only know what Pastor Hansen told me when I went to confirmation. He explained that religion meant this and that. When I get away from all this and can think things out on my own, that's one of the questions I want to look into. I want to find out whether what Pastor Hansen said was right – or anyway, whether it is right for me.

HELMER. But it's unheard of for so young a woman to behave like this! If religion cannot guide you, let me at least appeal to your conscience. I presume you have some moral feelings left? Or – perhaps you haven't? Well, answer me.

NORA. Oh, Torvald, that isn't an easy question to answer. I simply don't know. I don't know where I am in these matters. I only know that these things mean something quite different to me from what they do to you. I've learned now that certain laws are different from what I'd imagined them to be; but I can't accept that such laws can be right. Has a woman really not the right to spare her dying father pain, or save her husband's life? I can't believe that.

HELMER. You're talking like a child. You don't understand how society works.

NORA. No, I don't. But now I intend to learn. I must try to satisfy myself which is right, society or I.

HELMER. Nora, you're ill. You're feverish. I almost believe you're out of your mind.

NORA. I've never felt so sane and sure in my life.

HELMER. You feel sure that it is right to leave your husband and your children?

NORA. Yes. I do.

HELMER. Then there is only one possible explanation.

NORA. What?

HELMER. That you don't love me any longer.

NORA. No, that's exactly it.

HELMER. Nora! How can you say this to me?

NORA. Oh, Torvald, it hurts me terribly to have to say it, because you've always been so kind to me. But I can't help it. I don't love you any longer.

HELMER (*controlling his emotions with difficulty*). And you feel quite sure about this, too?

NORA. Yes, absolutely sure. That's why I can't go on living here any longer.

HELMER. Can you also explain why I have lost your love?

NORA. Yes, I can. It happened this evening, when the miracle failed to happen. It was then that I realized you weren't the man I'd thought you to be.

HELMER. Explain more clearly. I don't understand you.

NORA. I've waited so patiently, for eight whole years – well, good heavens, I'm not such a fool as to suppose that miracles occur every day. Then this dreadful thing happened to me, and then I *knew*: 'Now the miracle will take place!' When Krogstad's letter was lying out there, it never occurred to me for a moment that you would let that man trample over you. I *knew* that you would say to him: 'Publish the facts to the world!' And when he had done this –

HELMER. Yes, what then? When I'd exposed my wife's name to shame and scandal –

NORA. Then I was certain that you would step forward and take all the blame on yourself, and say: 'I am the one who is guilty!'

HELMER. Nora!

NORA. You're thinking I wouldn't have accepted such a sacrifice from you? No, of course I wouldn't! But what would my word have counted for against yours? That was the miracle I was hoping for, and dreading. And it was to prevent it happening that I wanted to end my life.

HELMER. Nora, I would gladly work for you night and day, and endure sorrow and hardship for your sake. But no man can be expected to sacrifice his honour, even for the person he loves.

NORA. Millions of women have done it.

HELMER. Oh, you think and talk like a stupid child.

NORA. That may be. But you neither think nor talk like the man I could share my life with. Once you'd got over your fright – and you weren't frightened of what might threaten me, but only of what threatened you – once the danger was past, then as far as you were concerned it was exactly as though nothing had happened. I was your little songbird just as before – your doll whom henceforth you would take particular care to protect from the world because she was so weak and fragile. (*Gets up.*) Torvald, in that moment I realized that for eight years I had been living here with a complete stranger, and had borne him three children – ! Oh, I can't bear to think of it! I could tear myself to pieces!

HELMER (*sadly*). I see it, I see it. A gulf has indeed opened between us. Oh, but Nora – couldn't it be bridged?

NORA. As I am now, I am no wife for you.

HELMER. I have the strength to change.

NORA. Perhaps – if your doll is taken from you.

HELMER. But to be parted – to be parted from you! No, no, Nora, I can't conceive of it happening!

NORA (*goes into the room, right*). All the more necessary that it should happen.

She comes back with her outdoor things and a small travelling-bag, which she puts down on a chair by the table.

HELMER. Nora, Nora, not now! Wait till tomorrow!

NORA (*puts on her coat*). I can't spend the night in a strange man's house.

HELMER. But can't we live here as brother and sister, then – ?

NORA (*fastens her hat*). You know quite well it wouldn't last. (*Puts on her shawl.*) Goodbye, Torvald. I don't want to see the children. I know they're in better hands than mine. As I am now, I can be nothing to them.

HELMER. But some time, Nora – some time – ?

NORA. How can I tell? I've no idea what will happen to me.

HELMER. But you are my wife, both as you are and as you will be.

NORA. Listen, Torvald. When a wife leaves her husband's house, as I'm doing now, I'm told that according to the law he is freed of any obligations towards her. In any case, I release you from any such obligations. You mustn't feel bound to me in any way however small, just as I shall not feel bound to you. We must both be quite free. Here is your ring back. Give me mine.

HELMER. That too?

NORA. That too.

HELMER. Here it is.

NORA. Good. Well, now it's over. I'll leave the keys here. The servants know about everything to do with the house – much better than I do. Tomorrow, when I have left town, Christine will come to pack the things I brought here from home. I'll have them sent on after me.

HELMER. This is the end, then! Nora, will you never think of me any more?

NORA. Yes, of course. I shall often think of you and the children and this house.

HELMER. May I write to you, Nora?

NORA. No. Never. You mustn't do that.

HELMER. But at least you must let me send you –

NORA. Nothing. Nothing.

HELMER. But if you should need help – ?

NORA. I tell you, no. I don't accept things from strangers.

HELMER. Nora – can I never be anything but a stranger to you?

NORA (*picks up her bag*). Oh, Torvald! Then the miracle of miracles would have to happen.

HELMER. The miracle of miracles!

NORA. You and I would both have to change so much that – oh, Torvald, I don't believe in miracles any longer.

HELMER. But I want to believe in them. Tell me. We should have to change so much that – !

NORA. That life together between us two could become a marriage. Goodbye.

   She goes out through the hall.

HELMER (*sinks down on a chair by the door and buries his face in his hands*). Nora! Nora! (*Looks round and gets up.*) Empty! She's gone! (*A hope strikes him.*) The miracle of miracles – ?

   The street door is slammed shut downstairs.

Note on the Translation

A Doll's House presents fewer problems to the translator than any other of Ibsen's plays, except perhaps *An Enemy of the People*. It is simply and directly written, and for nearly all the time the characters say what they mean, instead of talking at a tangent to their real meaning. Torvald Helmer utters several stuffy Victorianisms, and Krogstad sometimes speaks the language of melodrama, but both work well in performance. Here, as in all the plays, I have retained certain turns of phrase which look Victorian on the printed page but are effective in the theatre when spoken by an actor or actress in nineteenth-century clothes in a nineteenth-century room.

An Enemy of the People

Introduction

Ibsen wrote *An Enemy of the People* in Rome between March and June 1882, less than six months after completing *Ghosts*. It is probable that he had begun to plan it as early as 1880, for on 26 November of that year he wrote to Edmund Gosse that he was 'busy pondering a new play which I hope to complete during the summer', and both Lorentz Dietrichson and Kristofer Janson report conversations that they had with Ibsen around this time in which he expressed many of the opinions which he was later to put into Dr Stockmann's mouth. But he had put this project aside in order to write *Ghosts*, 'a theme' (he wrote to his publisher, Hegel of Gyldendal) 'which has long occupied my thoughts and which at length forced itself upon me so insistently that I could no longer ignore it.'

The extremely hostile reception which *Ghosts* had received in Scandinavia on its appearance in December 1881 drove Ibsen into a fury. 'What is one to say of the attitude taken by the so-called liberal press?' he wrote to Georg Brandes on 3 January 1882. 'These leaders who talk and write of freedom and progressiveness and at the same time allow themselves to be the slaves of the supposed opinions of their subscribers! I become more and more convinced that there is something demoralising about involving oneself in politics and attaching oneself to a party. Under no circumstances will I ever link myself with any party that has the majority behind it. Bjœrnson says: "The majority is always right." As a practising politician I suppose he has to say that. But I say: "The minority is always right." I am of course not thinking of the minority of reactionaries who have been left astern by the big central party which we call liberal; I mean the minority which forges ahead in territory which the majority has not yet reached. I believe that he is right who is most closely attuned to the future ... For me liberty is the first condition of life, and the highest. At home people don't bother much about liberty but only about liberties – a few more or a few less, according to the party standpoint. I feel most painfully affected by this vulgarity, this plebeianism in our public discussion. In the course of their undeniably worthy efforts to turn our country into a democratic community, people have unwittingly gone a good way towards turning us into a mob community. The aristocracy of the intellect seems to be in short supply in Norway.'

Later the same month (24 January 1882) he wrote to Olaf Skavlan: 'I myself am responsible for what I write, and I alone. I cannot possibly embarrass any party, for I belong to none. I want to act as a lone *franc-tireur* in the outposts and operate on my own ... Is it only in the political field that men are to be allowed to work for freedom in Norway? Is it not first and foremost man's spirit that needs to be set free? Such spiritual slaves as we are cannot even use the freedoms we already have. Norway is a free country inhabited by serfs.'

Normally, Ibsen allowed eighteen months to elapse between completing one play and beginning another;[1] but on 16 March he surprised Hegel by writing: 'I am able to tell you that I am now fully occupied with preparations for my new play. This time it will be a peaceful work which can be read by cabinet ministers and wholesale merchants and their ladies, and from which the theatres will not need to shrink. I should have no difficulty in polishing it off, and I will try to have it ready quite early in the autumn.' For once he found himself ahead of schedule, for on 21 June he was able to write to Hegel, still from Rome: 'Yesterday I completed my new play. It is entitled *An Enemy of the People*, and is in five acts. I am still a little uncertain whether to call it a comedy or simply a play; it has much of the character of a comedy, but there is also a serious basic theme ... In a few days I shall start on the fair copy, which should be ready at the latest by the end of July. I will send you the manuscript in stages, as usual.'

Unfortunately no working notes or preliminary draft of *An Enemy of the People* have survived, so that we do not know, as we do with most of his other plays, exactly how long he took to write each act and what alterations he made from his original conception.

At the beginning of August he left Rome for Gossensass in the Tyrol, and from there, on 28 August, he sent Hegel the fair copy of the first four acts. 'The fifth,' he explained, 'will follow in a few days, as I have already done half of it. The reason the manuscript

---

[1] Between 1877, when he finished *The Pillars of Society*, and 1896, when he wrote *John Gabriel Borkman*, *An Enemy of the People* provides the only exception to this rule. *When We Dead Awaken*, Ibsen's last play, came three years after *John Gabriel Borkman*, but this was largely because 1898 was much taken up with preparations for the celebration of Ibsen's seventieth birthday.

is arriving somewhat later than I implied in my previous letter is that I have fair-copied the whole play twice to achieve the maximum perfection in the dialogue.' On 9 September he posted the final act. 'It has been fun', he wrote, 'working on this play, and I feel a sense of deprivation and emptiness at being parted from it. Dr Stockmann and I got on most excellently; we agree about so many things; but the Doctor has a more muddled head on his shoulders than I have, and he has besides certain characteristics which will permit people to tolerate various things from his lips which they might not accept so readily if they had issued from mine. If you have begun to read the manuscript, I think you will share this opinion.'

An Enemy of the People was published by Gyldendal of Copenhagen on 28 November 1882, in an edition (despite the calamitous sales of *Ghosts*) of 10,000 copies. Its reception was mixed; not surprisingly, Dr Stockmann's hard remarks about political parties offended all the reviewers who belonged to either. Liberal circles were particularly cool; Strindberg dismissed it as 'insufferably aesthetic' (the modern word would be 'uncommitted'). The theatres, however, seized eagerly on the play. The Christiania Theatre and the Royal Theatres of Copenhagen and Stockholm, all of which had rejected *Ghosts* as unfit for public presentation, immediately acquired the production rights of *An Enemy of the People*, apparently insensitive to the fact that the theme of the latter play was the unworthiness of those who 'do not dare,' and its conclusion: 'The strongest man is he who stands most alone.' It was performed at the Christiania Theatre on 13 January 1883; at Bergen on 24 January; at Gothenburg in February, and in Stockholm and Copenhagen in March. In all three countries it was cordially, but not over-enthusiastically received. Strangely, in view of the popularity of *The Pillars of Society* and *A Doll's House*, and the sensation caused by the publication of *Ghosts*, it was not performed in Germany until 1887.

In 1892, *An Enemy of the People* was acted in New York, in German;[1] and the following year Lugné-Poe staged it in Paris at the Théâtre de L'Oeuvre. 'On the first night,' writes Archer, 'it was preceded by a lecture by M. Laurent Tailhade, which consisted not so much of an exposition of the play, as of a violent attack upon all the "leading men" in French literature and politics.

---

[1] Several of the first American performances of Ibsen were in a language other than English, owing to the high proportion, in those days, of first-generation European immigrants. The world première of *Ghosts* took place in Chicago in Norwegian (or in a mixture of Norwegian and Danish).

Beside it, Dr Stockmann's harangue in the fourth act seems mode-rate and almost mealy-mouthed ... The audience listened, not without protest, to M. Tailhade's diatribe, until he thought fit to describe the recent Franco-Russian fêtes as an act of collective insanity. At this point a storm of indignation burst forth, which lasted without pause for a quarter of an hour, and was not allayed by an attempt at intervention on the part of M. Lugné-Poe. The lecture closed amid wild confusion, and altogether the preliminary scene in the auditorium was like a spirited rehearsal of the meeting at Captain Horster's.'

In 1893 *An Enemy of the People* was produced in England by Herbert Beerbohm Tree at the Haymarket Theatre – the first Ibsen play to attract the attention of a fashionable actor-manager and receive the full West End treatment. Archer found the text 'monstrously mutilated' and the production 'distinctly below the level of the so-called "scratch" performances to which we have been accustomed'. Bernard Shaw thought that Tree's own per-formance 'though humorous and entertaining in its way, was, as a character creation, the polar opposite of Ibsen's Stockmann'. But the production was a success; Tree revived it several times, and in 1895 took it to America, where its success was repeated. Yet, for reasons which will be discussed later, apart from a single matinée in 1928 to celebrate the centenary of Ibsen's birth, Central London has seen only one production of *An Enemy of the People* since Tree's, in 1939, when Tyrone Guthrie directed it at the Old Vic with Roger Livesey as Stockmann and Edward Chapman as the Mayor. Joan Littlewood staged it at Stratford East in 1954, with Howard Goorney as Stockmann and Harry Corbett as the Mayor, setting the action in Lancashire; but, as T. C. Worsley commented, the Theatre Workshop company was 'less happy in the naturalistic mode than in some others'.

In 1905 *An Enemy of the People* was the instance of a demonstra-tion even more remarkable than that which it had caused in Paris. The venue was the Moscow Arts Theatre, and Konstantin Stanis-lavsky, who was playing Dr Stockmann, has described the occasion vividly in his autobiography, *My Life and Art*:

'In that time of political unrest – it was but a little while before the first revolution – the feeling of protest was very strong in all spheres of society. They waited for the hero who could tell the truth strongly and bravely in the very teeth of the government. It is not to be wondered at that the image of Dr Stockmann became popular at once in Moscow, and especially so in Petrograd. *An Enemy of the*

People became the favourite play of the revolutionists, notwithstanding the fact that Stockmann himself despised the solid majority and believed in individuals to whom he would entrust the conduct of life. But Stockmann protested, Stockmann told the truth, and that was considered enough.

'On the day of the well-known massacre in Kazansky Square, *An Enemy of the People* was on the boards of our theatre. The average run of spectators that night was from the intelligentsia, the professors and learned men of Petrograd. I remember that the orchestra was filled almost entirely with grey heads. Thanks to the sad events of the day, the auditorium was very excited and answered even the slightest hints about liberty in every word of Stockmann's protest. In the most unexpected places in the play the thunder of applause would break in on the performance. . . . The atmosphere in the theatre was such that we expected arrests at any minute and a stop to the performance. Censors, who sat at all the performances of *An Enemy of the People* and saw to it that I, who played Dr Stockmann, should use only the censored text, and raised trouble over every syllable that was not admitted by the censorship, were on this evening even more watchful than on other occasions. I had to be doubly careful. When the text of a role is cut and re-cut many times it is not hard to make a mistake and say too much or too little. In the last act of the play, Dr Stockmann, putting into order his room which has been stoned by the crowd, finds in the general chaos his black coat,[1] in which he appeared at the meeting the day before. Seeing a rent in the cloth, Stockmann says to his wife: "One must never put on a new coat when one goes to fight for freedom and truth."

'The spectators in the theatre connected this sentence with the massacre in Kazansky Square, where more than one new coat must have been torn in the name of freedom and truth. Unexpectedly, my words aroused such a pandemonium that it was necessary to stop the performance, into which a real mob scene was interpolated by impromptu. There had taken place the unification of the actor and the spectators, who took on themselves the role of chief actor in the theatre, that same mob action of which so much is said by the theoreticians of art. The entire audience rose from its seats and threw itself towards the footlights. Thanks to the fact that the stage was very low and there was no orchestra before it, I saw hundreds of hands stretched towards me, all of which I was forced to shake. The younger people in the audience jumped on to the stage and

[1] More accurately, his trousers.

embraced Dr Stockmann. It was not easy to establish order and to continue with the play. That evening I found out through my own experience what power the theatre could exercise'.[1]

Although the public reception of *Ghosts* was the immediate inspiration of *An Enemy of the People*, the opinions to which Ibsen gave expression in the latter play were not new to him; we find them continually cropping up in his earlier correspondence, especially in his letters to the Danish critic Georg Brandes. As early as 1871, eleven years before he began *An Enemy of the People*, he had declared to Brandes: 'I shall never be able to regard liberty as synonymous with political liberty. What you call liberty I call liberties, and what I call the fight for freedom is nothing but the eternal and living quest for the idea of freedom. He who possesses freedom otherwise than as an object to be sought possesses something dead and soulless. For the quintessence of freedom is the fact that, as one acquires it, it grows, so that if anyone stops during the battle and says: "Now I have it!" he reveals, by this very statement, that he has lost it.'

On 21 March 1872, he asserted to Fredrik Gjertsen his 'fundamental principle, in every context and situation, namely, that the minority is always right.' And the following month he wrote to Brandes: 'My dear friend, the liberals are the worst enemies of freedom. Spiritual and intellectual freedom flourish best under absolutism; that has been proved in France, and later in Germany, and it is now being proved in Russia ... As regards this agitation which is being worked up against you, with its lies and back-biting and so forth, let me give you a piece of advice which from my own experience I know to be sovereign. Be an aristocrat [*fornem*]! Aristocracy is the only weapon against this kind of thing. Appear indifferent; never write a word of reply in the newspapers; if you polemise in your writings, never direct your polemic against this or that specific attack; never write a single word which could make it seem that your enemies have found their mark; in short, act as though you had no idea that anyone was opposed to you.'

[1] Similarly, on the occasion of the Paris premiere, which occurred at the time of the Dreyfus affair, everyone, according to Lugné-Poe, identified Stockmann with Emile Zola. The play was deliberately chosen for the first Ibsen production in Spain (in Barcelona on 14 April 1893) to help organized opposition to the established order in government and industry, and for the first Japanese production (in Tokyo in 1898) as a protest against dangerous effusion from a chemical factory.

On 19 December 1879, a fortnight after the publication of *A Doll's House*, he wrote to Lorentz Dietrichson: 'It seems to me doubtful whether it is practicable to obtain better artistic conditions in our country before the intellectual soil has been thoroughly turned up, and cleansed and drained of all its swamp-like filth.' This was a metaphor to which he was to return in *An Enemy of the People*. And Kristofer Janson, the writer who was a part-original of Hjalmar Ekdal in *The Wild Duck*, reports a conversation he had with Ibsen on New Year's Eve, 1880, when Ibsen is thought to have been making his first plans for *An Enemy of the People*. 'Ibsen flared up. "The majority? What is the majority? The ignorant mass! The intelligence is always in the minority. How many of the majority do you think are qualified to hold an opinion? Most of them are just sheepdogs!"'[1]

'When my new play reaches you,' Ibsen wrote to Brandes on 21 September 1882, shortly after he had finished *An Enemy of the People*, 'you will perhaps be able to understand what interest and, I may add, fun it has given me to recall the many scattered and casual remarks I have made in my letters to you.' Nine months later, to the same correspondent, he added a provocative postcript to the play. 'An intellectual pioneer', he declared, 'can never gather a majority about him. In ten years the majority may have reached the point where Dr Stockmann stood when the people held their meeting. But during those ten years the Doctor has not remained stationary; he is still at least ten years ahead of the others. The majority, the masses, the mob, will never catch him up; he can never rally them behind him. I myself feel a similarly unrelenting compulsion to keep pressing forward. A crowd now stands where I stood when I wrote my earlier books. But I myself am there no longer. I am somewhere else – far ahead of them – or so I hope. At present I am struggling with the draft of a new play in four acts . . .' This new play, the successor to *An Enemy of the People*, was to be *The Wild Duck*.

The plot of *An Enemy of the People* had its origin in two actual incidents to which Ibsen's attention had been drawn. Alfred

---

[1] He also once remarked to Janson: 'The only people with whom I really have any sympathy are the nihilists and the socialists. They want something wholeheartedly, and they are consistent.' Ibsen did not object when, in 1890, Bernard Shaw identified 'Ibsenism' with socialism – indeed, he protested when some newspapers asserted that he had nothing to do with socialism.

Meissner, a young German poet whom he knew in Munich, told him how, when his father had been medical officer at the spa of Teiplitz in the eighteen-thirties, there had occurred an outbreak of cholera which the latter felt it his duty to make public. As a result, the season was ruined, and the citizens of Teiplitz became so enraged that they stoned the Doctor's house and forced him to flee the town.

Then there had been the case in Norway of a chemist named Harald Thaulow. For nearly ten years Thaulow had furiously attacked the Christiania Steam Kitchens for neglecting their duty towards the city's poor. He had delivered a violent speech on the subject in 1874, when Ibsen was revisiting Norway; and on 23 February 1881, only a fortnight before he died, Thaulow had attempted to read a prepared speech at the annual general meeting of the Steam Kitchens. The chairman of the meeting tried to prevent him from speaking, and eventually the audience forced him, amid commotion, to remain silent. Ibsen read a report of this meeting in *Aftenposten* just at the time when his indignation at the reception of *Ghosts* was reaching its climax, and he must have recognized in the eccentric old chemist a spirit very kindred to his own. The newspaper account is worth quoting:

THAULOW. I will not stop, you have no right to stop me, Mr Chairman.

(*Continues*). Point number ten –

CONSUL HEFTYE. Mr Thaulow must be stopped!

THAULOW *continues. Several of the public show their displeasure by walking about the hall.* THE CHAIRMAN *asks the meeting whether they recognize his right to bar* MR THAULOW *from the floor. Unanimous 'Ayes'.* THE CHAIRMAN *again asks* MR THAULOW *to stop reading.*

THAULOW. I will not be silenced.

THE CHAIRMAN. In that case, I shall –

THAULOW. I'll keep it quite short. (*Reads on.*)

CONSUL HEFTYE. Is he to be allowed to continue?

THAULOW (*continues reading*). The glorious achievements of the Christiania Steam Kitchens – I'll soon be through –

CONSUL HEFTYE. If this goes on the meeting can't continue.

CHAIRMAN. I regret that I must interrupt Mr Thaulow. You have not the floor –

THAULOW *reads on.*

CONSUL HEFTYE. Be quiet, or you'll be thrown out.

THAULOW. Oh, very well.

> THAULOW *sits down at last. After* THE CHAIRMAN *had read his report for some minutes –*

THAULOW. ... It's too much. It's no use trying to oppose the mob –

CONSUL HEFTYE. Did the Chairman hear Mr Thaulow refer to us as the mob? ...

> *At length* MR THAULOW *left the meeting in a rage, saying*: I'll have no more to do with you. I won't cast my pearls into the sand. This is a damned insult being inflicted on a free people in a free society. Now I'll go! Stand in the dunce's corner and be ashamed of yourselves!

An English Member of Parliament may also have contributed something to the play. Charles Bradlaugh, having narrowly escaped imprisonment for his part in a pamphlet advocating birth control (he had actually been sentenced, but had escaped on appeal), had been elected Radical M.P. for Northampton in 1880, but had been barred from taking his seat on the ground that, since he was a confessed free-thinker, the oath would not bind him. New elections were held in Northampton, and he was returned each time, but was still excluded; in 1881, he was forcibly removed from the House by ten policemen, and it was not until 1886 that a new Speaker granted him the right to take the oath and sit. 'You should hear Ibsen on Bradlaugh – he has the most vivid sympathy for him', wrote William Archer to his brother Charles on 14 March 1882, when Ibsen was about to start writing *An Enemy of the People*; and Bradlaugh has an obvious deal in common with Dr Stockmann.

Stockmann himself, however, was primarily based on two old acquaintances of Ibsen, both distinguished writers – Jonas Lie and Bjœrnsterne Bjœrnson. Ibsen had re-encountered Lie in Berchtesgaden the previous summer (1880) and had found him as confused, warm-hearted, inconsistent and impatient as ever. Bjœrnson shared the same warm-heartedness and impatience, plus eloquence, a strong family feeling, and an infinite capacity for moral indignation. But one must not forget, when considering the origins of Stockmann, that Ibsen himself had, as a younger man, been a fiery and eloquent speaker on causes that touched him. Lorentz Dietrichson has described him addressing a gathering of the Scandinavian community in Rome in 1864, on the subject of the Danish–German war. 'All the bitterness which had for so long been stored up within him, all the fiery indignation and passion for the Scandinavian cause which he had bottled up for so long, found an outlet. His voice began to ring, and in the evening dusk one saw only his burning eyes. When he had finished, no one cried bravo or raised his glass, but I think we all felt that that evening the Marseillaise of the North had rung out into the Roman night air'. That is not very far from the Dr Stockmann of Act Four; and it is worth remembering that the house in Skien in which Ibsen had been born was called Stockmannsgaarden.

One of the characters in *An Enemy of the People*, Aslaksen the printer, had already appeared in *The League of Youth*, completed in 1869. There he had been a sad little drunk; in the later play he has become a pillar of respectability and moderation. Morten Kiil, 'the Badger,' had been planned as a character for *The Pillars of Society*. He appears in the rough notes for that play, but never got into the final draft. Ibsen, like the Button Moulder's description of The Master in *Peer Gynt*, was

> a thrifty man . . .
> He never rejects as worthless anything
> Which he can use again as raw material.

As recently as October 1964 a number of previously unpublished letters of Ibsen were privately printed in a limited edition,[1] and among them are three of particular interest in which Ibsen discusses in detail the characters of *An Enemy of the People*. Hans Schrœder, the director of the Christiania Theatre who had rejected *Ghosts* – a memory which the unfortunate man was to carry with him for the rest of his days – had telegraphed Ibsen in Rome for permission to give the first public performance of *An Enemy of the People*. Ibsen agreed, stinging them for a lump payment of 4,000 crowns (he had let them have *A Doll's House* for 2,500), and a week later, on 14 December 1882, he wrote to Schrœder from Rome:

> Permit me to address to you a few lines concerning the forthcoming production of *An Enemy of the People*. It is not my intention or wish to attempt to influence *in absentio* either the staging or the casting; but the expression of certain feelings which I hold regarding various aspects of the play can do no

[1] *Henrik Ibsens Brevveksling med Christiania Theater 1878–1899*, edited with a commentary by Oeyvind Anker (Gyldendal Norsk Forlag, Oslo, 1964).

harm. I trust I may assume that Mrs Wolf will play Mrs Stockmann. ... If for the role of Hovstad you have an otherwise
suitable actor of not too heroic build, that is the kind of man you
should choose. Hovstad is the son of poor people, has grown up
in a dirty home on wretched and inadequate food, has frozen and
toiled horribly throughout his childhood, and subsequently, as a
poverty-stricken young man, has continued to undergo considerable privation. Such living conditions leave their mark not only
on a man's spirit but also on his outward appearance. Men of
heroic exterior are an exception among the plebs. Whatever the
circumstances Hovstad must always wear a depressed appearance,
somewhat shrunken and stooping, and uncertain in his move-
ments; all, of course, portrayed with complete naturalism. Billing's lines are so worded that they require an east-coast and not,
e.g., a Bergen dialect. He is, essentially, an east-coast character.
Captain Horster has been ridiculously misunderstood by a
Danish critic. He characterizes Horster as an old man, Dr Stockmann's old friend, etc. This is, of course, utterly wrong. Horster
is a young man, one of the young people whose healthy appetite
delights the Doctor, though he is an infrequent visitor at the
house because he dislikes the company of Hovstad and Billing.
Already in Act One, Horster's interest in Petra must subtly and
delicately be indicated, and during the brief exchanges between
him and her in Act Five we must sense that they now stand at
the threshold of a deep and passionate relationship.

Both the boys must be carefully instructed so that the difference
in their characters is clearly established. And I must beg that in
Act Four every possible actor at your disposal be used. The stage
director must here enjoin the greatest possible naturalism and
strictly forbid any caricaturing or exaggeration. The more realistic characters you can work into the crowd the better.

Throughout the play the stage director must inexorably insist
that none of the players alter his or her lines. They must be
spoken exactly as they stand in the text. A lively tempo is desirable. When I was last at the Christiania Theatre the speech
seemed to me very slow. But above all, truthfulness to nature –
the illusion that everything is real and that one is sitting and
watching something that is actually taking place in real life. *An
Enemy of the People* is not easy to stage. It demands exceptionally
well-drilled ensemble playing, i.e., protracted and meticulously
supervised rehearsals. But I rely upon the good will of all
concerned. ...

Ten days later, on Christmas Eve, Ibsen had occasion to write again to Schrœder: '*Morgenbladet* has published an announcement about the casting for *An Enemy of the People*, in consequence of which I must further inconvenience you with a few lines. I see that Gundersen is to play the Mayor. This actor's appearance hardly suggests a man who cannot bear to eat hot food in the evening, has a bad stomach and an uncertain digestion, and lives on weak tea. Nor is it well suited to a man who is characterized as neat, refined, and fastidious. But these shortcomings can partly be countered by the right clothes and make-up. Mr Gundersen must therefore pay careful attention to these two points. Nor does Mr Reimers's physique fit such a temperament as Dr Stockmann's; hot-headed people are in general more slightly built. The same advice accordingly applies to Mr Reimers as that which I have suggested for Mr Gundersen. He must make himself as thin and small as possible.'

On 31 December 1882, Ibsen wrote again: 'I fear I must once again trouble you with a few lines. From your kind letter which reached me yesterday I gather it is intended to have both the boys in my play acted by girls. This has somewhat disturbed me, since it seems to imply that sufficient attention has not been paid to the spirit in which this play was written and in which it requires to be staged. To allow boys' parts to be taken by women may sometimes be excusable in operetta, vaudeville, or the so-called romantic drama; for in these the prime requirement is unqualified illusion; every member of the audience is fully conscious throughout the evening that he is merely sitting in a theatre and watching a theatrical performance. But this should not be the case when *An Enemy of the People* is being acted. The spectator must feel as though he were invisibly present in Dr Stockmann's living-room; everything here must seem real; the two boys included. Consequently they cannot be played by actresses dressed up in wigs and stays; their feminine figures will not be able to be concealed by their costume of shirt and trousers, and they will never make any spectator believe that he is looking at two real schoolboys from some small town. How in any case can a grown woman make herself look like a ten-year-old child? Both parts must therefore be played by children, or at worst by a couple of small girls whose figures are not yet fully developed; and then damn the corsets and let them have big boys' boots on their legs. They must also, of course, be taught the way boys behave.

'It is stated in the play that at the public meeting Dr Stockmann is to be dressed in black; but his clothes must not be new or elegant, and his white cravat should sit a little crooked.'

Of all the roles, by any author, that Konstantin Stanislavsky played, Dr Stockmann was his favourite. 'I felt myself more at home on the stage in the role of Stockmann', he wrote in *My Life and Art*, 'than in any other role of my repertoire . . . For me Stockmann was not a politician, not an orator at meetings, not a *raisonneur*, but a man of ideals, the true friend of his country and his people. He was the best and purest citizen of his motherland.' Stanislavsky goes on to speak of: 'the inner image with all its peculiarities and details; the short-sighted eyes which spoke so eloquently of his inner blindness to human faults, the childlike and youthful manner of movement, the friendly relations with his children and family, the happiness, the love of joking and play, the gregariousness and attractiveness which forced all who came in touch with him to become purer and better, and to show the best sides of their natures in his presence . . . I had only to think of the thoughts and cares of Stockmann and the signs of short sight would come of themselves, together with the forward stoop of the body, the quick step, the eyes that looked trustfully into the soul of the man or object on the stage with me, the index and middle fingers of the hand stretched forward of themselves for the sake of greater persuasiveness, as if to push my own thoughts, feelings and words, into the soul of my listener'.[1]

An Enemy of the People is less frequently performed today than most of Ibsen's mature plays, for two principal reasons. One is, simply, the size of the cast. A crowd costs money, and without a crowd the great fourth act loses much of its impact (Shakespeare's *Julius Caesar* presents a similar problem). The other difficulty is ideological. Some of the opinions expressed by Dr Stockmann, especially his demands for 'aristocrats', his contempt for the masses, and his assertion that 'the minority is always right', strike an illiberal note in modern ears. On these points Ibsen was in fact expressing a commonly shared attitude; Mill, Tocqueville, Dickens and most liberal thinkers of the time distrusted the tyranny of the commonplace majority. 'Those whose opinions go by the name of public opinion . . . are always a mass, that is to say, collective

[1] Stanislavsky based his physical appearance in the role on that of Rimsky-Korsakov, and borrowed several gestures and characteristics from Gorki. The actor L. M. Leonidov observed that 'Stockmann's loneliness was of the same nature as Stanislavsky's loneliness'.

mediocrity', wrote Mill in his great essay *On Liberty*. 'No government by a democracy or a numerous aristocracy, either in its political acts or in the opinions, qualities, and tone of mind which it fosters, ever did or could rise above mediocrity, except in so far as the sovereign Many have let themselves be guided (which in their best times they always have done) by the counsels and influence of a more highly gifted and instructed One or Few. The initiation of all wise or noble things comes and must come from individuals; generally at first from some one individual'. That is precisely Dr Stockmann's message. But it is an unfashionable viewpoint to put forward in an age of universal suffrage.

The play has, also, suffered worse than most from the dead hand of academic criticism. The kind of commentator that dismisses *Emperor and Galilean* as 'stone-cold', *Brand* as 'ambiguous', and *Little Eyolf* as 'a falling-off' (to quote from a recent and embarrassing English book intended as a vindication of Ibsen), has tended to reject *An Enemy of the People* as 'thin'. It lacks, indeed, the extra density and overtones of Ibsen's later works; but there are precious few other plays outside the Greeks, Shakespeare and Chekhov with which it need fear comparison. Nor can it be glibly dismissed as a *jeu d'esprit*. Even adequately performed, it is one of the most accessible and compulsive of Ibsen's plays, and Dr Stockmann is one of the half-dozen greatest male parts he wrote. The truths it expresses have not dated, and are not likely to as long as there are town councils and politicians. There will always, somewhere in the world, be a Kazansky Square.

MICHAEL MEYER

This translation of An Enemy of the People *was first performed on 3 April 1962 at the Playhouse, Nottingham, with the following cast:*

DR THOMAS STOCKMANN, *medical officer at the Baths*	John Stratton
MRS STOCKMANN, *his wife*	Dorothy Primrose
PETRA, *their daughter, a schoolteacher*	Anne Stallybrass
EILIF ⎱ *their sons, aged 13 and 10* MORTEN ⎰	Terry Smith Paul Nugent
PETER STOCKMANN, *the Doctor's elder brother, Mayor and Chief Constable, Chairman of the Baths Committee, etc.*	Alan MacNaughtan
MORTEN KIIL, *master tanner, foster father to Mrs Stockmann*	Stafford Byrne
HOVSTAD, *editor of the People's Tribune*	Roland Curram
BILLING, *an employee of the newspaper*	Roger Jerome
HORSTER, *a sea captain*	Ronald Magill
ASLAKSEN, *a printer*	Bartlett Mullins
PEOPLE *at a public meeting – men of all classes, a few women and a bunch of schoolboys*	Vanessa Forsyth, Pauline Mason, Ethel Farrugia, Michael Colefax, Paul Silber, John Tordoff, Roy Greenwood, Christopher Ackhurst, Roger Dyason, Edmund Thomas, Herbert Simpson

Directed by Allan Davis

The action takes place in a coastal town in Southern Norway.

ACT ONE

Evening in DR STOCKMANN'S *living-room. It is humbly but neatly furnished and decorated. In the wall to the right are two doors, of which the further leads out to the hall and the nearer to the* DOCTOR'S *study. In the opposite wall, facing the hall door, is a door that leads to the other rooms occupied by the family. In the middle of this wall stands a tiled stove; further downstage is a sofa with a mirror above it. In front of the sofa is an oval table with a cloth on it. Upon this table stands a lighted lamp with a shade. Upstage, an open door to the dining-room, in which can be seen a table laid for the evening meal, with a lamp on it.*

At this table BILLING *is seated, a napkin tucked beneath his chin.* MRS STOCKMANN *is standing by the table, offering him a plate with a large joint of beef on it. The other places around the table are empty, and the table is in the disorder of a meal that has been finished.*

MRS STOCKMANN. There, Mr Billing! But if you will come an hour late, you'll have to put up with cold.

BILLING (*eating.*) Oh, but this is capital. Absolutely capital!

MRS STOCKMANN. Well you know how punctually my husband always likes to eat –

BILLING. It doesn't bother me. I enjoy eating alone, without having to talk to anyone.

MRS STOCKMANN. Oh. Well, as long as you're *enjoying* it, that's – (*Listens towards the hall.*) Ah, this must be Mr Hovstad.

BILLING. Very likely.

MAYOR PETER STOCKMANN *enters wearing an overcoat and his official hat, and carrying a stick.*

MAYOR. Good evening to you, my dear sister-in-law.

MRS STOCKMANN (*goes into the living-room*). Why, good

evening! Fancy seeing you here! How nice of you to come and call on us!

MAYOR. I just happened to be passing, so – (*Glances towards the dining-room.*) But I hear you have company.

MRS STOCKMANN (*a little embarrassed*). Oh, no, no, that's no one. (*Quickly.*) Won't you have something, too?

MAYOR: I? No, thank you! Good heavens, a cooked meal at night! My digestion would never stand that!

MRS STOCKMANN. Oh, but surely just for once –

MAYOR. No, no! It's very kind of you, but I'll stick to my tea and sandwiches. It's healthier in the long run; and a little less expensive.

MRS STOCKMANN (*smiles*). You speak as though Thomas and I were spendthrifts!

MAYOR. Not you, my dear sister-in-law. Such a thought was far from my mind. (*Points towards the* DOCTOR's *study.*) Isn't he at home?

MRS STOCKMANN. No, he's gone for a little walk with the boys.

MAYOR. I wonder if that's wise so soon after a meal? (*Listens.*) Ah, this must be he.

MRS STOCKMANN. No, I don't think it can be, yet. (*A knock on the door.*) Come in!

HOVSTAD, *the editor of the local newspaper, enters from the hall.*

MRS STOCKMANN. Oh – Mr Hovstad –?

HOVSTAD. Yes. Please excuse me, I was detained down at the printer's. Good evening, Your Worship.

MAYOR (*greets him somewhat stiffly*). Good evening. I suppose you are here on business?

HOVSTAD. Partly. About an article for my newspaper –

MAYOR. I guessed as much. I hear my brother is a regular contributor to the *People's Tribune*.

HOVSTAD. Yes, he usually drops us a line when he thinks the truth needs to be told about something.

MRS STOCKMANN (*to* HOVSTAD, *pointing towards the dining-room*). But – won't you –?

MAYOR. Great heavens, you mustn't think I blame him for writing for the kind of public he's most likely to find sympathetic to his ideas. Besides, I have no reason to bear your newspaper any ill will, Mr Hovstad –

HOVSTAD. I should hope not.

MAYOR. On the whole I think I may say that an admirable spirit of tolerance reigns in our town. A fine communal spirit! And the reason for this is that we have this great common interest that binds us together – an interest which is the close concern of every right-minded citizen –

HOVSTAD. You mean the Baths?

MAYOR. Exactly! Our magnificent new Baths! Mark my words, sir! These Baths will prove the very heart and essence of our life! There can be no doubt about it.

MRS STOCKMANN. Yes, that's just what Thomas says.

MAYOR. It's really astounding the strides this place has made during the past two or three years! The town is becoming prosperous. People are waking up and beginning to live. Buildings and ground rents are increasing in value every day.

HOVSTAD. And unemployment is going down.

MAYOR. Yes, there's that too. The burden upon the propertied classes of poor relief has been most gratifyingly reduced – and will be still more if only we have a really good summer this year, with plenty of visitors. What we want most is invalids. They'll give the Baths a good name.

HOVSTAD. And I hear the indications are promising.

MAYOR. They are indeed. Enquiries about accommodation are pouring in every day.

HOVSTAD. Well then, the Doctor's article will be most opportune.

MAYOR. Oh, has he written something new?

HOVSTAD. No, it's something he wrote last winter; a eulogy of the Baths and the excellent health facilities of the town. But I decided to hold it over.

MAYOR. Ah, there was a snag somewhere?

HOVSTAD. No, it wasn't that. I just thought it would be better to wait till the spring. Now people are thinking about where to spend their summer holidays –

MAYOR. Quite right! Quite right, Mr Hovstad!

MRS STOCKMANN. Thomas never stops thinking about those Baths.

MAYOR. Well, he *is* employed there.

HOVSTAD. Yes, and he was the one who really created it all, wasn't he?

MAYOR. Was he? Really? Yes, I have heard that certain people do hold that opinion. I must say I was labouring under the delusion that I had had some modest share in promoting the enterprise.

MRS STOCKMANN. That's what Thomas is always telling people.

HOVSTAD. No one denies that, Your Worship. You got it going and saw to all the practical details – we all know that. I only meant that the idea originated with the Doctor.

MAYOR. Yes, my brother's always been full of ideas – unfortunately. But when things have to be done, another kind of man is needed, Mr Hovstad. And I should have thought that least of all in this house would –

MRS STOCKMANN. But my dear brother-in-law –!

HOVSTAD. Surely Your Worship doesn't –?

MRS STOCKMANN. Do go inside and get yourself something to· eat, Mr Hovstad. My husband will be here any moment.

HOVSTAD. Thank you – just a bite, perhaps. (*Goes into the dining-room.*)

MAYOR (*lowers his voice slightly*). It's extraordinary about people of peasant stock. They never learn the meaning of tact.

MRS STOCKMANN. But is it really anything to bother about? Can't you and Thomas share the honour as brothers?

MAYOR. Well, I should have thought so. But it seems not everyone is content to share.

MRS STOCKMANN. Oh, nonsense! You and Thomas always get on so well together. Ah, this sounds like him.

Goes over and opens the door leading to the hall.

DR STOCKMANN (*laughing and boisterous*). Hullo, Catherine! I've another guest for you here! The more the merrier, what? Come in, Captain Horster! Hang your overcoat up there on the hook. No, of course, you don't wear an overcoat, do you? Fancy, Catherine, I bumped into him in the street! Had the devil of a job persuading him to come back with me!

    CAPTAIN HORSTER *enters and shakes hands with* MRS STOCKMANN.

DR STOCKMANN (*in the doorway*). Run along in now, lads. (*To* MRS STOCKMANN.) They're hungry again already! This way, Captain Horster, you're going to have the finest roast beef you ever –!

    Drives HORSTER *into the dining-room.* EILIF *and* MORTEN *go in too.*

MRS STOCKMANN. Thomas! Don't you see who's –?

DR STOCKMANN (*turns in the doorway*). Oh, hullo, Peter! (*Goes over and shakes his hand.*) Well, it's good to see you!

MAYOR. I'm afraid I can only spare a few minutes –

DR STOCKMANN. Rubbish! We'll be having some hot toddy soon. You haven't forgotten the toddy, Catherine?

MRS STOCKMANN. No, of course not. I've got the kettle on – (*Goes into the dining-room.*)

MAYOR. Hot toddy too –!

DR STOCKMANN. Yes. Now sit down, and we'll have a good time.

MAYOR. Thank you. I never partake in drinking parties.

DR STOCKMANN. But this isn't a party.

MAYOR. Well, but –! (*Glance towards the dining-room.*) It's really extraordinary the amount they eat!

DR STOCKMANN (*rubs his hands*). Yes, there's nothing better than to see young people tuck in, is there? Always hungry! That's the way it should be! They've got to have food! Gives them strength! They're the ones who've got to ginger up the future, Peter.

MAYOR. May one ask what it is that needs to be 'gingered up',
as you put it?

DR STOCKMANN. You must ask the young ones that – when the
time comes. We can't see it, of course. Obviously – a couple of
old fogeys like you and me –

MAYOR. Well, really! That's a most extraordinary way to describe
us –

DR STOCKMANN. Oh, you mustn't take me too seriously, Peter.
I feel so happy and exhilarated, you see! It's so wonderful to be
alive at a time like this, with everything germinating and burst-
ing out all around us! Oh, it's a glorious age we live in! It's as
though a whole new world were coming to birth before our eyes!

MAYOR. Do you really feel that?

DR STOCKMANN. Yes. Of course, you can't see it as clearly as I
do. You've spent your life in this background, so it doesn't
make the same impression on you as it does on me. But I've
had to spend all these years sitting up there in that damned
northern backwater, hardly ever seeing a new face that had a
stimulating word to say to me. To me it's as though I had
moved into the heart of some pulsing metropolis –

MAYOR. Hm; metropolis –!

DR STOCKMANN. Oh, I know it must seem small in comparison
with lots of other cities. But there's life here – promise – so
many things to work and fight for! And that's what matters.
(*Shouts.*) Catherine, hasn't the post come yet?

MRS STOCKMANN (*from the dining-room*). No, not yet.

DR STOCKMANN. And to be making a decent living, Peter!
That's something one learns to appreciate when one's been
living on the edge of starvation, as we have –

MAYOR. Oh, surely –!

DR STOCKMANN. Oh yes, I can tell you we were often pretty
hard pressed up there. But now, we can live like lords! Today,
for instance, we had roast beef for dinner! *And* there was
enough left over for supper! Won't you have a bit? Let me
show it to you anyway. Come on, have a look –

MAYOR. No, really –

DR STOCKMANN. Well, look at this, then! Do you see? We've got a tablecloth!

MAYOR. Yes, I've noticed it.

DR STOCKMANN. And a lampshade too! See? All from what Catherine's managed to save! It makes the room so cosy, don't you think? Come and stand here – no, no, no, not there! There, now! Look! See how the light sort of concentrates downwards? I really think it looks very elegant, don't you?

MAYOR. Well, if one can indulge in that kind of luxury –

DR STOCKMANN. Oh, I think I can permit myself that now. Catherine says I earn almost as much as we spend.

MAYOR. Almost!

DR STOCKMANN. Well, a man of science ought to live in a little style. I'm sure any magistrate spends far more in a year than I do.

MAYOR. Yes, I should think so! After all, a magistrate is an important public official –

DR STOCKMANN. Well, a wholesale merchant, then. A man like that spends much more –

MAYOR. His circumstances are different.

DR STOCKMANN. Oh, it isn't that I'm wasteful, Peter. I just can't deny myself the pleasure of having people around me! I need that, you know. I've been living outside the world for so long, and for me it's a necessity to be with people who are young, bold and cheerful, and have lively, liberal minds – and that's what they are, all the men who are sitting in there enjoying a good meal! I wish you knew Hovstad a little better –

MAYOR. That reminds me, Hovstad told me he's going to print another article by you.

DR STOCKMANN. An article by me?

MAYOR. Yes, about the Baths. Something you wrote last winter.

DR STOCKMANN. Oh, that. No, I don't want them to print that now.

MAYOR. Not? But I should have thought now would be the most suitable time.

DR STOCKMANN. I dare say it would under ordinary circumstances. (*Walks across the room.*)

MAYOR (*watches him*). And what is extraordinary about the circumstances now?

DR STOCKMANN (*stops*). I'm sorry, Peter, I can't tell you that yet. Not this evening, anyway. There may be a great deal that's extraordinary; or there may be nothing at all. It may be my imagination –

MAYOR. I must say you're making it all sound very mysterious. Is there something the matter? Something I mustn't be told about? I should have thought that I, as Chairman of the Baths Committee –

DR STOCKMANN. And I should have thought that I, as – well, let's not start flying off the handle.

MAYOR. Heaven forbid. I'm not in the habit of flying off the handle, as you phrase it. But I must absolutely insist that all arrangements be made and executed through the proper channels [and through the authorities legally appointed for that purpose].[1] I cannot permit any underhand or backdoor methods.

DR STOCKMANN. Have I ever used underhand or backdoor methods?

MAYOR. You will always insist on going your own way. And that's almost equally inadmissible in a well-ordered community. The individual must learn to fall in line with the general will – or, to be more accurate, with that of the authorities whose business it is to watch over the common good.

DR STOCKMANN. I dare say. But what the hell has that to do with me?

MAYOR. Because that, my dear Thomas, is what you seem never to be willing to learn. But take care. You'll pay for it some time. Well, I've warned you. Good-bye.

[1] Square brackets in the text indicate suggested cuts for performance.

DR STOCKMANN. Are you raving mad? You're barking completely up the wrong tree –

MAYOR. I'm not in the habit of doing that. Well, if you'll excuse me – (*Bows towards the dining-room.*) Good-bye, sister-in-law. Good day, gentlemen. (*Goes.*)

MRS STOCKMANN (*comes back into the living-room*). Has he gone?

DR STOCKMANN. Yes, Catherine, and in a damned bad temper.

MRS STOCKMANN. Oh, Thomas, what have you done to him now?

DR STOCKMANN. Absolutely nothing. He can't expect me to account to him until the time comes.

MRS STOCKMANN. Account to him? For what?

DR STOCKMANN. Hm; never mind, Catherine. Why the devil doesn't the post come?

> HOVSTAD, BILLING *and* HORSTER *have got up from the dining table and come into the living-room.* EILIF *and* MORTEN *follow a few moments later.*

BILLING (*stretches his arms*). Ah, a meal like that makes one feel like a new man! By Jingo, yes!

HOVSTAD. His Worship wasn't in a very cheerful mood tonight.

DR STOCKMANN. Oh, that's his stomach. He's got a bad digestion.

HOVSTAD. I expect we radical journalists stuck in his gullet.

MRS STOCKMANN. I thought you were getting on rather well with him.

HOVSTAD. Oh, it's only an armistice.

BILLING. That's it! The word epitomizes the situation in a nutshell!

DR STOCKMANN. Peter's a lonely man, poor fellow. We must remember that. He has no home where he can relax; only business, business. And all that damned tea he pours into himself! Well, lads, pull up your chairs! Catherine, where's that toddy?

MRS STOCKMANN (*goes into the dining-room*). It's just coming.

DR STOCKMANN. You sit down here on the sofa with me, Captain Horster. You're too rare a guest in this house! Sit, sit, gentlemen!

THE GENTLEMEN *sit at the table.* MRS STOCKMANN *brings a tray with a kettle, decanters, glasses, etc.*

MRS STOCKMANN. Here you are. This is arrack, and this is rum; and there's the brandy. Now everyone must help himself.

DR STOCKMANN (*takes a glass*). Don't you worry about that! (*As the toddy is mixed.*) But where are the cigars? Eilif, you know where the box is. Morten, you can bring me my pipe. (*The* BOYS *go into the room on the right.*) I've a suspicion Eilif pinches a cigar once in a while, but I pretend I don't know! (*Shouts.*) And my smoking cap, Morten! Catherine, can't you tell him where I've put it? Oh, good, he's found it. (*The* BOYS *return with the things he asked for.*) Help yourselves, my friends! I stick to my pipe, you know; this old friend's been my companion on many a stormy round up there in the north. (*Clinks his glass with theirs.*) Skoal! Ah, I must say it's better to be sitting here, warm and relaxed.

MRS STOCKMANN (*who is sitting, knitting*). Will you be sailing soon, Captain Horster?

HORSTER. I expect to be off next week.

MRS STOCKMANN. It's America this time, isn't it?

HORSTER. That's the idea.

BILLING. But then you won't be able to vote in the next council elections!

[HORSTER. Is there going to be a new election?

BILLING. Didn't you know?

HORSTER. No, such things don't interest me.

BILLING. But you must care about public affairs?]

HORSTER. No, I don't understand these matters.

BILLING. All the same, one ought at least to vote.

HORSTER. Even if one doesn't understand what it's about?

BILLING. Understand? What's that got to do with it? Society's like a shop. Everyone's got to lend a hand at the rudder.

HORSTER. Not in my ship!

[HOVSTAD. It's curious how little sailors bother about what goes on in their own country.

BILLING. Most abnormal.]

DR STOCKMANN. Sailors are like birds of passage; wherever they happen to be, they regard that as home. Which means the rest of us must be all the more active, Mr Hovstad. Have you anything salutary to offer us in the *People's Tribune* tomorrow?

HOVSTAD. Nothing of local interest. But the day after, I thought of printing your article –

DR STOCKMANN. Oh God, yes, that article! No, look, you'll have to sit on that.

HOVSTAD. Oh? We've plenty of space just now; and I thought this would be the most suitable time –

DR STOCKMANN. Yes, yes, I dare say you're right, but you'll have to wait all the same. I'll explain later –

> PETRA, *in hat and cloak, with a pile of exercise books under her arm, enters from the hall.*

PETRA. Good evening.

DR STOCKMANN. Hullo, Petra, is that you?

> *The others greet her, and she them. She puts down her cloak, hat and books on a chair by the door.*

PETRA. And you're all sitting here having a party while I've been out working!

DR STOCKMANN. Well, come and have a party too.

BILLING. May I mix you a tiny glass?

PETRA (*comes over to the table*). Thanks, I'll do it myself; you always make it too strong. Oh, by the way, father, I've a letter for you.

> *Goes over to the chair on which her things are lying.*

DR STOCKMANN. A letter? Who from?

PETRA (*looks in her coat pocket*). The postman gave it to me just as I was going out –

DR STOCKMANN (*gets up and goes over to her*). Why on earth didn't you let me have it before?

PETRA. I really didn't have time to run up again. Here it is.

DR STOCKMANN (*seizes the letter*). Let me see it, child, let me see it! (*Looks at the envelope.*) Yes, this is it!

MRS STOCKMANN. Is this what you've been waiting for so anxiously, Thomas?

DR STOCKMANN. It is indeed. I must go and read it at once. Where can I find a light, Catherine? Is there no lamp in my room again?

MRS STOCKMANN. Yes, there's one burning on your desk.

DR STOCKMANN. Good, good. Excuse me a moment –
      Goes into the room on the right.

PETRA. What on earth can that be, Mother?

MRS STOCKMANN. I don't know. These last few days he's done nothing but ask about the post.

BILLING. Probably some patient out of town –

PETRA. Poor father! He'll soon find he's bitten off more than he can chew. (*Mixes herself a glass.*) Ah, that tastes good!

HOVSTAD. Have you been at evening classes tonight, too?

PETRA (*sips her drink*). Two hours.

BILLING. And four hours this morning at the technical college –

PETRA (*sits at the table*). Five hours.

MRS STOCKMANN. And you've got exercises to correct tonight, I see.

PETRA. Yes, lots.

HORSTER. You seem to have bitten off more than you can chew too, by the sound of it.

PETRA. Yes, but I like it. It makes you feel so wonderfully tired.

BILLING. Wonderfully?

PETRA. Yes. One sleeps so soundly afterwards.

MORTEN. You must be very wicked, Petra.

PETRA. Wicked?

MORTEN. Yes, if you work so much. Dr Roerlund says work is a punishment for our sins.

EILIF (*sniffs*). Silly! Fancy believing stuff like that!

MRS STOCKMANN. Now, now, Eilif!

BILLING (*laughs*). Ha! Very good!

HOVSTAD. Don't you want to work hard too, Morten?

MORTEN. No! Not me!

HOVSTAD. But surely you want to become something?

MORTEN. I want to be a Viking!

EILIF. But then you'll have to be a heathen.

MORTEN. All right, I'll be a heathen!

BILLING. I'm with you there, Morten! That's just the way I feel!

MRS STOCKMANN (*makes a sign*). I'm sure you don't really, Mr Billing.

BILLING. By Jingo, I do! I *am* a heathen and I'm proud of it! Before long we'll all be heathens. Just you wait and see.

MORTEN. Shall we be able to do anything we like then?

BILLING. Yes, Morten! You see –

MRS STOCKMANN. Hurry off now, boys. I'm sure you've some homework to do.

EILIF. I can stay a few minutes longer –

MRS STOCKMANN. No, you can't. Be off, the pair of you!

The BOYS *say good night and go into the room on the left.*

HOVSTAD. Do you really think it can do the boys any harm to hear this kind of thing?

MRS STOCKMANN. Well, I don't know. I just don't like it.

PETRA. Oh, really, mother! I think you're being very stupid.

MRS STOCKMANN. Perhaps I am; but I don't like it. Not here in the home.

PETRA. Oh, there's so much fear of the truth everywhere! At home and at school. Here we've got to keep our mouths shut, and at school we have to stand up and tell lies to the children.

HORSTER. Lie to them?

PETRA. Yes, surely you realize we have to teach them all kinds of things we don't believe in ourselves.

BILLING. I fear that is all too true!

PETRA. If only I had the money, I'd start a school of my own. And there things would be different.

BILLING. Ah! Money!

HORSTER. If you mean that seriously, Miss Stockmann, I could gladly let you have a room at my place. My father's old house is almost empty; there's a great big dining-room downstairs –

PETRA (*laughs*). Thank you! But I don't suppose it'll ever come to anything.

HOVSTAD. No, I think Miss Petra will probably turn to journalism. By the way, have you found time to look at that English novel you promised to translate for us?

PETRA. Not yet. But I'll see you get it in time.

> DR STOCKMANN *enters from his room with the letter open in his hand.*

DR STOCKMANN (*waves the letter*). Here's news that's going to set this town by the ears, believe you me!

BILLING. News?

MRS STOCKMANN. Why, what's happened?

DR STOCKMANN. A great discovery has been made, Catherine!

HOVSTAD. Really?

MRS STOCKMANN. By you?

DR STOCKMANN. Precisely! By me! (*Walks up and down.*) Now let them come as usual and say it's all madman's talk and I'm imagining things! But they'll have to watch their step this time! (*Laughs.*) Yes, I fancy they'll have to watch their step!

PETRA. Father, for Heaven's sake tell us what it is!

DR STOCKMANN. Yes, yes, just give me time and you'll hear everything. Oh, if only I had Peter here now! Well, it only goes to show how blindly we mortals can form our judgments –

HOVSTAD. What do you mean by that, Doctor?

DR STOCKMANN (*stops by the table*). Is it not popularly supposed that our town is a healthy place?

HOVSTAD. Yes, of course.

DR STOCKMANN. A quite unusually healthy place? A place which deserves to be recommended in the warmest possible terms both for the sick and for their more fortunate brethren?

MRS STOCKMANN. Yes, but my dear Thomas – !

DR STOCKMANN. And we ourselves have praised and recommended it, have we not? I have written thousands of words of eulogy both in the *People's Tribune*, and in pamphlets –

HOVSTAD. Yes, well, what of it?

DR STOCKMANN. These Baths, which have been called the artery of the town, and its central nerve and – and God knows what else –

BILLING. 'The pulsing heart of our city' is a phrase I once, in a festive moment, ventured to –

DR STOCKMANN. No doubt. But do you know what they really are, these beloved Baths of ours which have been so puffed up and which have cost so much money? Do you know what they are?

HOVSTAD. No, what are they?

DR STOCKMANN. Nothing but a damned cesspit!

PETRA. The Baths, father?

MRS STOCKMANN (*simultaneously*). Our Baths!

HOVSTAD (*simultaneously*). But, Doctor – !

BILLING. Absolutely incredible!

DR STOCKMANN. These Baths are a whited sepulchre – and a poisoned one at that. Dangerous to health in the highest degree! All that filth up at Moelledal – you know, that stinking refuse from the tanneries – has infected the water in the pipes that feed the Pump Room. And that's not all. This damnable muck has even seeped out on to the beach –

HORSTER. Where the sea baths are?

DR STOCKMANN. Exactly!

HOVSTAD. But how can you be so sure about all this, Doctor?

DR STOCKMANN. I've investigated the whole thing most thoroughly. Oh, I've long suspected something of the kind. Last year there were a lot of curious complaints among visitors who'd come for the bathing – typhoid, and gastric troubles –

MRS STOCKMANN. Yes, so there were.

DR STOCKMANN. At the time we thought these people had

brought the disease with them. But later, during the winter, I began to have other thoughts. So I set to work to analyse the water as closely as I was able.

MRS STOCKMAN. So that's what you've been toiling so hard at!

DR STOCKMANN. Yes, you may well say I have toiled, Catherine. But of course I lacked the proper scientific facilities. So I sent specimens of both the drinking water and the sea water to the University to have them analysed by a chemist.

HOVSTAD. And now you have that analysis?

DR STOCKMANN (*shows the letter*). Here it is! It establishes conclusively that the water here contains putrid organic matter – millions of bacteria! It is definitely noxious to the health even for external use.

MRS STOCKMANN. What a miracle you found this out in time!

DR STOCKMANN. You may well say that, Catherine.

HOVSTAD. And what do you intend to do now, Doctor?

DR STOCKMANN. Put the matter right, of course.

HOVSTAD. Can that be done?

DR STOCKMANN. It must be done! Otherwise the Baths are unusable – and all our work has been wasted. But don't worry. I'm pretty sure I know what needs to be done.

MRS STOCKMANN. But, my dear Thomas, why have you kept all this so secret?

DR STOCKMANN. Did you expect me to go round the town talking about it before I was certain? No, thank you, I'm not that mad.

PETRA. You might have told us –

DR STOCKMANN. I wasn't going to tell anyone. But tomorrow you can run along to the Badger and –

MRS STOCKMANN. Thomas, really!

DR STOCKMANN. Sorry, I mean your grandfather. It'll shock the old boy out of his skin. He thinks I'm a bit gone in the head anyway – oh, and there are plenty of others who think the same! I know! But now these good people shall see! Now they shall see! (*Walks around and rubs his hands.*) There's going to be such a to-do in this town, Catherine! You've no idea! The whole water system will have to be relaid.

HOVSTAD (*gets up*). The whole of the water system –?

DR STOCKMANN. Of course. The intake is too low. It'll have to be raised much higher up.

PETRA. Then you were right after all!

DR STOCKMANN. Yes, Petra, do you remember? I wrote protesting against the plans when they were about to start laying it. But no one would listen to me then. Well, now I'll give them a real broadside. Of course, I've written a full report to the Baths Committee; it's been ready for a whole week, I've only been waiting to receive this. (*Shows the letter.*) But now I shall send it to them at once! (*Goes into his room and returns with a sheaf of papers.*) Look at this! Ten foolscap pages – closely written! I'm sending the analysis with it. A newspaper, Catherine! Get me something to wrap these up in. Good! There, now! Give it to – to –! (*Stamps his foot.*) What the devil's her name? You know, the maid! Tell her to take it straight down to the Mayor.

MRS STOCKMANN *goes out through the dining-room with the parcel.*

PETRA. What do you think Uncle Peter will say, father?

DR STOCKMANN. What can he say? He must be grateful that so important a fact has been brought to light.

HOVSTAD. May I have your permission to print a short piece about your discovery in the *People's Tribune*?

DR STOCKMANN. I'd be very grateful if you would.

HOVSTAD. I think it's desirable that the community should be informed as quickly as possible.

DR STOCKMANN. Yes, yes, of course.

MRS STOCKMANN (*comes back*). She's gone with it now.

BILLING. You'll be the first citizen in the town, Doctor, by Jingo, you will!

DR STOCKMANN (*walks round contentedly*). Oh, nonsense, I've really done nothing except my duty. I dug for treasure and struck lucky, that's all. All the same –!

BILLING. Hovstad, don't you think the town ought to organize a torchlight procession in honour of Dr Stockmann?

HOVSTAD. I'll suggest it, certainly.

BILLING. And I'll have a word with Aslaksen.

DR STOCKMANN. No, my dear friends, please don't bother with that nonsense. I don't want any fuss made. And if the Baths Committee should decide to raise my salary, I won't accept it! It's no good, Catherine, I won't accept it!

MRS STOCKMANN. Quite right, Thomas.

PETRA (*raises her glass*). Skoal, father!

HOVSTAD }
BILLING } Skoal, skoal, Doctor!

HORSTER (*clinks his glass with the* DOCTOR'S). Here's hoping your discovery will bring you nothing but joy!

DR STOCKMANN. Thank you, my dear friends, thank you! I'm so deeply happy! Oh, it's good to know that one has the respect of one's fellow-citizens! Hurrah, Catherine!

> *Seizes her round the neck with both hands and whirls round with her.* MRS STOCKMANN *screams and struggles. Laughter, applause, and cheers for the* DOCTOR. *The* BOYS *stick their heads in through the door.*

ACT TWO

The DOCTOR's *living-room. The door to the dining-room is shut.*
Morning.

MRS STOCKMANN (*enters from the dining-room with a sealed*
letter in her hand, goes over to the door downstage right and peeps
in). Are you at home, Thomas?

DR STOCKMANN (*offstage*). Yes, I've just come in. (*Enters.*)
What is it?

MRS STOCKMANN. A letter from your brother. (*Hands it to him.*)

DR STOCKMANN. Aha, let's see what he says. (*Opens the envelope*
and reads): 'I return herewith the manuscript you sent me –'
(*Reads on, mumbling.*) Hm –!

MRS STOCKMANN. Well, what does he say?

DR STOCKMANN (*puts the papers in his pocket*). No, he just
writes that he'll be coming up here to see me towards noon.

MRS STOCKMANN. You must remember to stay at home, then.

DR STOCKMANN. Oh, that'll be all right. I've finished my round
for today.

MRS STOCKMANN. I'm very curious to know how he's taken it.

DR STOCKMANN. You'll see. He won't like the fact that I made
this discovery and not he.

MRS STOCKMANN. Doesn't it worry you? It does me.

DR STOCKMANN. Well, he'll be happy at heart, of course. The
trouble is, Peter gets so damned angry at the idea of anyone
but himself doing anything for the good of the town.

MRS STOCKMANN. You know, Thomas, I really think you ought
to share the honour with him. Couldn't you say it was he who
started you thinking along these lines –?

DR STOCKMANN. Gladly, as far as I'm concerned. As long as I
get the matter put right, I –

OLD MORTEN KIIL (*puts his head in through the door leading from the hall, looks around inquiringly, chuckles to himself and asks slyly*). Is it – is it true?

MRS STOCKMANN. Why, father!

DR STOCKMANN. Hullo, father-in-law! Good morning, good morning!

MRS STOCKMANN. Well, aren't you going to come in?

MORTEN KIIL. I will if it's true. If not, I'll be off –

DR STOCKMANN. If what's true?

MORTEN KIIL. This nonsense about the water system. Is it true, eh?

DR STOCKMANN. Of course it's true. But how did you hear about it?

MORTEN KIIL (*comes in*). Petra looked in on her way to school –

DR STOCKMANN. Oh, did she?

MORTEN KIIL. Mm. And she told me. I thought she was just pulling my leg. But that's not like Petra.

DR STOCKMANN. How could you think she'd do a thing like that?

MORTEN KIIL. Never trust anyone. That's my motto. You get made a fool of before you know where you are. So it is true, then?

DR STOCKMANN. Absolutely true. Sit down now, father. (*Coaxes him down on to the sofa.*) Isn't it a stroke of luck for the town?

MORTEN KIIL (*stifles a laugh*). Stroke of luck for the town?

DR STOCKMANN. That I made this discovery in time –

MORTEN KIIL (*as before*). Oh, yes, yes, yes! But I never thought you'd start playing monkey tricks with your own flesh and blood!

DR STOCKMANN. Monkey tricks?

MRS STOCKMANN. Father dear –?

MORTEN KIIL (*rests his hands and chin on the handle of his stick and winks slyly at the* DOCTOR). What was it, now? Didn't you say some animals had got into the water pipes?

DR STOCKMANN. Yes, bacteria.

MORTEN KIIL. Quite a number of them, so Petra told me.
Regular army!

DR STOCKMANN. Millions, probably.

MORTEN KIIL. But no one can see them. Isn't that right?

DR STOCKMANN. Of course one can't *see* them.

MORTEN KIIL (*chuckles silently*). Devil take me if this isn't the
best I've heard from you yet!

DR STOCKMANN. What do you mean?

MORTEN KIIL. But you'll never get the Mayor to believe a tale
like that.

DR STOCKMANN. We'll see.

MORTEN KIIL. Do you think he's that daft?

DR STOCKMANN. I hope the whole town will be that daft.

MORTEN KIIL. The whole town? That's perfectly possible!
Serve them right, it'll teach them a lesson! They hounded me
out of the Council – yes, that's what I call it, for they drove me
out like a dog, they did! But now they're going to pay for it!
You make fools of them, Stockmann!

DR STOCKMANN. But, father –

MORTEN KIIL. You make fools of them, my boy! (*Gets up.*)
If you can put the Mayor and his friends out of countenance,
I'll give a hundred crowns to the poor immediately!

DR STOCKMANN. That's very generous of you.

MORTEN KIIL. I'm not a rich man, mind! But if you do that,
I'll remember the poor to the tune of fifty crowns; at Christmas.

HOVSTAD *enters from the hall.*

HOVSTAD. Good morning! (*Stops.*) Oh, am I intruding?

DR STOCKMANN. No, come in, come in!

MORTEN KIIL (*chuckles again*). Him! Is he in with you on this?

HOVSTAD. What do you mean?

DR STOCKMANN. Indeed he is.

MORTEN KIIL. I might have guessed it! So it's to be in the
papers! Yes, you're a card all right, Stockmann! Well, you two
put your heads together. I'm off.

DR STOCKMANN. Oh, father, stay a little longer.

MORTEN KIIL. No, I'm off. Pull out all the tricks you know! By God, I'll see you don't lose by it! (*Goes.* MRS STOCKMANN *accompanies them out.*)

DR STOCKMANN (*laughs*). Imagine, Hovstad, the old man doesn't believe a word I say about the water system!

HOVSTAD. Oh, so *that* was –?

DR STOCKMANN. Yes, that's what we were talking about. I suppose that's why you've come too?

HOVSTAD. Yes. Can you spare me a moment or two, Doctor?

DR STOCKMANN. As long as you want, my dear fellow.

HOVSTAD. Have you heard anything from the Mayor?

DR STOCKMANN. Not yet. He'll be along shortly.

HOVSTAD. I've been thinking a lot about this since last night.

DR STOCKMANN. Yes?

HOVSTAD. You're a doctor and a man of science, and to you this business of the water is something to be considered in isolation. I think you don't perhaps realize how it's tied up with a lot of other things.

DR STOCKMANN. I don't quite understand you. [Let's sit down my dear chap. No, over there on the sofa.]

    HOVSTAD *sits on the sofa*, DR STOCKMANN *in an armchair on the other side of the table.*

DR STOCKMANN. Well?

HOVSTAD. You said yesterday that the pollution of the water was the result of impurities in the soil.

DR STOCKMANN. Yes, we're pretty certain that filthy swamp up at Moelledal is the cause of the evil.

HOVSTAD. Forgive me, Doctor, but I believe the real cause of all the evil is to be found in quite a different swamp.

DR STOCKMANN. Which one?

HOVSTAD. The swamp in which our whole communal life is slowly rotting.

DR STOCKMANN. Damn it, Mr Hovstad, what kind of talk is this?

HOVSTAD. Little by little all the affairs of this town have fallen into the hands of a small clique of bureaucrats.

DR STOCKMANN. Oh, come, you can't group them all under that description.

HOVSTAD. No, but the ones who don't belong to it are the friends and hangers-on of the ones who do. It's the rich men, the ones with names – they're the people who rule our life.

DR STOCKMANN. They're shrewd and intelligent men.

HOVSTAD. Did they show shrewdness or intelligence when they laid the water pipes where they are now?

DR STOCKMANN. No, that was very stupid, of course. But it's going to be put right now.

HOVSTAD. You think they'll enjoy doing that?

DR STOCKMANN. Enjoy it or not, they'll be forced to do it.

HOVSTAD. If the press is allowed to use its influence.

DR STOCKMANN. That won't be necessary, my dear fellow. I'm sure my brother will –

HOVSTAD. I'm sorry, Doctor, but I intend to take this matter up myself.

DR STOCKMANN. In the newspaper?

HOVSTAD. When I took over the *People's Tribune* I did so with the fixed purpose of breaking up this ring of obstinate bigots who hold all the power in their hands.

DR STOCKMANN. But you told me yourself what happened as a result. The paper almost had to close down.

HOVSTAD. We had to play it easy then, that's true. There was a risk that if these men fell, the Baths might not be built. But now we have them, and these fine gentlemen have become dispensable.

DR STOCKMANN. Dispensable, perhaps. But we owe them a debt all the same.

HOVSTAD. Oh, that'll be handsomely acknowledged. But a radical writer like me can't let an opportunity like this pass unused. We must destroy the myth of these men's infallibility. It must be rooted out like any other kind of superstition.

DR STOCKMANN. Ah, I'm with you there! If it is a superstition, then away with it!

HOVSTAD. I'd prefer not to attack the Mayor, since he's your brother. But I know you feel as strongly as I do that truth must precede all other considerations.

DR STOCKMANN. Of course. (*Bursts out.*) But –! But –!

HOVSTAD. You mustn't think ill of me. I'm not more ambitious or self-seeking than most men.

DR STOCKMANN. But my dear fellow, who suggests you are?

HOVSTAD. I'm the son of poor people, as you know, and I've had the chance to see what's needed most in the lower strata of society. It's to have a share in the control of public affairs. That's what develops ability, and knowledge, and human dignity.

DR STOCKMANN. I appreciate that.

HOVSTAD. And then I think a journalist has a lot to answer for if he neglects an opportunity to achieve emancipation for the masses – [– the small and the oppressed]. Oh, I know – the big boys will call me a demagogue and all that – but I don't care. As long as my conscience is clear, I –

DR STOCKMANN. That's the point, yes! That's exactly it, Mr Hovstad! All the same – damn it – (*A knock at the door.*) Come in!

ASLAKSEN, *the printer, appears in the doorway leading from the hall. He is humbly but decently dressed in black, with a white and somewhat crumpled cravat, gloves, and a silk hat in his hand.*

ASLAKSEN (*bows*). I trust you'll forgive me for being so bold, Doctor –

DR STOCKMANN (*gets up*). Why, hullo! Aren't you Aslaksen the printer?

ASLAKSEN. I am indeed, Doctor.

HOVSTAD (*gets up*). Are you looking for me, Aslaksen?

ASLAKSEN. No, I'd no idea I'd see you here. It was the Doctor himself I –

DR STOCKMANN. Well, what can I do for you?

ASLAKSEN. Is it true what Mr Billing tells me, that you're thinking of getting us a better water system?

DR STOCKMANN. Yes, for the Baths.

ASLAKSEN. Ah, yes, I see. Well, I just came to say that I'm right behind you!

HOVSTAD (*to* DR STOCKMANN). You see!

DR STOCKMANN. I'm most grateful; but –

ASLAKSEN. You might find it useful to have us tradespeople behind you. We form a pretty solid majority in this town – when we choose to, mind! And it's always good to have the majority behind you, Doctor.

DR STOCKMANN. True enough. But I don't see that any special effort is necessary here. Surely it's a perfectly straightforward matter –

ASLAKSEN. Yes, but you might be glad of us all the same. I know these local authorities. The boys in power don't like accepting suggestions from outside. So I thought it might not be out of place if we organized a little demonstration.

HOVSTAD. That's just what I feel.

DR STOCKMANN. Demonstration? In what way will you demonstrate?

ASLAKSEN. Oh, with restraint, Doctor. I always insist on restraint. Restraint is the primary virtue of every citizen. That's my opinion, anyway.

DR STOCKMANN. Yes, yes, Mr Aslaksen. Your views are well known –

ASLAKSEN. Yes, I fancy they are. Now this business of the water system is very important to us tradespeople. It looks as though the Baths are going to prove as you might say a little goldmine for the town. We'll all be depending on the Baths for our livelihood, especially us property owners. That's why we want to give the project every support we can. And seeing as I'm Chairman of the Property Owners' Association –

DR STOCKMANN. Yes?

ASLAKSEN. And seeing as I'm also on the Council of the Temperance Society – you do know I'm a temperance worker –?

DR STOCKMANN. Yes, yes.

ASLAKSEN. Well, so it stands to reason I come into contact with a lot of people. And seeing as I'm known to be a level-headed and law-abiding citizen, as you said yourself, it means I have a certain influence in the town – I wield a little power – though I say it myself.

DR STOCKMANN. I'm well aware of that, Mr Aslaksen.

ASLAKSEN. Yes, well – so it'd be an easy matter for me to arrange an address, if the occasion should arise.

DR STOCKMANN. An address?

ASLAKSEN. Yes, a kind of vote of thanks from the citizens of this town to you for having carried this important matter to a successful conclusion. Of course, it stands to reason the wording's got to be restrained, so it won't offend the authorities and the other people as has the power. And so long as we're careful about that, I don't think anyone can take offence, can they?

HOVSTAD. Well, even if they don't particularly like it, they –

ASLAKSEN. No, no, no! We mustn't offend authority, Mr Hovstad! We can't afford to defy the people on whom our lives depend. I've seen plenty of that in my time, and no good ever came out of it. But the sober expression of liberal sentiments can cause no affront.

DR STOCKMANN (*shakes his hand*). My dear Aslaksen, I can't tell you how deeply happy I am to find all this support among my fellow citizens. I am most moved, most moved. Well, now! What about a small glass of sherry?

ASLAKSEN. No, thank you! I never touch spirits.

DR STOCKMANN. A glass of beer, then? What do you say to that?

ASLAKSEN. No, thank you, not that either, Doctor. I never touch anything so early in the day. And now I must be getting back to town to talk to some of the other property owners and prepare the atmosphere.

DR STOCKMANN. It's really most kind of you, Mr Aslaksen. But I simply cannot get it into my head that all this fuss is really necessary. I should have thought the matter would solve itself.

ASLAKSEN. The authorities move somewhat ponderously, Doctor. Heaven knows I don't intend any reflection on them –!

HOVSTAD. We'll give them a drubbing in print tomorrow, Mr Aslaksen.

ASLAKSEN. But no violence, Mr Hovstad! Proceed with restraint! Otherwise you'll get nowhere with them. You can rely on my judgment, for I have culled my knowledge in the school of life. Yes, well, I must say good-bye. You know now that we trades-people stand behind you like a wall, Doctor. You have the solid majority on your side, whatever else may happen.

DR STOCKMANN. Thank you, my dear Mr Aslaksen. (*Shakes his hand.*) Good-bye, good-bye!

ASLAKSEN. Are you coming down to the press too, Mr Hovstad?

HOVSTAD. I'll follow later. I've a few things to arrange first.

ASLAKSEN. Yes, yes.

Bows and goes out. DR STOCKMANN *accompanies him out into the hall.*

HOVSTAD (*as the* DOCTOR *returns*). Well, what do you say to that, Doctor? Don't you think it's time this town was shaken out of its torpidity and its weak-kneed half-heartedness?

DR STOCKMANN. You mean Aslaksen?

HOVSTAD. Yes, I do. Oh, he's honest enough in some respects, but he's stuck in the swamp. And most of the others are the same. They swing this way and that, and spend so much time looking at every side of the question that they never make a move in any direction.

DR STOCKMANN. But Aslaksen seemed very well-meaning, I thought.

HOVSTAD. There's something I regard as more important than that. To know your own mind and have the courage of your convictions.

DR STOCKMANN. Yes, you're right there.

HOVSTAD. That's why I'm so keen to seize this opportunity and see if I can't get these well-meaning idiots to act like men for once. All this grovelling to authority has got to be stopped. This blunder they've made about the water system is quite indefensible, and that fact's got to be drummed into the ears of every citizen who's got the right to vote.

DR STOCKMANN. Very well. If you think it's for the communal good, go ahead. But not till I've talked with my brother.

HOVSTAD. I'll get my editorial written anyway. And if the Mayor refuses to take action, then –

DR STOCKMANN. Oh, but that's unthinkable.

HOVSTAD. It's a possibility. And if it should happen –?

DR STOCKMANN. If it does, I promise you that – yes, you can print my report. Print the whole damned thing!

HOVSTAD. Is that a promise?

DR STOCKMANN (*hands him the manuscript*). Here it is. Take it with you. It won't do any harm for you to read through it; and you can give it back to me afterwards.

HOVSTAD. Right, I'll do that. Well, good-bye, Doctor.

DR STOCKMANN. Good-bye, good-bye! Don't you worry, Mr Hovstad – everything's going to go quite smoothly. Quite smoothly!

HOVSTAD. Hm. We shall see.

   Nods and goes out through the hall.

DR STOCKMANN (*goes over to the dining-room and looks in*). Catherine –! Oh, hullo, Petra, are you here?

PETRA (*enters*). Hasn't he come yet?

DR STOCKMANN. Peter? No. But I've been having a long talk with Hovstad. He's quite excited about this discovery of mine. It seems it has a much wider significance than I'd supposed. So he's placed his newspaper at my disposal, if I should need it.

MRS STOCKMANN. But do you think you will?

DR STOCKMANN. Oh no, I'm sure I won't. But it's good to know that one has the free press on one's side – the mouthpiece of liberal opinion. And what do you think? I've had a visit from the Chairman of the Property Owners' Association!

MRS STOCKMANN. Oh? And what did he want?

DR STOCKMANN. He's going to support me too. They're all going to support me, if there's any trouble. Catherine, do you know what I have behind me?

MRS STOCKMANN. Behind you? No, what have you behind you?

DR STOCKMANN. The solid majority.

MRS STOCKMANN. I see. And that's a good thing, is it?

DR STOCKMANN. Of course it's a good thing! (*Rubs his hands and walks up and down.*) How splendid to feel that one stands shoulder to shoulder with one's fellow citizens in brotherly concord!

PETRA. And that one's doing so much that's good and useful, father.

DR STOCKMANN. Yes, and for one's home town too!

MRS STOCKMANN. There's the doorbell.

DR STOCKMANN. Ah, this must be him! (*A knock on the inner door.*) Come in!

MAYOR (*enters from the hall*). Good morning.

DR STOCKMANN (*warmly*). Hullo, Peter!

MRS STOCKMANN. Good morning, brother-in-law. How are you?

MAYOR. Oh, thank you; so-so. (*To the* DOCTOR.) Last night, after office hours, I received a thesis from you regarding the state of the water at the Baths.

DR STOCKMANN. Yes. Have you read it?

MAYOR. I have.

DR STOCKMANN. Well! What do you think?

MAYOR (*glances at the others*). Hm –

MRS STOCKMANN. Come, Petra.

She and PETRA *go into the room on the left.*

MAYOR (*after a pause*). Was it necessary to conduct all these investigations behind my back?

DR STOCKMANN. Well, until I was absolutely certain, I –

MAYOR. And now you are?

DR STOCKMANN. Yes. Surely you must be convinced –?

MAYOR. Is it your intention to place this document before the Baths Committee as an official statement?

DR STOCKMANN. Of course! Something must be done. And quickly.

MAYOR. I find your phraseology in this document, as usual, somewhat extravagant. Amongst other things, you say that all we have to offer our visitors at present is a permanent state of ill-health.

DR STOCKMANN. Peter, how else can you describe it? Just think! That water's poisonous even if you bathe in it, let alone drink it! And we're offering this to unfortunate people who are ill and who have turned to us in good faith, and are paying us good money, in order to get their health back!

MAYOR. And your conclusion is that we must build a sewer to drain away these aforesaid impurities from the swamp at Moelledal, and that the whole water system must be relaid.

DR STOCKMANN. Can you think of any other solution? I can't.

MAYOR. This morning I called upon the town engineer. In the course of our discussion I half jokingly mentioned these proposals as a thing we might possibly undertake some time in the future.

DR STOCKMANN. Some time in the future?

MAYOR. He smiled at what he obviously regarded as my extravagance – as I knew he would. Have you ever troubled to consider what these alterations you suggest would cost? According to the information I received, the expense would probably run into several hundred thousand crowns.

DR STOCKMANN. Would it be that much?

MAYOR. Yes. But that's not the worst. The work would take at least two years.

DR STOCKMANN. Two years, did you say? Two whole years?

MAYOR. At least. And what do we do with the Baths in the meantime? Close them? Yes, we'd be forced to. You don't imagine anyone would come here once the rumour got around that the water was impure?

DR STOCKMANN. But, Peter, it is!

MAYOR. [And for this to happen just now, when the whole enterprise is coming to fruition!] There are other towns around with qualifications to be regarded as health resorts. Do you think they won't start trying to attract the market? Of course they will! And there we shall be! We'll probably have to abandon the whole expensive scheme, and you will have ruined the town [that gave you birth].

DR STOCKMANN. I – ruined –!

MAYOR. It's only as a health resort – a Spa – that this town has any future worth speaking of. Surely you realize that as well as I do.

DR STOCKMANN. But what do you propose we do?

MAYOR. Your report has not completely convinced me that the situation is as dangerous as you imply.

DR STOCKMANN. Oh, Peter, if anything it's worse! Or at least it will be in the summer, once the hot weather starts.

MAYOR. As I said, I believe that you are exaggerating the danger. [A capable medical officer must be able to take measures. He must know how to forestall such unpleasantnesses, and how to remedy them if they should become obvious.

DR STOCKMANN. Go on.]

MAYOR. The existing water system at the Baths is a fact, and must be accepted as such. However, in due course I dare say the Committee might not be inflexibly opposed to considering whether, without unreasonable pecuniary sacrifice, it might not be possible to introduce certain improvements.

DR STOCKMANN. And you think I'd lend my name to such chicanery?

MAYOR. Chicanery!

DR STOCKMANN. That's what it would be! A fraud, a lie, a crime against the community, against the whole of society!

MAYOR. As I have already pointed out, I have not succeeded

in convincing myself that any immediate or critical danger exists.

DR STOCKMANN. Oh, yes you have! [You must have! My arguments are irrefutable – I know they are! And you know that as well as I do, Peter!] But you won't admit it, because it was you who forced through the proposal that the Baths and the water pipes should be sited where they are, and you refuse to admit that you made a gross blunder. Don't be such a fool, do you think I don't see through you?

MAYOR. And suppose you were right? If I do guard my reputation with a certain anxiety, it is because I have the welfare of our town at heart. Without moral authority I cannot guide and direct affairs as I deem most fit for the general good. For this, and diverse other reasons, it is vital to me that your report should not be placed before the Baths Committee. It must be suppressed for the general good. At a later date I shall bring the matter up for discussion, and we shall discreetly do the best we can. But nothing, not a single word, about this unfortunate matter must come to the public ear.

DR STOCKMANN. Well, it can't be stopped now, my dear Peter.

MAYOR. It must and shall be stopped.

DR STOCKMANN. It can't, I tell you. Too many people know.

MAYOR. Know? Who knows? You don't mean those fellows from the *People's Tribune* –?

DR STOCKMANN. [Oh, yes, they too.] The free press of our country will see to it that you do your duty.

MAYOR (*after a short pause*). You're an exceedingly foolish man, Thomas. Haven't you considered what the consequences of this action may be for you?

DR STOCKMANN. Consequences? Consequences for me?

MAYOR. Yes. For you and for your family.

DR STOCKMANN. What the devil do you mean by that?

MAYOR. I think I have always shown myself a good brother to you, whenever you've needed help.

DR STOCKMANN. You have, and I thank you for it.

MAYOR. I'm not asking for thanks. To a certain extent I've been forced to do it – for my own sake. [I always hoped I might be able to curb you a little if I could help to improve your economic position.

DR STOCKMANN. What! So it was only for your own sake that you –

MAYOR. Partly, I said.] It's painful for a public servant to see his next-of-kin spend his entire time compromising himself.

DR STOCKMANN. And you think I do that?

MAYOR. Unfortunately you do, without knowing it. You have a restless, combative, rebellious nature. And then you've this unfortunate passion for rushing into print upon every possible – and impossible – subject. The moment you get an idea you have to sit down and write a newspaper article or a whole pamphlet about it.

DR STOCKMANN. Surely if a man gets hold of a new idea it's his duty as a citizen to tell it to the public?

MAYOR. People don't want new ideas. They're best served by the good old accepted ideas they have already.

DR STOCKMANN. And you can say that to my face!

[MAYOR. Yes, Thomas. I'm going to speak bluntly to you for once. Up to now I've tried to avoid it, because I know how hasty you are; but now I've got to tell you the truth. You've no idea how much harm you do yourself by this impulsiveness of yours. You abuse the authorities, and even the government – you throw mud at them, you claim you've been cold-shouldered and persecuted. But what else can you expect, when you're such a difficult person?

DR STOCKMANN. Oh, so I'm difficult too, am I?]

MAYOR. Oh, Thomas, you're impossible to work with. [I've discovered that for myself.] You never consider anyone else's feelings. You even seem to forget it's me you have to thank for getting you your job at the Baths –

DR STOCKMANN. It was mine by right! I was the first person to see that this town could become a flourishing watering place!

[And I was the only person who did see it at that time!] For many years I fought alone for this idea! I wrote, and wrote –

MAYOR. No one denies that. But the time wasn't ripe then. [Of course you weren't to know that, tucked away in your northern backwater.] But as soon as the right moment arrived, I – and others – took the matter up –

DR STOCKMANN. Yes, and made a mess of my wonderful plan! Oh yes, it's becoming very clear now what brilliant fellows you were!

MAYOR. As far as I can see, all you're looking for now is just another excuse for a fight. You've always got to pick a quarrel with your superiors – it's your old failing. You can't bear to have anyone in authority over you. [You look askance at anyone who occupies a position higher than yours. You regard him as a personal enemy – and then, as far as you're concerned, one weapon of attack is as good as another.] But now I've shown you what's at stake, for the whole town, and for myself too. And I'm not prepared to compromise.

DR STOCKMANN. What do you mean?

MAYOR. Since you have been so indiscreet as to discuss this delicate matter, which you ought to have kept a professional secret, the affair obviously cannot be hushed up. All kinds of rumours will spread around, and the malicious elements among us will feed these rumours with details of their own invention. It is therefore necessary that you publicly deny these rumours.

DR STOCKMANN. I don't understand you.

MAYOR. I feel sure that on further investigation you will convince yourself that the situation is not nearly as critical as you had at first supposed.

DR STOCKMANN. Aha; you feel sure, do you?

MAYOR. I also feel sure you will publicly express your confidence that the Committee will [painstakingly and conscientiously take all necessary measures to] remedy any possible defects which may exist.

DR STOCKMANN. But you can't remedy the defect by just patching things up! I'm telling you, Peter, unless you start again from scratch, it's my absolute conviction that –

MAYOR. As an employee you have no right to any independent conviction.

DR STOCKMANN (*starts*). No right!

MAYOR. As an employee. As a private person – well, heaven knows that's another matter. But as a subordinate official at the Baths, you have no right to express any opinion which conflicts with that of your superiors.

DR STOCKMANN. This is going too far! I, a doctor, a man of science, have no right –!

MAYOR. The question is not merely one of science. [The problem is complex.] The issues involved are both technical and economical.

DR STOCKMANN. I don't care how you define the bloody thing! I must be free to say what I think about anything!

MAYOR. Go ahead. As long as it isn't anything connected with the Baths. That we forbid you.

DR STOCKMANN (*shouts*). You forbid –! You –! Why, you're just a –

MAYOR. *I* forbid you – I, your chief! And when I forbid you to do something, you must obey!

DR STOCKMANN (*controls himself*). Peter – if you weren't my brother –!

PETRA (*throws open the door*). Father, don't put up with this!

MRS STOCKMANN (*follows her*). Petra, Petra!

MAYOR. Ha! Eavesdroppers!

MRS STOCKMANN. You were talking so loud – we couldn't help hearing –

PETRA. I was listening.

MAYOR. Well, I'm not altogether sorry –

DR STOCKMANN (*goes closer to him*). You spoke to me of forbidding and obeying?

MAYOR. You forced me to use that tone.

DR STOCKMANN. And you expect me to publicly swallow my own words?

MAYOR. We regard it as an unavoidable necessity that you issue a statement on the lines I have indicated.

DR STOCKMANN. And if I don't – obey?

MAYOR. Then we shall be forced to issue an explanation, to calm the public.

DR STOCKMANN. All right! But I shall write and refute you. I stick to my views. I shall prove that I am right and you are wrong. And what will you do then?

MAYOR. Then I shall be unable to prevent your dismissal.

DR STOCKMANN. What –!

PETRA. Father! Dismissal!

MRS STOCKMANN. Dismissal!

MAYOR. Dismissal from your post as public medical officer. I shall feel compelled to apply for immediate notice to be served on you, barring you from any further connection with the Baths.

DR STOCKMANN. You'd have the impudence to do that?

MAYOR. You're the one who's being impudent.

PETRA. Uncle, this is a disgraceful way to treat a man like father!

MRS STOCKMANN. Be quiet, Petra.

MAYOR (*looks at* PETRA). So we've opinions of our own already, have we? But of course! (*To* MRS STOCKMANN.) Sister-in-law, you seem to be the most sensible person in this house. Use what influence you have over your husband. Make him realize the consequences this will have both for his family and –

DR STOCKMANN. My family concerns no one but myself.

MAYOR. – both for his family, and for the town he lives in.

DR STOCKMANN. I'm the one who has the town's real interests at heart! I want to expose the evils that sooner or later must come to light. I'm going to prove to people that I love this town where I was born.

MAYOR. Oh, you're blind! All you're trying to do is to stop up the source of the town's prosperity.

DR STOCKMANN. That source is poisoned, man! Are you mad? We live by hawking filth and disease! And all this communal life you boast so much about is based upon a lie!

MAYOR. That's pure imagination – if nothing worse. The man who casts such foul aspersions against the town he lives in is an enemy of society.

DR STOCKMANN (*goes towards him*). You dare to –!

MRS STOCKMANN (*throws herself between them*). Thomas!

PETRA (*grasps her father by the arm*). Keep calm, father!

MAYOR. I shall not expose myself to violence. You've been warned. Consider what is your duty to yourself and your family. Good-bye. (*Goes.*)

DR STOCKMANN (*walks up and down*). And in my own house too, Catherine!

MRS STOCKMANN. Yes, Thomas. It's a shame and a scandal –

PETRA. I'd like to get my hands on him –!

DR STOCKMANN. It's my own fault. I ought to have exposed them long ago! I should have bared my teeth; and used them! Calling me an enemy of society! By God, I'm not going to take that lying down!

MRS STOCKMANN. But, Thomas dear, might is right –

DR STOCKMANN. I'm the one who's right!

MRS STOCKMANN. What's the good of being right if you don't have the might?

PETRA. Mother, how can you speak like that?

[DR STOCKMANN. So it's no use in a free society to have right on one's side? Don't be absurd, Catherine. Besides – don't I have the free press in front of me – and the solid majority behind me? That's might enough, I should have thought!

MRS STOCKMANN. For heaven's sake, Thomas, surely you're not thinking of setting yourself up against your brother?

DR STOCKMANN. What the devil else do you expect me to do? Don't you want me to stand up for what I believe to be right?

PETRA. Yes, father, you must!

MRS STOCKMANN. It'll do you no good. If they won't, they won't.]

DR STOCKMANN (*laughs*). Oh, Catherine, just give me time. You'll see! I'm going to fight this war to the end.

MRS STOCKMANN. Yes, and the end will be that you'll lose your job. [You'll see.

DR STOCKMANN. At least I shall have done my duty to the community; my duty to society. And they call me an enemy of society –!]

MRS STOCKMANN. What about your family, Thomas? [And your home? Do you think you'll be doing your duty to the ones who depend on you?]

PETRA. Oh, mother, don't always think only of us.

MRS STOCKMANN. It's easy for you to talk. You can stand on your own feet, if need be. But think of the boys, Thomas! [And think of yourself too – and me –

DR STOCKMANN. You must be mad, Catherine! If I give in like a coward to Peter and his wretched gang, do you think I'd ever have another moment of happiness in my life?

MRS STOCKMANN. I don't know about that. But God preserve us from the happiness we're likely to enjoy if you go on digging your heels in. You'll have no means of livelihood, no regular income. Didn't we have enough of that in the old days? Remember that, Thomas. Think what it'll mean.

DR STOCKMANN (*writhes, fighting with himself, and clenches his fists*). And these office lackeys can do this to a free and honourable man! Isn't it monstrous, Catherine?

MRS STOCKMANN. Yes, they've behaved very wickedly to you, that's true. But heaven knows, there's so much injustice one has to put up with in this world. There are the boys, Thomas.] Look at them! What's to become of them? [No, no, you can't have the heart.]

  EILIF *and* MORTEN *have meanwhile entered, carrying their schoolbooks.*

DR STOCKMANN. My sons! (*Suddenly stands erect, his mind*

made up.) Even if my whole world crashes about me, I shall never bow my head. (*Goes towards his room.*)

MRS STOCKMANN. Thomas, what are you going to do?

DR STOCKMANN (*in the doorway*). I want to have the right to look my sons in the eyes when they grow up into free men! (*Goes into his room.*)

MRS STOCKMANN (*bursts into tears*). Oh, God help us!

[PETRA. Father's right, mother! He'll never give in.]

The boys ask in bewilderment what is the matter. PETRA *signs to them to go.*

ACT THREE

The editorial office of the People's Tribune. *On the left in the background is the entrance door; to the right in the same wall is another door with glass panes through which the composing room is visible. Another door is in the wall on the right. In the middle of the room is a big table covered with papers, newspapers and books. Downstage left is a window; by it is a writing desk with a high stool. Two armchairs stand by the table, and there are other chairs along the walls. The room is gloomy and uncomfortable; the furniture is old, the armchairs dirty and torn. In the composing room one or two* COMPOSITORS *are at work. Beyond them, a hand-press is being operated.*

HOVSTAD *sits writing at the desk. After a few moments,* BILLING *enters right, with the* DOCTOR's *manuscript in his hand.*

BILLING. I say, I say, I say!

HOVSTAD (*writing*). Have you read it?

BILLING (*puts the manuscript on the desk*). I should say I have!

HOVSTAD. Pretty forceful, isn't it?

BILLING. Forceful? He'll butcher them, by Jingo! Every paragraph's a knock-out!

HOVSTAD. Those fellows won't give in at the first blow, though.

BILLING. That's true. But we'll go on bashing them, punch after punch, till their whole damned oligarchy falls to the ground! As I sat in there reading this, it was as though I saw the revolution dawning from afar!

HOVSTAD (*turns*). Hush, don't let Aslaksen hear.

BILLING (*lowers his voice*). Aslaksen's a coward, a jellyfish! He hasn't the guts of a man! But you'll have your way? You will publish the Doctor's article?

HOVSTAD. Yes, unless the Mayor backs down –

BILLING. That'd be a damned nuisance!

HOVSTAD. Whichever way it turns out we can exploit the situation. If the Mayor doesn't agree to the Doctor's proposal, he'll have all the tradespeople down on him – the Property Owners' Association, and the rest. And if he does agree to it he'll antagonize all the big shareholders in the Baths who up to now have been his chief supporters –

BILLING. Of course! They'll have to fork out a pile of money –

HOVSTAD. You bet they will. And then the clique will be broken, and day after day we'll drum it into the public that the Mayor's incompetent in more respects than one, and that [all the responsible offices in the town,] the whole municipal authority, ought to be handed over to people of liberal opinions.

BILLING. By Jingo, that's the truth! I see it! I see it! We stand on the threshold of a revolution!

A knock on the door.

HOVSTAD. Quiet! (*Shouts.*) Come in.

DR STOCKMANN *enters through the door upstage left.*

HOVSTAD (*goes to greet him*). Ah, here is the Doctor! Well?

DR STOCKMANN. Print away, Mr Hovstad!

HOVSTAD. So it's come to that?

BILLING. Hurrah!

DR STOCKMANN. Print away, I say! Yes, it's come to that all right. Well, now they shall have it the way they want it. It's war now, Mr Billing!

BILLING. War to the death, I hope! Give it to them, Doctor!

DR STOCKMANN. This report is only the beginning. My head's already teeming with ideas for four or five other articles. Where's Aslaksen?

BILLING (*calls into the composing-room*). Aslaksen, come here a moment!

HOVSTAD. Four or five other articles, did you say? On the same theme?

DR STOCKMANN. No – oh, good heavens no, my dear fellow! No, they'll be about quite different things. But it all stems from this business of the water system and the sewer. One thing leads to another, you know. It's like when you start to pull down an old building. Exactly like that.

BILLING. By Jingo, that's true! You suddenly realize you'll never be finished till you've pulled down the whole rotten structure!

ASLAKSEN (*from the composing-room*). Pulled down! You're surely not thinking of pulling the Baths down, Doctor?

HOVSTAD. No, no, don't get frightened.

DR STOCKMANN. No, we were talking about something else. Well, Mr Hovstad, what do you think of my report?

HOVSTAD. I think it's an absolute masterpiece –

DR STOCKMANN. Do you think so? That makes me very happy – very happy.

HOVSTAD. It's so clear and to the point; you don't have to be a specialist to follow the argument. I'm sure you'll have every enlightened person on your side.

ASLAKSEN. Every discriminating one too, I trust?

BILLING. Discriminating or not – you'll have the whole town behind you.

ASLAKSEN. Well then, I don't think we need be afraid to print it.

DR STOCKMANN. I should damn well hope not.

HOVSTAD. It'll be in tomorrow morning.

DR STOCKMANN. Good God, yes, we can't afford to waste a single day. Oh, Mr Aslaksen, there was one thing I wanted to ask you. You must take charge of this manuscript yourself.

ASLAKSEN. If you wish.

DR STOCKMANN. Treat it as though it was gold. No misprints! Every word is important. I'll drop back later; perhaps you'd let me look at a proof. I can't tell you how eager I am to see this thing in print – launched –!

BILLING. Launched, yes! Like a thunderbolt!

DR STOCKMANN. – and submitted to the judgment of every intelligent citizen. Oh, you'd never guess what I've had to put up with today! I've been threatened with God knows what. They want to rob me of my elementary rights as a human being –

BILLING. Your rights as a human being!

DR STOCKMANN. [They want to degrade me, reduce me to the level of a beggar.] They demand that I put my private interests above my most sacred and innermost convictions –

BILLING. By Jingo, that's going too far!

HOVSTAD. You can expect anything from that lot.

DR STOCKMANN. [But they won't get far with me!] I'll give it to them in black and white! I'll grapple with them every day in the *People's Tribune*! I'll sweep them with one broadside after another –!

ASLAKSEN. Yes, but remember –

BILLING. Hurrah! It's war, it's war!

DR STOCKMANN. I'll beat them to the ground, [I'll crush them,] I'll flatten their defences for every honest man to see! [By God I will!]

ASLAKSEN. But do it soberly, Doctor. Act with restraint –

BILLING. No, no! Don't spare your powder!

DR STOCKMANN (*continues imperturbably*). You see, it isn't just a question of the water system and the sewer. This whole community's got to be cleansed and decontaminated –

BILLING. That's the very word!

DR STOCKMANN. All these skimpers and compromisers have got to be thrown out! There's got to be a clean sweep! [Oh, such endless vistas have been opened up before my eyes today! I don't see my way quite clearly yet. But I will!] We need fresh standard-bearers, my friends! Young men! Our advance posts must be manned by new captains!

BILLING. Hear, hear!

DR STOCKMANN. As long as we stick together, [it'll all happen so easily! –] the whole revolution will glide into existence like a ship from the stocks! Don't you agree?

HOVSTAD. I think we've every prospect now of getting the helm into the right hands.

ASLAKSEN. As long as we proceed with restraint, I don't think there can be any danger.

DR STOCKMANN. Who the hell cares about danger? I'm doing this in the name of truth and of my conscience!

HOVSTAD. You're a man who deserves support, Doctor.

ASLAKSEN. Yes, the Doctor's a true friend of the town, that's certain. I'll go further; he's a friend of society!

BILLING. By Jingo, Mr Aslaksen, Dr Stockmann is a friend of the people!

[ASLAKSEN. I think the Property Owners' Association might be able to use that phrase.]

DR STOCKMANN (*moved, presses their hands*). Thank you, my dear, good friends – thank you! It's so refreshing for me to hear this. My brother described me in vastly different terms. By God, I'll give it back to him with interest! Now I must go and see a poor devil of a patient. But I'll be back! Take good care of that manuscript, Mr Aslaksen. And for heaven's sake don't cut out any of the exclamation marks! If anything, put in a few more! Good, good! Well, good-bye! Good-bye, good-bye!

He shakes hands with them as they accompany him to the door and he goes out.

HOVSTAD. He's going to be bloody useful to us.

ASLAKSEN. As long as he sticks to the Baths. But if he tries to go further, we'd be unwise to stay with him.

HOVSTAD. Hm; that all depends –

BILLING. You're such a damned coward, Aslaksen!

ASLAKSEN. Coward? Yes, when it's a question of fighting local authorities, I am a coward, Mr Billing. That's a lesson I have learned in the school of life. But elevate me into the field of high politics, confront me with the Government, and then see if I am a coward!

BILLING. No, no, I'm sure you're not. But that's just where you're so inconsistent.

ASLAKSEN. Because I know my responsibilities as a citizen! Throwing stones at the government can't harm society. It doesn't bother those fellows – they stay put. But local authorities can be overthrown, and then you may get inexperience at the helm. [With disastrous results for property owners and the like.]

HOVSTAD. But what about the education of people through self-government?

ASLAKSEN. When a man has interests to protect he can't think of everything, Mr Hovstad.

HOVSTAD. Then I hope to God I never have any interests to protect.

BILLING. Hear, hear!

HOVSTAD. I'm not a trimmer, and I never will be.

ASLAKSEN. A politician should never commit himself, Mr Hovstad. And you, Mr Billing, you ought to put a reef or two in your sails if you want that job of clerk to the council.

BILLING. I –!

HOVSTAD. *You*, Billing?

BILLING. Of course I only applied for it to put their backs up, you understand.

ASLAKSEN. Well, it's no business of mine. But since I'm being accused of cowardice and inconsistency, I'd like to make this clear. My political record is open for anyone to investigate. I've never changed my standpoint – apart from having learned more restraint. My heart still belongs with the people; but I don't deny that my head keeps one ear cocked towards the authorities. The local ones, anyway. (*Goes into the composing-room.*)

BILLING. Couldn't we change to some other printer, Hovstad?

HOVSTAD. Do you know anyone else who'd give us credit [for printing and paper]?

BILLING. It's a damned nuisance not having any capital!

HOVSTAD (*sits at the desk*). Yes, if we only had *that* –

BILLING. Ever thought of trying Dr Stockmann?

HOVSTAD (*glancing through his papers*). What'd be the use of that? He hasn't a bean.

BILLING. No; but he's got a good man behind him. Old Morten Kiil – the fellow they call the Badger –

HOVSTAD (*writing*). Do you really think he's got much?

BILLING. By Jingo, of course he has! And part of it must go to the Stockmanns. He's bound to provide for – well, the children, anyway.

HOVSTAD (*half turns*). Are you banking on that?

BILLING. Banking? I never bank on anything.

HOVSTAD. You'd better not. And don't bank on becoming clerk to the council either, because I can promise you you won't.

BILLING. Do you think I don't know? *Not* to get it is just what I want! A snub like that puts you on your mettle. It gives you a fresh supply of gall, and you need that in a backwater like this, where hardly anything really infuriating ever happens.

HOVSTAD (*writing*). Yes, yes.

BILLING. Well, they'll soon hear from me! I'll go and write that appeal for funds to the Property Owners' Association. (*Goes into the room on the right.*)

HOVSTAD (*sitting at the desk, chews his pen and says slowly*). Hm! So that's the way the wind blows! (*There is a knock on the door.*) Come in!

PETRA *enters through the door upstage left.*

HOVSTAD (*gets up*). Why, hullo! Fancy seeing you here!

PETRA. Please forgive me –

HOVSTAD (*pushes forward an armchair*). Won't you sit down?

PETRA. No, thank you. I'm only staying a moment.

HOVSTAD. Is it something from your father –?

PETRA. No, something from me. (*Takes a book from her coat pocket.*) Here's that English novel.

HOVSTAD. Why are you giving it back to me?

PETRA. I don't want to translate it.

HOVSTAD. But you promised –

PETRA. I hadn't read it then. You can't have, either!

HOVSTAD. No – you know I don't understand English. But –

PETRA. Exactly. That's why I wanted to tell you – you'll have to find something else to serialize. (*Puts the book on the table.*) You can't possibly print this in the *People's Tribune*.

HOVSTAD. Why not?

PETRA. Because it's diametrically opposed to what you believe.

HOVSTAD. Oh, that's the reason?

PETRA. I don't think you understand. Its theme is that there's a supernatural power which takes care of all the so-called good people in this world, and works things so that in the end everything turns out well for them and all the so-called bad people get punished.

HOVSTAD. Yes, well, that's all right. That's just what people want to read.

PETRA. But do you want to be the one who provides it for them? You don't believe a word of that! You know quite well it doesn't happen like that in real life.

HOVSTAD. Of course not. But an editor can't always do as he wishes. One often has to bow to people's feelings in minor matters. After all, politics are the most important things in life – for a newspaper, anyway. And if I want to win people over to my views about freedom and progress, I mustn't frighten them away. If they find a moral story like this in the back pages of the newspaper they're more likely to go along with what we print on the front page. It reassures them.

PETRA. Oh, really! You're not as crafty as that. I don't see you as a spider spinning webs to catch your readers!

HOVSTAD (*smiles*). Thank you for holding such a high opinion of me. No, actually this was Billing's idea, not mine.

PETRA. Billing's!

HOVSTAD. Yes. He was talking on those lines here the other day. He's the one who's so keen that we should publish this novel. I'd never heard of the book.

PETRA. But Billing holds such progressive views –

HOVSTAD. Oh, there's more in Billing than meets the eye. I've just heard he's applied for the post of clerk to the council.

PETRA. I don't believe that, Mr Hovstad. How could he reconcile himself to doing a thing like that?

HOVSTAD. You'd better ask him.

PETRA. I'd never have thought that of Billing.

HOVSTAD (*looks more closely at her.*) Wouldn't you? Does it so surprise you?

PETRA. Yes. Perhaps not, though. I don't really know –

HOVSTAD. We journalists aren't worth much, Miss Stockmann.

PETRA. How can you say that?

HOVSTAD. I sometimes think it.

PETRA. In the ordinary run of events, perhaps not – that I can understand. But now, when you've taken up such an important cause –

[HOVSTAD. This business with your father, you mean?

PETRA. Yes, that.] Now surely you must feel you're worth more than most men.

HOVSTAD. Yes, today I do feel a bit like that.

PETRA. It's true, isn't it! You do! Oh, it's a wonderful vocation you've chosen! To be able to pioneer neglected truths and brave new doctrines – the mere fact of standing fearlessly forth to defend a man who's been wronged –

HOVSTAD. Especially when this man who's been wronged is – hm – how shall I say –?

PETRA. When he is a man of such honour and integrity?

HOVSTAD (*more quietly*). I was about to say: especially when he is your father.

PETRA (*astounded*). Mr Hovstad!

HOVSTAD. Yes, Petra – Miss Petra –

PETRA. Is that what seems important to you? Not the issue itself. Not the truth – or the fact that this means everything to Father –

HOVSTAD. Yes – yes, of course – those things too –

PETRA. No, thank you. You let the cat out of the bag there, Mr Hovstad. Now I shall never believe you again. About anything.

HOVSTAD. Does it make you so angry that I've done this for your sake?

PETRA. I'm angry because you haven't been honest with Father. You've been talking to him as though truth and the good of the people were what mattered most to you. You've been fooling both of us. You're not the man you've been pretending you are. And that I'll never forgive you – never!

HOVSTAD. You shouldn't speak so sharply to me, Miss Petra. Least of all just now.

PETRA. Why not now?

HOVSTAD. Because your father needs my help.

PETRA. So that's the sort of man you are!

HOVSTAD. No, no, I didn't mean that. Please believe me –!

PETRA. I know what to believe. Good-bye.

ASLAKSEN (*hurries in furtively from the composing-room*). For God's sake, Mr Hovstad –! (*Sees* PETRA.) Oh, dear, that's unlucky –!

PETRA. There's the book. You can give it to someone else. (*Goes towards the door.*)

HOVSTAD (*goes after her*). But, Miss Petra –!

PETRA. Good-bye. (*Goes.*)

ASLAKSEN. Mr Hovstad, listen, please!

HOVSTAD. Yes, yes, what is it?

ASLAKSEN. The Mayor's standing outside there in the composing-room!

HOVSTAD. The Mayor?

ASLAKSEN. Yes. He wants to talk to you. He came in the back way – didn't want to be seen, I suppose.

HOVSTAD. What can he want? No, wait, I'd better – (*Goes to the door of the composing-room, opens it, bows and invites the* MAYOR *to enter.*)

HOVSTAD. Keep a look out, Aslaksen, and make sure no one –

ASLAKSEN. Of course. (*Goes into the composing-room*).

MAYOR. You weren't expecting to see me here.

HOVSTAD. No, frankly, I wasn't.

MAYOR (*looks round*). You've done this up quite nicely. Very pleasant.

HOVSTAD. Oh –

MAYOR. And here I am, coming along and making demands on your time.

HOVSTAD. Not at all, sir. What can I do for you? Please allow me – (*Takes the* MAYOR'S *hat and stick and puts them on a chair.*) Won't you sit down?

MAYOR (*sits at the table*). Thank you.

    HOVSTAD *also sits at the table.*

MAYOR. Something – something extremely irritating has happened to me today, Mr Hovstad.

HOVSTAD. Really? Of course, Your Worship has so many responsibilities –

MAYOR. This particular matter concerns the medical officer at the Baths.

HOVSTAD. Oh – the Doctor –?

MAYOR. He's written a sort of – report to the Baths Committee regarding some supposed defects in the Baths.

HOVSTAD. You amaze me.

MAYOR. Hasn't he told you? I thought he said –

HOVSTAD. Oh yes, that's true, he did say something –

ASLAKSEN (*from the composing-room*). I'd better have that manuscript –

HOVSTAD (*irritated*). Hm – it's there on the desk –

ASLAKSEN (*finds it*). Good.

MAYOR. Why, surely that's it!

ASLAKSEN. Yes, this is the Doctor's article, Your Worship.

HOVSTAD. Oh, is this what you were talking about?

MAYOR. The very thing. What do you think of it?

HOVSTAD. Of course I'm not a specialist, and I've only glanced through it –

MAYOR. But you're going to print it?

HOVSTAD. I can't very well refuse a signed contribution –

ASLAKSEN. I have no say in the contents of the paper, Your Worship –

MAYOR. Of course not.

ASLAKSEN. I only print what's put into my hands.

MAYOR. Absolutely.

ASLAKSEN. So if you'll excuse me – (*Goes towards the composing-room.*)

MAYOR. No, wait a moment, Mr Aslaksen. With your permission, Mr Hovstad –

HOVSTAD. Of course, Your Worship.

MAYOR. You're an intelligent and discriminating man, Mr Aslaksen.

ASLAKSEN. I'm glad Your Worship thinks so.

MAYOR. And a man of wide influence in more circles than one.

ASLAKSEN. Oh – mostly among humble people –

MAYOR. The small taxpayers are the most numerous, here as elsewhere.

ASLAKSEN. Yes, that's true.

MAYOR. And I've no doubt you know how most of them feel. Don't you?

ASLAKSEN. Yes, I think I may say I do, Your Worship.

MAYOR. Well then, since the less affluent of the citizens of this town are so laudably disposed to make this sacrifice, I –

ASLAKSEN. What!

HOVSTAD. Sacrifice –?

MAYOR. It's a fine token of public spirit. A remarkably fine token. I was about to confess I hadn't expected it. But you know the mood of the people better than I do.

ASLAKSEN. But, Your Worship –

MAYOR. And it will probably be no mean sacrifice that the ratepayers will be called upon to make.

HOVSTAD. The ratepayers?

ASLAKSEN. But I don't understand – surely the shareholders –?

MAYOR. According to a provisional estimate, the alterations that the medical officer at the Baths regards as desirable will cost some two to three hundred thousand crowns.

ASLAKSEN. That's a lot of money; but –

MAYOR. We shall of course be forced to raise a municipal loan.

HOVSTAD (*gets up*). You surely don't mean that the ordinary citizens –?

ASLAKSEN. You mean you'd charge it on the rates! Empty the pockets of the tradespeople –?

MAYOR. Well, my dear Mr Aslaksen, where else is the money to come from?

ASLAKSEN. That's the business of the gentlemen who own the Baths.

MAYOR. The Committee cannot see their way towards authorizing any further expenditure.

ASLAKSEN. Is that quite definite, Your Worship?

MAYOR. I have gone into the matter very thoroughly. If the people want all these comprehensive alterations, then the people themselves will have to pay for them.

ASLAKSEN. But, good God Almighty – oh, I beg Your Worship's pardon! – but this puts a completely different face on the situation, Mr Hovstad.

HOVSTAD. It certainly does.

MAYOR. The worst of the matter is that we shall be compelled to close the Baths for two to three years.

HOVSTAD. Close them? You mean – close them completely?

ASLAKSEN. For two years?

MAYOR. That's how long the work will take, at the lowest calculation.

ASLAKSEN. But, good heavens, we'll never be able to stand that, Your Worship! How are we property owners to live in the meantime?

MAYOR. I'm afraid that's a very difficult question to answer, Mr Aslasken. But what do you expect us to do? Do you imagine we shall get a single visitor here if we start spreading the idea that the water is contaminated, that we are living over a cesspit, that the whole town –?

ASLAKSEN. And all this is just pure speculation?

MAYOR. With the best will in the world I have been unable to convince myself that it is anything else.

ASLAKSEN. But if that's the case it's monstrous of Dr Stockmann to have – I beg Your Worship's pardon, but –

MAYOR. I deplore your observation, Mr Aslaksen, but I'm afraid it represents the truth. My brother has unfortunately always been an impulsive man.

ASLAKSEN. And you still want to support him in this action, Mr Hovstad?

HOVSTAD. But who could have possibly guessed that –?

MAYOR. I have written a brief *résumé* of the situation as it appears to an impartial observer; and in it I have suggested how any possible flaws in the existing arrangements could safely be remedied by measures within the financial resources at present possessed by the Baths.

HOVSTAD. Have you that document with you, Your Worship?

MAYOR (*feels in his pocket*). Yes, I brought it with me just in case you –

ASLAKSEN (*quickly*). Oh, my goodness, there he is!

MAYOR. Who? My brother?

HOVSTAD. Where – where?

ASLAKSEN. He's just coming through the composing-room.

MAYOR. Most unfortunate! I don't want to meet him here, and I've something else I wanted to speak to you about.

HOVSTAD (*points towards the door, right*). Go in there till he's gone.

MAYOR. But –?

HOVSTAD. There's only Billing there.

ASLAKSEN. Quick, quick, Your Worship! He's coming now!

MAYOR. Very well. But get rid of him as soon as you can.

    Goes out through the door on the right, which ASLAKSEN
    opens and closes for him.

HOVSTAD. Find something to do, Aslaksen.

He sits down and writes. ASLAKSEN *starts looking through a pile of newspapers on a chair to the right.*

DR STOCKMANN (*enters from the composing-room*). Well, here I am again! (*Puts down his hat and stick.*)

HOVSTAD (*writing*). Already, Doctor? Aslaksen, hurry up with that thing we were talking about. We're badly behindhand today.

DR STOCKMANN (*to* ASLAKSEN). No proofs yet, by the sound of it?

ASLAKSEN (*without turning*). No, surely you didn't think they'd be ready yet.

DR STOCKMANN. That's all right. I'm just impatient, as I know you'll appreciate. I can't rest till I've seen that thing in print.

HOVSTAD. Hm – it'll be a good time yet. Won't it, Aslaksen?

ASLAKSEN. I'm afraid so.

DR STOCKMANN. Very well, my dear friends. I'll be back later. I don't mind making the journey twice if need be! [In such a vital matter, with the welfare of the whole town at stake, one mustn't grudge a little extra effort!] (*Is about to go, but stops and comes back.*) Oh, by the way, there's one more thing I must speak to you about.

HOVSTAD. I'm sorry, but couldn't it wait till another time –?

DR STOCKMANN. I can tell you in two words. It's just this – [when people read my article in the paper tomorrow and discover I've been racking my brains all winter working silently for the welfare of the town –

HOVSTAD. But, Doctor –

DR STOCKMANN. I know what you're going to say! You think it was no more than my damned duty – my job as a citizen. Yes, of course – I know that as well as you do. But] my fellow citizens, you see – oh dear, those good people, they're so fond of me –

ASLAKSEN. Yes, the people of this town have been very fond of you, Doctor, up to today.

[DR STOCKMANN. Yes, and that's exactly why I'm frightened that – what I mean is – when they read this – especially the poorer people – as a clarion call bidding them take the government of their town into their own hands –

HOVSTAD (*gets up*). Look, Doctor, I don't want to hide anything from you –

DR STOCKMANN. Ah, something's already afoot! I might have guessed! But I don't want it! If anything like that's being organized, I –

HOVSTAD. Like what?]

DR STOCKMANN. Well, if anything like a torchlight procession or a banquet or – a subscription for some little token of thanks is being organized, you must promise me solemnly you'll squash the idea. And you too, Mr Aslaksen! You hear?

HOVSTAD. I'm sorry, Doctor, but we might as well tell you the truth now as later –

   MRS STOCKMANN, *in hat and cloak, enters through the door upstage, left.*

MRS STOCKMANN (*sees the* DOCTOR). I knew it!

HOVSTAD (*goes towards her*). You here too, Mrs Stockmann?

DR STOCKMANN. What the devil do you want here, Catherine?

MRS STOCKMANN. Surely you can guess.

HOVSTAD. Won't you sit down? [Or perhaps –?]

MRS STOCKMANN. Thank you, you needn't bother. And you mustn't take offence at my coming here to fetch my husband, for I'm the mother of three children, I'd have you realize.

DR STOCKMANN. Oh really, Catherine, we know all this.

MRS STOCKMANN. Well, it doesn't seem you've much thought for your wife and children today, or you wouldn't have come here to cause all of us misery.

DR STOCKMANN. Are you quite mad, Catherine? Simply because a man has a wife and children, is he to be forbidden to proclaim the truth – to be a useful and active citizen – to serve the town he lives in?

MRS STOCKMANN. Oh, Thomas, if only you'd use some restraint.

ASLAKSEN. That's exactly what I say. Restraint in all things.

MRS STOCKMANN. And as for you, Mr Hovstad, it's not right for you to persuade my husband to leave his house and home and trick him into involving himself in all this –

HOVSTAD. I haven't tricked anyone –

DR STOCKMANN. Tricked! You think *I* allow myself to be tricked?

MRS STOCKMANN. Yes, you do. Oh, I know you're the cleverest man in the town, but you're so dreadfully easy to fool, Thomas. (*To* HOVSTAD.) And don't forget he'll lose his job at the Baths if you print that thing he's written –

ASLAKSEN. What!

HOVSTAD. But Doctor – I –

DR STOCKMANN (*laughs*). Just let them try! Oh no, Catherine – they'll watch their step! You see, I have the majority behind me!

MRS STOCKMANN. Yes, that's just the trouble. They're an ugly thing to have behind you.

DR STOCKMANN. Rubbish, Catherine! You go home now and take care of the house, and let me take care of society. How can you be frightened when I feel so calm and happy? (*Rubs his hands and walks up and down.*) Truth and the people will win this battle, never you fear! Oh, I can see every liberal-minded citizen in this town marching forward in an unconquerable army –! (*Stops by a chair.*) What – the devil is *this*?

ASLAKSEN (*looks at it*). Oh dear!

DR STOCKMANN. The crown of authority! (*Takes the* MAYOR's *hat carefully in his fingers and holds it in the air.*)

MRS STOCKMANN. The Mayor's hat!

DR STOCKMANN. And his marshal's baton too. How in the name of hell –?

HOVSTAD. Well –

DR STOCKMANN. Ah, I see! He's been here to talk you over!

(*Laughs.*) He came to the wrong men! And then he saw me in the composing-room – (*Roars with laughter.*) Did he run away, Mr Aslaksen?

ASLAKSEN (*quickly*). Oh yes, Doctor, he ran away.

DR STOCKMANN. Ran away leaving his stick and –? Rubbish! Peter never left anything behind in his life! But where the devil have you put him? Ah, yes, of course – in there! Now, Catherine, you watch!

MRS STOCKMANN. Thomas, I beg you –!

ASLAKSEN. Don't do anything rash, Doctor!

DR STOCKMANN *has put the* MAYOR's *hat on his head and taken his stick. Then he goes across, throws the door open and brings his hand up to the hat in salute. The* MAYOR *enters, red with anger.* BILLING *follows him.*

MAYOR. What is the meaning of this disorderly scene?

DR STOCKMANN. A little more respect if you please, my dear Peter. I am the supreme authority in this town now. (*He walks up and down.*)

MRS STOCKMANN (*almost in tears*). Thomas, please!

MAYOR (*follows him*). Give me my hat and stick!

DR STOCKMANN (*as before*). You may be Chief of Police, but I'm the Mayor! I'm master of this whole town, I am!

MAYOR. Take off that hat, I tell you! Remember that that hat is an official emblem –

DR STOCKMANN. Rubbish! Do you think the awakening lion of public opinion is going to let itself be frightened by a hat? We're starting a revolution tomorrow, I'd have you know! You threatened to sack me, but now I'm going to sack you – sack you from all your positions of responsibility! You think I can't? You're wrong, Peter! I have as my allies the conquering forces of social revolution! Hovstad and Billing will thunder in the *People's Tribune*, and Mr Aslaksen will march forth at the head of the entire Property Owners' Association –

ASLAKSEN. No, Doctor, I won't.

DR STOCKMANN. Indeed you will!

MAYOR. Aha! But perhaps Mr Hovstad will support this uprising!

HOVSTAD. No, Your Worship.

ASLAKSEN. Mr Hovstad isn't so mad as to ruin himself and his newspaper for the sake of an hallucination.

DR STOCKMANN (*looks around*). What the devil –?

HOVSTAD. You have presented your case in a false light, Doctor; and therefore I cannot support you.

BILLING. No, after what His Worship has had the grace to tell me in there, I shouldn't –

DR STOCKMANN. Lies! I'll answer for the truth of my report! You just print it. I shan't be frightened to defend it.

HOVSTAD. I'm not printing it. I can't and I won't and I dare not print it.

DR STOCKMANN. Dare not? What nonsense is this? You're the editor, and it's the editors who rule the press.

ASLAKSEN. No, Doctor. It's the subscribers.

MAYOR. Fortunately.

ASLAKSEN. It's public opinion, the educated reader, the property owners and so forth – they're the ones who rule the press.

DR STOCKMANN (*calmly*). And all these forces are ranged against me?

ASLAKSEN. They are. If your report got printed, it would mean ruin for the entire community.

DR STOCKMANN. I see.

MAYOR. My hat and stick!

　　DR STOCKMANN *takes off the hat and puts it on the table together with the stick.*

MAYOR (*takes them both*). Your little reign didn't last long.

DR STOCKMANN. It isn't over yet. (*To* HOVSTAD.) You refuse absolutely, then, to print my report in the *People's Tribune*?

HOVSTAD. Absolutely. Out of consideration for your family, if for no other reason.

MRS STOCKMANN. Never you mind his family, Mr Hovstad.

MAYOR (*takes a paper from his pocket*). This will give the public full possession of the facts. It's an official statement. Mr Hovstad –

HOVSTAD (*takes the paper*). Right. I'll see it's set up at once.

DR STOCKMANN. But not mine! You think you can gag me and stifle the truth! But it won't be as easy as you think. Mr Aslaksen, take this manuscript of mine and print it immediately as a pamphlet – at my own expense! I'll publish it myself! I want four hundred copies – five – no, make it six hundred copies!

ASLAKSEN. I wouldn't give you the use of my press if you offered me gold, Doctor. I daren't. Public opinion wouldn't allow me. You won't find a printer to take it anywhere in this town.

DR STOCKMANN. Give it back to me then.

HOVSTAD *hands him the manuscript.*

DR STOCKMANN (*takes his hat and stick*). I'll see the contents are made known all the same. I'll summon a public meeting and read it! All my fellow citizens shall know the truth!

MAYOR. You won't find anyone in this town who'll lease you a hall for such a purpose.

ASLAKSEN. Not one. I'm sure of that.

BILLING. By Jingo, you won't.

MRS STOCKMANN. This is too disgraceful! Why are they all against you?

DR STOCKMANN (*hotly*). I'll tell you why! It's because in this town all the men are old women! Like you, they just think of their families and not of the community.

MRS STOCKMANN (*grasps his arm*). Then I'll show them that an – an old woman can be a man – for once. I'm sticking with you, Thomas.

DR STOCKMANN. Well said, Catherine! The truth shall be told – by God it will! If I can't lease a hall, I'll hire a drummer to march through the town with me, and I'll read it out at every street corner!

MAYOR. You can't be so crazy as to do that!

DR STOCKMANN. I am!

ASLAKSEN. You won't find a single man in the whole town who'll go with you.

BILLING. No, by Jingo!

MRS STOCKMANN. Don't you give in, Thomas! I'll ask the boys to go with you.

DR STOCKMANN. That's a splendid idea!

MRS STOCKMANN. Morten will love to do it. And so will Eilif, I'm sure.

DR STOCKMANN. Yes, and Petra, too! And you, Catherine!

MRS STOCKMANN. No, no, not me. But I'll stand at the window and watch you. I'll do that.

DR STOCKMANN (*throws his arms around her and kisses her*). Thank you! Well, my fine gentlemen, let the trumpets sound! Let's see whether meanness and mediocrity have the power to gag a man who wants to clean up society!

   DR *and* MRS STOCKMANN *go out through the door upstage left.*

MAYOR (*shakes his head thoughtfully*). Now he's driven her mad, too!

ACT FOUR

A big, old-fashioned room in CAPTAIN HORSTER's *house. In the background an open double-leaved door leads to a lobby. In the left-hand wall are three windows. Against the middle of the opposite wall has been placed a dais, on which stands a small table with two candles, a water carafe, a glass and a bell. The room is further illuminated by bracket lamps between the windows. Downstage left stands a table with a candle on it, and a chair. Downstage right is a door, with a few chairs by it.*

A large gathering of CITIZENS, *of all classes. Here and there,* WOMEN *can be seen among the crowd, and there are a few* SCHOOLBOYS. *More and more people gradually stream in from the back, filling the room.*

A CITIZEN (*to another, as he bumps against him*). Hullo, Lamstad! You here too this evening?

SECOND CITIZEN. I never miss a public meeting.

THIRD CITIZEN (*standing near them*). Brought your whistle, I hope?

SECOND CITIZEN. Course I have. Haven't you?

THIRD CITIZEN. You bet! And Skipper Evensen said he'd bring a bloody great horn!

SECOND CITIZEN. He's a card, old Evensen!

Laughter among the CROWD.

FOURTH CITIZEN (*joins them*). I say, what's this meeting about?

SECOND CITIZEN. Dr Stockmann's going to deliver a lecture attacking the Mayor.

FOURTH CITIZEN. But the Mayor's his brother.

FIRST CITIZEN. That don't matter. Dr Stockmann ain't afraid of no one.

THIRD CITIZEN. But he's in the wrong. It said so in the *People's Tribune*.

SECOND CITIZEN. Yes, he must be in the wrong this time. The Property Owners wouldn't let him use their hall, nor the People's Club neither.

FIRST CITIZEN. He couldn't even get the hall at the Baths.

SECOND CITIZEN. Well, what do you expect?

FIRST CITIZEN. Which one do you think we ought to support?

FOURTH CITIZEN. Just keep your eye on old Aslaksen, and do as he does.

BILLING (*with a portfolio under his arm, pushes his way through the* CROWD). Excuse me, please, gentlemen! Can I get through, please? I'm reporting the meeting for the *People's Tribune*. Thank you! (*Sits down at the table, left.*)

[A WORKER. Who was that?

ANOTHER WORKER. Don't you know? It's that chap Billing, who works on Aslaksen's paper.]

CAPTAIN HORSTER *escorts* MRS STOCKMANN *and* PETRA *in through the door downstage right.* EILIF *and* MORTEN *are with them.*

CAPTAIN HORSTER. I thought you might sit here. You can slip out easily if anything should happen.

MRS STOCKMANN. Do you think there'll be trouble?

CAPTAIN HORSTER. One never knows, with a crowd like this. But sit down, and don't worry.

MRS STOCKMANN (*sits*). It was very kind of you to offer my husband this room.

CAPTAIN HORSTER. Well, no one else would, so I –

PETRA (*who has sat down too*). It was brave of you, too, Captain Horster.

CAPTAIN HORSTER. Oh, that didn't call for much courage.

HOVSTAD *and* ASLAKSEN *come through the crowd, at the same time but separately.*

ASLAKSEN (*goes over to* CAPTAIN HORSTER). Hasn't the Doctor come yet?

CAPTAIN HORSTER. He's waiting in there.

There is a stir among the CROWD *near the door backstage.*

HOVSTAD (*to* BILLING). There's the Mayor! See?

BILLING. Yes, by Jingo! So he's come after all!

The MAYOR *gently pushes his way through the* CROWD, *greeting people politely, and stations himself against the wall on the left. A few moments later* DR STOCKMANN *enters through the door downstage right. He is dressed in black, with a frock-coat and a white cravat. A few people clap uncertainly, but are countered by subdued hissing. Silence falls.*

DR STOCKMANN (*in a low voice*). How do you feel, Catherine?

MRS STOCKMANN. I'm all right. (*More quietly.*) Now don't lose your temper, Thomas!

DR STOCKMANN. Oh, I'll control myself, don't you worry. (*Looks at his watch, steps up on to the dais and bows.*) It's a quarter past, so I'll begin – (*Takes out his manuscript.*)

ASLAKSEN. Surely a Chairman ought to be elected first?

DR STOCKMANN. No, no, there's no need for that.

SEVERAL MEN (*shout*). Yes, yes!

MAYOR. I really think we should have someone in the chair.

DR STOCKMANN. But, Peter, I've called this meeting to deliver a lecture!

MAYOR. The Doctor's lecture may possibly give rise to divergent expressions of opinion.

SEVERAL VOICES FROM THE CROWD. A Chairman! A Chairman!

HOVSTAD. Public opinion seems to demand a Chairman.

DR STOCKMANN (*controlling himself*). Very well. Let public opinion have its way.

ASLAKSEN. Would His Worship the Mayor be willing to under-take that function?

THREE MEN (*clap*). Bravo! Hear, hear!

MAYOR. For reasons which I'm sure you will appreciate, I must decline that honour. But fortunately we have among us a man whom I think we can all accept. I refer to the Chairman of the Property Owners' Association, Mr Aslaksen.

MANY VOICES. Yes, yes! Good old Aslaksen! Hurrah for As-laksen.

DR STOCKMANN *picks up his manuscript and descends from the dais.*

ASLAKSEN. If my fellow citizens want to express their trust in me, I won't refuse their call.

Applause and cheers. ASLAKSEN *steps up on to the dais.*

BILLING (*writes*). 'Mr Aslaksen was chosen amid acclamation . . .'

ASLAKSEN. Now that I stand here, may I crave permission to say a few brief words? I'm a mild and peace-loving man who believes in sensible discretion, and in – and in discreet good sense. Everyone who knows me knows that.

MANY VOICES. Yes! That's right, Aslaksen!

ASLAKSEN. Experience in the school of life has taught me that the most valuable virtue for any citizen is restraint –

MAYOR. Hear, hear!

ASLAKSEN. [And that discretion and restraint are the best ser-vants of society.] I would therefore suggest to our respected fellow-citizen who has summoned this meeting that he endeav-our to keep himself within the bounds of temperance.

DRUNKEN MAN (*by the entrance door*). Three cheers for the Temperance Society! Jolly good health!

A VOICE. Shut your bloody trap.

MANY VOICES. Hush, hush!

ASLAKSEN. No interruptions, gentlemen, please! Does anyone wish to say anything before I –?

MAYOR. Mr Chairman!

ASLAKSEN. Your Worship!

MAYOR. As everyone here is doubtless aware, I have close ties of relationship with the present medical officer at the Baths, and would consequently have preferred not to speak this evening. But my official position on the Committee of that organization, and my anxiety for the best interests of the town, force me to table a resolution. I hope I may assume that no citizen here present would regard it as desirable that dubious and exagger-

ated allegations concerning the sanitary conditions at the Baths
should circulate outside this town.

MANY VOICES. No, no, no! Certainly not! We protest!

MAYOR. I therefore move that this meeting refuse the aforesaid
medical officer permission to read or dilate upon his theories
concerning the matter in question.

DR STOCKMANN (*explosively*). Refuse permission? What the
devil –?

    MRS STOCKMANN *coughs*.

DR STOCKMANN (*composes himself*). Very well. You refuse permission.

MAYOR. In my statement to the *People's Tribune* I have acquainted
the public with the essential facts so that every intelligent citizen
can form his own judgment. Amongst other things I pointed out
that the medical officer's proposals – quite apart from the fact
that they amount to a vote of no confidence in the leading citizens of this town – will burden the ratepayers with the unnecessary expenditure of at least a hundred thousand crowns.

    Groans and a few whistles.

ASLAKSEN (*rings his bell*). Order please, gentlemen! I beg leave
to second His Worship's motion. I would add that in my view
the Doctor has had an ulterior motive, no doubt unconscious,
in stirring up this agitation; [he talks about the Baths, but]
what he's really aiming at is a revolution. He wants to transfer
authority into other hands. No one doubts the honesty of the
Doctor's intentions. [Heaven knows, there can be no two opinions about that!] I too believe in popular self-government, so
long as it doesn't impose too heavy an expense upon the tax-
payer. But that's just what would happen here; so I'm blowed,
if you'll excuse the expression, if I can support Dr Stockmann
in this matter. One can pay too high a price for gold; that's my
opinion.

    Lively expressions of assent from all sides.

HOVSTAD. I too feel impelled to explain my position. Dr Stockmann's agitation won considerable sympathy at first, and I

myself supported it as impartially as I was able. But then we found we had allowed ourselves to be misled by a false picture of the facts –

DR STOCKMANN. That's a lie!

HOVSTAD. A not completely reliable picture, then. His Worship's statement has proved that. I hope no one here doubts the liberality of my views. The *People's Tribune*'s attitude on major political questions is well known to you all. But I have learned from men of discretion and experience that in local matters it is the duty of a newspaper to observe a certain caution.

ASLAKSEN. Exactly my feelings.

HOVSTAD. Now in the matter under discussion it's quite clear that Dr Stockmann has popular opinion against him. Well, I ask you, gentlemen, what is the primary duty of an editor? Is it not to reflect the opinions of his readers? Has he not been entrusted with what might be described as an unspoken mandate to advance the cause of those who hold the same views as himself, with all the eloquence of which he is capable? Or am I mistaken?

MANY VOICES. No, no, no! Mr Hovstad is right!

HOVSTAD. It has caused me much heartsearching to break with a man under whose roof I have lately been a not infrequent guest – a man who has until this day rejoiced in the undivided affection of his fellow citizens – a man whose only, or anyway principal fault is that he follows his heart rather than his head.

SCATTERED VOICES. That's true. Hurrah for Dr Stockmann!

HOVSTAD. But my duty towards society left me no alternative. And there's one further consideration which forces me to oppose him, in the hope of halting him on the inauspicious road he has now begun to tread – consideration for his family –

DR STOCKMANN. Stick to the water system and the sewer!

HOVSTAD. – consideration for his wife and the children he has abandoned.

MORTEN. Does he mean us, Mother?

MRS STOCKMANN. Hush!

ASLAKSEN. I shall now put His Worship's resolution to the vote.

DR STOCKMANN. Don't bother! I won't say a word about those damned Baths. No. I've something else to tell you tonight.

MAYOR (*in a low voice*). What the devil's this?

A DRUNKEN MAN (*near the entrance door*). I pay my taxes! So I'm entitled to express my opinion! And it's my absolute 'n unintelligible opinion that –

SEVERAL VOICES. Keep quiet there!

OTHERS. He's drunk! Throw him out!

> *The* DRUNK MAN *is removed.*

DR STOCKMANN. Have I the floor?

ASLAKSEN (*rings his bell*). Dr Stockmann has the floor.

DR STOCKMANN. A few days ago, if anyone had tried to gag me like this I'd have fought like a lion for my sacred human rights! But now that doesn't matter. Now I have more important things to talk about.

> THE CROWD *moves closer around him.* MORTEN KIIL *can be seen among them.*

DR STOCKMANN (*continues*). I've been thinking a great deal these past few days. I've brooded so deeply that in the end my head began to spin –

MAYOR (*coughs*). Hm –!

DR STOCKMANN. But then everything began to fall into place. [I saw the whole picture of things quite clearly. And that's why I'm standing here this evening.] I'm going to make a mighty revelation to you, my friends! I'm going to tell you about a discovery that is infinitely more important than the fiddling little fact that our water system is poisoned and our health baths sited above a cesspit!

MANY VOICES (*shout*). Leave the Baths alone! Don't talk about them! We won't listen!

DR STOCKMANN. This great discovery that I have made during

these last few days is that all our spiritual sources are poisoned, and that the whole of our vaunted social system is founded upon a cesspit of lies!

ASTONISHED VOICES (*mutter in low tones*). What's that? What did he say?

MAYOR. These are ridiculous insinuations –

ASLAKSEN (*his hand on the bell*). I must request the speaker to moderate his language.

DR STOCKMANN. [I have loved this birthplace of mine as dearly as any man can love the place where he spent his youth.] I was young when I left home, and distance, hunger and memory threw, as it were, a brighter lustre over this place and the people who dwelt here.

Some applause and cheers are heard.

DR STOCKMANN. For years I lived in a dreadful backwater far up in the north. [As I wandered among those people who lived scattered over the mountains, I often thought it would have been better for those poor degraded creatures if they'd had a vet instead of a man like me!

Murmurs.

BILLING (*puts down his pen*). By Jingo, I've never heard the like of that –!

HOVSTAD. That's a filthy slander against a worthy community!

DR STOCKMANN. Wait a moment! I don't think anyone could say that I forgot my birthplace up there. I sat there brooding like a duck on an egg; and the chick I hatched was – the plan for these Baths.

Clapping, and murmurs of disapproval.

DR STOCKMANN.] Then at long last fate smiled upon me and allowed me to return. [And then, my fellow-citizens, then I thought I had nothing left to wish for in this world. No –] I had one ambition left – a burning desire to work with all my heart and soul for the welfare of my home and my community.

MAYOR (*gazing into space*). You've a strange way of showing it!

DR STOCKMANN. I went around here revelling blindly in my

new-found happiness. But yesterday morning – no, it was the previous night, actually – my eyes were opened, and the first thing that greeted them was the stupendous imbecility of the authorities –

Noise, shouting and laughter. MRS STOCKMANN *coughs loudly.*

MAYOR. Mr Chairman!

ASLAKSEN (*rings his bell*). As Chairman of this meeting, I –

DR STOCKMANN. Oh, let's not start quibbling about words, Mr Aslaksen. I only mean that I suddenly realized how really revoltingly our politicians had behaved down there at the Baths. I can't stand politicians! I've had all I can take of them. They're like goats in a plantation of young trees! They destroy everything! They block the way for a free man, however much he may twist and turn – and I'd like to see them rooted out and exterminated, like other vermin –

Commotion in the hall.

MAYOR. Mr Chairman, are such calumnies to be permitted?

ASLAKSEN (*his hand on the bell*). Dr Stockmann –!

DR STOCKMANN. I can't understand why I'd never had a proper look at these gentlemen before. I'd had a prime example right in front of my eyes all the time – my brother Peter – procrastinating and purblind –!

Laughter, confusion and whistling. MRS STOCKMANN *sits and coughs.* ASLAKSEN *rings his bell loudly.*

THE DRUNK MAN (*who has come back*). Are you referring to me? My name's Petersen, but don't you bloody well –

ANGRY VOICES. Throw that drunk out! Get rid of him!

The DRUNK MAN *is thrown out again.*

MAYOR. Who was that person?

A BYSTANDER. I don't know, Your Worship.

ASLAKSEN. The man was obviously intoxicated with German beer. Continue, Doctor; but please try to use restraint!

DR STOCKMANN. Well, my fellow-citizens, I won't say anything more about our politicians. If anyone imagines from what I've just said that I've come here this evening to crucify these gentlemen, he's wrong – quite wrong. [For I cherish the comforting belief that these laggards, these survivors from a dying world, are studiously cutting their own throats. They need no doctor's help to hasten their demise. And anyway, it isn't they who are the chief danger to society!] They aren't the ones who are most active in poisoning the sources of our spiritual life [and contaminating the ground on which we tread]! It isn't they who are the most dangerous enemies of truth and freedom in our society!

SHOUTS FROM ALL SIDES. Who, then? Who is? Name them!

DR STOCKMANN. Don't worry, I'll name them! Because this is the great discovery I've made today! (*Raises his voice.*) The most dangerous enemies of truth and freedom are the majority! Yes, the solid, liberal, bloody majority – they're the ones we have to fear! Now you know!

Complete uproar. Nearly everyone is shouting, stamping and whistling. Some of the older men exchange covert glances and seem to be enjoying the situation. MRS STOCKMANN *gets up anxiously.* EILIF *and* MORTEN *go threateningly over to the schoolboys, who are making a commotion.* ASLAKSEN *rings his bell and calls for silence.* HOVSTAD *and* BILLING *are both talking, but neither can be heard. At last silence is restored.*

ASLAKSEN. As Chairman I call upon the speaker to withdraw those mischievous observations.

DR STOCKMANN. Never, Mr Aslaksen! It's the majority in this community that is depriving me of my freedom and trying to forbid me to proclaim the truth.

HOVSTAD. The majority is always right.

BILLING. And speaks the truth, by Jingo!

DR STOCKMANN. The majority is never right! Never, I tell you! That's one of those community lies that free, thinking men have got to rebel against! Who form the majority – in any country? The wise, or the fools? I think we'd all have to agree that the fools are in a terrifying, overwhelming majority all over the world! But in the name of God it can't be right that the fools should rule the wise! (*Uproar and shouting.*) Yes, yes, you can shout me down! But you can't say I'm wrong! The majority has the power – unfortunately – but the majority is not right! The ones who are right are a few isolated individuals like me! The minority is always right! (*Uproar again.*)

HOVSTAD. So Dr Stockmann's turned aristocrat since the day before yesterday!

DR STOCKMANN. I've already said I don't want to waste words on the little flock of short-winded sheep puffing along in the rear! Life has nothing exciting left to offer them. But I'm thinking of the few, the individuals amongst us, who have adopted the new, fresh, burgeoning truths as their watchword! These men stand at the outposts, so far forward that the compact majority hasn't yet arrived – and there they are fighting for those truths which are still too new to man's conscious mind to have any majority behind them.

HOVSTAD. I see, so you've become a revolutionary!

DR STOCKMANN. Yes, Mr Hovstad, by God I have! I intend to start a revolution against the lie that truth is a monopoly of the majority! What are these truths to which the majority clings? They're the truths which are so old that they're on the way to becoming decrepit! But when a truth's as old as that, gentlemen, it's also well on the way to becoming a lie!

Laughter and jeers.

DR STOCKMANN. Yes, yes, you can believe me or not, as you wish; but truths aren't such long-lived Methuselahs as people imagine. A normal truth lives for – what shall I say? – seventeen to eighteen years on an average – twenty years at the most – seldom longer. But truths as old as that are always dreadfully thin. [All the same, it isn't until then that the majority cottons on to them, and commends them to society as sound spiritual fodder. But] there's no great nourishment in that sort of food, I can promise you [that; and as a doctor, I know about these things.] All these majority truths are like last year's salt pork; they're hams that have gone sour and green and tainted. And they're the cause of all the moral scurvy that's rotting our society!

ASLAKSEN. It seems to me that the honourable speaker has strayed somewhat from his text.

MAYOR. I warmly endorse the Chairman's observation.

DR STOCKMANN. Oh, really, Peter, I think you must be quite mad! I'm sticking as close to my text as any man could! My whole point is precisely this, that it's the masses, the mob, this damned majority – they're the thing that's poisoning the sources of our spiritual life and contaminating the ground we walk on!

HOVSTAD. And the great progressive majority does this simply by being sensible enough to believe in those truths which are indisputable and generally acknowledged?

DR STOCKMANN. Oh, my good Mr Hovstad, don't talk to me about indisputable truths. The truths that the masses and the mob acknowledge are the ones that were held by advanced thinkers in our grandparents' time. We outrunners of today don't acknowledge them any longer. I really believe there's only one indisputable truth. It is that no society can live a healthy life if it feeds on truths that are old and marrowless.

HOVSTAD. Instead of all this generalizing why don't you give us a few examples of these old and marrowless truths on which we're living?

Murmurs of agreement from several quarters.

DR STOCKMANN. Oh, I could reel you off a whole list of the beastly things; but to start with I'll limit myself to one 'acknowledged' truth which is really a damned lie, but which Mr Hovstad and the *People's Tribune* and all the hangers-on of the *People's Tribune* feed on all the same.

HOVSTAD. And that is –?

DR STOCKMANN. That is the doctrine which you have inherited from your forefathers and which you continue thoughtlessly to proclaim far and wide – the doctrine that the plebs, the masses, the mob, are the living heart of the people – that they *are* the people – and that the common man, all those ignorant and incompetent millions, have the same right to sanction and condemn, to advise and to govern, as the few individuals who are intellectually aristocrats.

BILLING. Now, really, by Jingo –!

HOVSTAD (*simultaneously, shouts*). Mark that, fellow citizens!

FURIOUS VOICES. Oh-ho, so we're not the people, aren't we? So it's only the aristocrats who have the right to rule?

A WORKER. Throw him out if he talks like that!

OTHERS. Chuck him through the door!

A CITIZEN (*shouts*). Blow that horn, Evensen!

Loud blasts are heard. Whistles and furious uproar in the hall.

DR STOCKMANN (*when the noise has abated somewhat*). Can't you be reasonable? Can't you bear to hear the truth just for once? I'm not asking you all to agree with me immediately! But I did expect Mr Hovstad would admit I was right once he'd given the matter a little thought. After all, Mr Hovstad claims to be a freethinker –

SURPRISED VOICES (*murmur*). Freethinker, did he say? What? Is Mr Hovstad a freethinker?

HOVSTAD (*shouts*). Prove that, Dr Stockmann! When have I said so in print?

DR STOCKMANN (*thinks*). No, by Jove, you're right! You've never had the guts to admit it publicly. Well, I won't corner you, Mr Hovstad. Let me be the freethinker, then. From my knowledge of natural science I shall now reveal to you all that the *People's Tribune* is deceiving you most shamefully when it tells you that you, the common millions, the masses, the mob, are the true heart and core of the people! That's just a newspaper lie! The masses are nothing but raw material which may, some day, be refined into individuals!

Growls, laughter and disturbances in the hall.

DR STOCKMANN. Well, isn't that the way life works with the rest of creation? [Look at the enormous difference there is between a breed of animal that's cultivated and one that is uncultivated! Just look at a common farmyard hen. What is such a stunted piece of rubbish worth as flesh? Not much! And what kind of eggs does it lay? Any common rook or crow can lay eggs just as good. But take a cultivated Spanish or Japanese hen, or take a fine pheasant or turkey, and see the difference!] Consider dogs, with which we human beings have so much in common! Think first of a simple mongrel – one of those filthy, ragged, common curs that lope along the streets and defile the walls of our houses. And then put that mongrel next to a greyhound[1] with a distinguished pedigree whose ancestors have been fed delicate meals for generations and have had the opportunity to listen to harmonious voices and music. Don't you think the brain of that greyhound is differently developed from that of the mongrel? You bet your life it is! It's the pups of these cultivated animals that trainers teach to perform the most amazing tricks. A common mongrel couldn't learn to do such things if you stood it on its head!

Noise and laughter.

A CITIZEN (*shouts*). So we're dogs too now, are we?

ANOTHER. We're not animals, Doctor!

DR STOCKMANN. Yes, my friend, we are animals! But [there aren't many aristocratic animals among us. And there's a terrifying difference between men who are greyhounds and men who are mongrels. And that's what's so absurd, that Mr Hovstad is quite at one with me as long as we're talking about four-legged animals –

HOVSTAD. Well, they're only beasts.

DR STOCKMANN. All right! But as soon as I start to apply the law to the ones who are two-legged, Mr Hovstad balks at the consequences; he turns his whole philosophy upside down, and proclaims in the *People's Tribune* that the street mongrel is the champion of the menagerie. But that's how it always is, as long as a man remains possessed by this blind worship of the mob and hasn't worked his way out of spiritual bondage into aristocracy.

[1] See page 223.

HOVSTAD. I don't want any kind of aristocracy. I come of simple peasant stock; and I'm proud that I have my roots deep down in the mob, whom you deride.

MANY WORKERS. Hurrah for Hovstad! Hurrah, hurrah!

DR STOCKMANN. The kind of mob I'm talking about isn't only to be found at the bottom of the barrel. It swarms and mills all around us, even among the high peaks of society. Just look at your own smug, sleek Mayor! My brother Peter's as good a mobster as ever walked in two shoes?

　　Laughter and hisses.

MAYOR. I protest against these personal insinuations.

[DR STOCKMANN (*unperturbed*). And that isn't because he stems like me from a villainous old pirate from Pomerania or somewhere down there – for we do –!

MAYOR. It's absurd, it's a myth! I deny it!]

DR STOCKMANN. Because he thinks what his superiors think, and his opinions are the opinions he's heard them express. The men who do that are spiritually of the mob; and that's why my noble brother Peter is so frighteningly unaristocratic in all essentials – and consequently so terrified of all things liberal.

MAYOR. Mr Chairman –!

HOVSTAD. So it's the aristocrats who are the liberals in this country? That really is a new discovery!

　　Laughter among the CROWD.

DR STOCKMANN. Yes, that's part of my discovery too. [And the reason is that liberality is almost exactly the same as morality.] And I say it's quite indefensible of the *Tribune* day after day to proclaim the false gospel that the masses, [the mob, the solid majority,] have a monopoly on liberality and morality, and that vice and corruption and every kind of spiritual filth are a kind of pus that oozes out of culture, just as all that beastly stuff in the Baths oozes down from the tanneries at Mœlledal!

　　Confusion and interruptions.

DR STOCKMANN (*unperturbed, laughs in his excitement*). [And yet this same *People's Tribune* can preach that the masses and the mob must be elevated to a higher standard of living! Good God Almighty, if what the *People's Tribune* teaches were true, then to elevate the masses would simply be to start them on the road to ruin!] But luckily the idea that culture demoralizes is an old inherited fairy tale. No, it's stupidity, poverty and foul living conditions that do the Devil's work! In a house where the rooms aren't aired and the floors swept every day – my wife Catherine says they ought to be scrubbed too, but there can be two opinions on that – in such a house, I say, within two or three years people lose the capacity for moral thought and moral action. Lack of oxygen debilitates the conscience. And there's a shortage of oxygen in many, many houses in this town, from the sound of things, if the whole of this damned majority can be so devoid of conscience as to want to build the prosperity of their town on a quagmire of deceit and lies.

ASLAKSEN. You can't cast an accusation like that against a whole community!

A MAN. I appeal to the Chairman to order the speaker to stand down.

EXCITED VOICES. Yes, yes! That's right. Make him stand down!

DR STOCKMANN (*explodes*). Then I'll shout the truth at every street corner! I'll write in the newspapers of other towns! The whole country shall be told what is happening here!

HOVSTAD. It sounds almost as though the Doctor wishes to destroy this town.

DR STOCKMANN. Yes, I love this town where I was born so dearly that I would rather destroy it than see it flourish because of a lie!

ASLAKSEN. Those are strong words.

   Shouts and whistling. MRS STOCKMANN *coughs in vain;* the
   DOCTOR *no longer hears her.*

HOVSTAD (*shouts through the uproar*). The man who can want to destroy a whole community must be a public enemy!

DR STOCKMANN (*with increasing excitement*). A community that lives on lies deserves to be destroyed! I say that the town that houses such a community should be levelled to the ground! All those who live by lies ought to be exterminated like vermin! You will end by contaminating the entire country! You will bring it to the pass where the whole land will deserve to be laid waste! And if things go that far, then I say with all my heart: 'Let the whole land be laid waste! Let the whole people be exterminated!'

A MAN. That's talking like an enemy of the people!

BILLING. There speaks the voice of the people, by Jingo!

THE WHOLE CROWD (*screams*). Yes, yes, yes! He's an enemy of the people! He hates his country! He hates the people!

ASLAKSEN. Both as a citizen and as a human being I am deeply shocked by what I have had to hear. Dr Stockmann has shown himself in his true colours – [in a manner of which I should never have dreamed him capable. I fear I must support the view expressed a moment ago by respected citizens; and] I move that [we embody this opinion in a resolution. I suggest the following:] 'This meeting declares [that it regards] the medical officer at the Baths, Dr Thomas Stockmann, an enemy of the people.'

> *Deafening cheers and applause. Many of the* CROWD *form a circle around* DR STOCKMANN *and whistle at him.* MRS STOCKMANN *and* PETRA *have got to their feet.* MORTEN *and* EILIF *are fighting with the other* SCHOOLBOYS, *who have been whistling too. Some* ADULTS *part them.*

DR STOCKMANN (*to the people who have been whistling.*) You fools! I tell you –!

ASLAKSEN (*rings his bell*). The Doctor no longer has the floor. A formal ballot will take place; [but to protect personal feelings the voting should be done in writing and anonymously.] Have you any clean paper, Mr Billing?

BILLING. I've both blue and white here –

ASLAKSEN (*descends from the dais*). Good, that'll save time. Tear it into squares; like that, yes. (*To the* CROWD.) Blue means no, white means yes. I'll collect the votes myself.

The MAYOR *leaves the hall.* ASLAKSEN *and a couple of other* CITIZENS *go around the* CROWD *with the pieces of paper in hats.*

FIRST CITIZEN (*to* HOVSTAD). What's come over the Doctor? What's one to think?

HOVSTAD. You know how impulsive he is.

SECOND CITIZEN (*to* BILLING). I say, you're a regular visitor in that house. Have you ever noticed – does the fellow drink?

BILLING. I don't know what to reply, by Jingo! There's always toddy on the table when anyone comes.

THIRD CITIZEN. I think he just goes off his head now and then.

FIRST MAN. Yes, don't they say there's madness in the family?

BILLING. Could be.

A FOURTH MAN. No, it's pure spite. Wants revenge for something or other.

BILLING. He did say something the other day about a rise in salary. But he didn't get it.

ALL THE MEN (*with one voice*). Ah, that explains it!

THE DRUNK MAN (*in the thick of the* CROWD). I want a blue one! And I want a white one too!

SHOUTS. There's the drunk man again! Throw him out!

MORTEN KIIL (*comes up to* DR STOCKMANN). Well, Stockmann, you see now what happens once you start playing monkey tricks?

DR STOCKMANN. I have done my duty.

MORTEN KIIL. What was that you were saying about the tanneries at Mœlledal?

DR STOCKMANN. You heard. I said that that's where all the filth comes from.

MORTEN KIIL. From my tannery too?

DR STOCKMANN. I'm afraid your tannery is the worst of all.

MORTEN KIIL. Are you going to print that in the papers?

DR STOCKMANN. I shall hide nothing.

MORTEN KIIL. That'll cost you dear, Stockmann. (*Goes.*)

A FAT MAN (*goes across to* CAPTAIN HORSTER, *without greeting the* LADIES). Well, Captain, so you lend your house to enemies of the people?

CAPTAIN HORSTER. I reckon I can do what I like with my own property.

FAT MAN. Then you won't object if I do the same with mine?

CAPTAIN HORSTER. What do you mean?

FAT MAN. You'll hear from me tomorrow. (*Turns and goes.*)

PETRA. Isn't that the man who owns your ship, Captain Horster?

CAPTAIN HORSTER. Yes.

ASLAKSEN (*with the voting papers in his hand, steps up on to the dais and rings his bell*). Gentlemen, allow me to inform you of the result. With only a single dissentient vote –

A YOUNG MAN. That's the drunk man!

ASLAKSEN. With only one dissentient vote, and that of a man not sober, this gathering of citizens unanimously declares the medical officer of the Baths, Dr Thomas Stockmann, an enemy of the people! (*Shouts and gestures of approval.*) Long live our ancient and noble community! (*More cheers.*) Long live our worthy and active Mayor, who has so loyally ignored the ties of blood! (*Cheers.*) The meeting is closed. (*He steps down.*)

BILLING. Three cheers for the Chairman!

WHOLE CROWD. Hurrah for Mr Aslaksen! Hurrah! Hurrah!

DR STOCKMANN. My hat and coat, Petra. Captain, have you room in your ship for passengers to the new world?

CAPTAIN HORSTER. For you and yours, Doctor, I'll make room.

DR STOCKMANN (*as* PETRA *helps him on with his coat*). Good! Come, Catherine! Come, boys! (*He takes his wife by the arm.*)

MRS STOCKMANN (*quietly.*) Thomas dear, let's go out the back way.

DR STOCKMANN. No back way for me, Catherine! (*Raises his voice.*) You'll hear from your enemy of the people before he shakes the dust of this town from his feet! I'm not so forgiving as a certain person. I don't say: 'I forgive ye, for ye know not what ye do!'

ASLAKSEN (*shouts*). That comparison's a blasphemy, Dr Stockmann!

BILLING. I'll say it is, by Go–! What a dreadful thing for respectable people to hear!

A COARSE VOICE. He's threatening us now!

EXCITED SHOUTS. Let's break his windows! Throw him in the fjord!

A MAN (*in the* CROWD). Blow your horn, Evensen! (*He imitates the sound of the horn twice.*)

> *Blasts on the horn, whistles and wild cries. The* DOCTOR *goes with his family towards the door.* CAPTAIN HORSTER *clears a way for them.*

THE WHOLE CROWD (*howls after them as they go*). Enemy of the people! Enemy of the people! Enemy of the people!

BILLING (*as he puts his notes in order*). I'm damned if I'll drink toddy with them tonight, by Jingo!

> *The* CROWD *swarms towards the door. The shouting spreads outside. From the street can be heard the cry: 'Enemy of the people! Enemy of the People! Enemy of the people!'*

ACT FIVE

DR STOCKMANN's *study. Bookshelves and cupboards containing medicine bottles, along the walls. In the background is the exit to the hall; downstage left is the door to the living-room. In the wall on the right are two windows, all the panes of which are smashed. In the middle of the room stands the* DOCTOR's *desk, covered with books and papers. The room is in disorder. It is morning.*

> DR STOCKMANN, *in dressing-gown and slippers and with his smoking-cap on his head, is crouched down raking under one of the cupboards with an umbrella. At length he pulls out a stone.*

DR STOCKMANN (*speaks through the open door into the living-room*). Catherine, I've found another!

MRS STOCKMANN (*from the living-room*). Oh, you'll find a lot more yet.

DR STOCKMANN (*puts the stone among a heap of others on the table*). I shall keep these stones as sacred relics. Eilif and Morten shall see them every day, and when they're grown up they shall inherit them from me. (*Rakes under a bookshelf.*) Hasn't – what the devil's her name? – you know, the maid – hasn't she gone for the glazier yet?

MRS STOCKMANN (*enters*). He said he didn't know if he'd be able to come today.

[DR STOCKMANN. The truth is, he doesn't dare.

MRS STOCKMANN. Yes.] Randine says he daren't because of the neighbours. (*Speaks into the living-room.*) What is it, Randine? Very well. (*Goes inside and returns immediately.*) Here's a letter for you, Thomas.

DR STOCKMANN. Give it to me. (*Opens it and reads.*) I see.

MRS STOCKMANN. Who's it from?

DR STOCKMANN. The landlord. He's giving us notice to quit.

MRS STOCKMANN. Is he really? He seems such a decent man –

DR STOCKMANN (*looks at the letter*). [He daren't do otherwise, he says.] He's very sorry, but [he daren't do otherwise] – his fellow-citizens – respect for public opinion – certain obligations – dare not offend certain persons of influence –

MRS STOCKMANN. There, Thomas, you see.

DR STOCKMANN. Yes, yes, I see. They're all cowards in this town. None of them dares do anything for fear of the others. (*Throws the letter on the table.*) But we don't have to worry, Catherine. We're off to the new world now –

MRS STOCKMANN. Thomas, do you really think it's a good idea, this going away?

DR STOCKMANN. Am I to stay here when they've pilloried me as an enemy of the people, branded me, broken my windows? And just look at this, Catherine! They've torn my trousers, too!

MRS STOCKMANN. Oh no! And they're your best!

DR STOCKMANN. One should never wear one's best trousers when one goes out to fight for freedom and truth. [Oh, I don't mind so much about the trousers – you can always patch them up for me. It's the fact that these riff-raff dare to threaten me as though they were my equals – that's the thing I can't damned well stomach!

MRS STOCKMANN. Yes, Thomas, they've behaved shockingly to you in this town. But does that mean we have to leave the country?

DR STOCKMANN. Do you think the rabble aren't just as insolent in other towns? Oh, yes, Catherine. There isn't twopence to choose between them. To hell with the curs, let them yelp. That's not the worst. The worst is that throughout this country all the people are just party slaves. Mind you, they're probably not much better in America. The majority's rampant there too, and liberal public opinion and all the rest of the rubbish. But the context is larger there, you see. They may kill you, but they

won't torture you slowly; they don't pin a free man in a vice
like they do here. And if you want to, you can stay independent
outside it all.] (*Walks across the room.*) If only I knew of some
primeval forest or a little South Sea island that was going
cheap –

[MRS STOCKMANN. But what about the boys, Thomas?

DR STOCKMANN (*stops*). How extraordinary you are, Catherine!
Would you rather they grew up in a society like this? You saw
for yourself last night that half the people are raving lunatics;
and if the other half haven't lost their wits it's only because
they're beasts that don't have any wits to lose.

MRS STOCKMANN. But, Thomas dear, you're so careless about
what you say.

DR STOCKMANN. What! Don't I tell them the truth? Don't they
turn every idea upside down? Don't they merge right and wrong
so that they can't tell the difference? Don't they call everything
a lie which I know to be true? But the maddest thing of all is
that you get grown men of liberal inclinations getting together
in groups and convincing themselves and other people that
they're progressive thinkers! Did you ever hear the like,
Catherine?

MRS STOCKMANN. Yes, yes, it's all very stupid, but –]
    PETRA *enters from the living-room.*

MRS STOCKMANN. Are you back from school already?

PETRA. I've got the sack.

MRS STOCKMANN. The sack?

DR STOCKMANN. You too!

PETRA. Mrs Busk gave me notice. So I thought I'd better leave
at once.

DR STOCKMANN. Quite right, by heaven!

MRS STOCKMANN. Who'd have thought Mrs Busk was such a
nasty woman?

PETRA. Oh, mother, she's not nasty. It was quite obvious she
didn't like doing it. But she said she dared not do otherwise.
So I got the sack.

DR STOCKMANN (*laughs and rubs his hands*). [Dared not do otherwise!] She too! Oh, that's splendid!

MRS STOCKMANN. Well, after those dreadful scenes last night, you can't –

PETRA. It wasn't only that. Listen to this, father.

DR STOCKMANN. Yes?

PETRA. Mrs Busk showed me no less than three letters she'd received this morning –

DR STOCKMANN. Anonymous, of course?

PETRA. Yes.

DR STOCKMANN. They daren't even sign their names, Catherine.

PETRA. Two of them stated that a gentleman who frequents this house announced in the Club last night that I held excessively free views on various subjects –

DR STOCKMANN. I hope you didn't deny that.

PETRA. Not on your life! [Mrs Busk expresses pretty free views herself when we're alone together; but now that this has come out about me, she didn't dare to keep me.]

MRS STOCKMANN. [Fancy – 'a gentleman who frequents this house'!] You see what thanks you get for your hospitality, Thomas!

DR STOCKMANN. We won't go on living in this jungle any longer. Pack the bags as quickly as you can, Catherine. The sooner we get away from here, the better.

MRS STOCKMANN. Hush! I think there's someone in the hall. Go and look, Petra.

PETRA (*opens the door*). Oh, is it you, Captain Horster? Please come in.

CAPTAIN HORSTER (*from the hall*). Good morning. I felt I had to come along and see how everything was.

DR STOCKMANN (*shakes his hand*). Thank you. It's extremely good of you.

MRS STOCKMANN. And thank you for seeing us safely back last night, Captain Horster.

PETRA. How did you manage to get home again?

CAPTAIN HORSTER. Oh, I managed; [I'm pretty strong, and] those fellows bark worse than they bite.

DR STOCKMANN. Yes, isn't it amazing what wretched cowards they are! [Come here, I'll show you something.] Look, here are all the stones they threw through our windows. Just look at them! Upon my soul, there aren't more than two decent rocks in the whole lot; the others are just pebbles – mere gravel! And yet they stood out there howling, and swearing they'd beat the life out of me – but action – action – no, you won't see much of that in this town.

CAPTAIN HORSTER. Just as well for you on this occasion, Doctor.

[DR STOCKMANN. Of course! But it annoys me all the same; for if it ever comes to a serious fight, in defence of our country, you'll see, Captain Horster – public opinion'll be for safety first, and this sacred majority'll run for their lives like a flock of sheep. That's what's so sad – it really hurts me to think of it – no, damn it, I'm just being stupid! They've said I'm an enemy of the people, so let me be an enemy of the people!

MRS STOCKMANN. You'll never be that, Thomas.

DR STOCKMANN. Don't be so sure, Catherine. An ugly word can be like the scratch of a needle on the lung. And that damned phrase – I can't forget it – it's got stuck down here in the pit of my stomach, and it's lying there chafing and corroding me like an acid. And there's no magnesia that will neutralize that.

PETRA. You must just laugh at them, father.

CAPTAIN HORSTER. People will think differently of you in time, Doctor.

MRS STOCKMANN. Yes, Thomas, that's as sure as you're standing here.]

DR STOCKMANN. [Perhaps, when it's too late.] Well, it's their funeral! [Let them live like beasts; they'll be sorry they drove a patriot into exile.] When do you sail, Captain Horster?

CAPTAIN HORSTER. Hm – that was what I came to talk to you about, as a matter of fact –

DR STOCKMANN. Why, has something happened to the ship?

CAPTAIN HORSTER. No. It's just that I shan't be going with her

PETRA. They surely haven't given you the sack?

CAPTAIN HORSTER (*smiles*). Indeed they have!

PETRA. You, too!

MRS STOCKMANN. There, Thomas, you see!

DR STOCKMANN. And just because I spoke the truth! Oh, if I'd ever dreamed that such a thing could happen –

CAPTAIN HORSTER. Don't worry about me. I'll find a job with a company somewhere else.

DR STOCKMANN. But that boss of yours is a rich man, he's completely independent! Oh, damn, damn!

CAPTAIN HORSTER. He's fair enough in the ordinary way. He said himself, he'd have liked to have kept me, if only he'd dared –

DR STOCKMANN (*laughs*). [But he didn't dare! No, of course not!]

CAPTAIN HORSTER. It isn't so easy, he said, when you belong to a party –

DR STOCKMANN. That's the truest word he ever uttered! A party is like a mincing machine. It grinds everyone's brains into a pulp, and all you're left with is human sausages, all identical!

MRS STOCKMANN. Thomas, really!

PETRA (*to* CAPTAIN HORSTER). If only you hadn't seen us home, this might never have happened.

CAPTAIN HORSTER. I don't regret it.

PETRA (*holds out her hand*). Thank you!

CAPTAIN HORSTER (*to* DR STOCKMANN). What I wanted to say was, if you still want to go, I have thought of another way –

DR STOCKMANN. Fine! As long as we can get away quickly –

MRS STOCKMANN. Hush – wasn't that a knock at the door?

PETRA. I think it's Uncle.

DR STOCKMANN. Aha! (*Shouts*). Come in!

MRS STOCKMANN. Now, Thomas dear, do promise me –

    The MAYOR *enters from the hall.*

MAYOR (*in the doorway*). Oh, you're engaged. I'll come back later –

DR STOCKMANN. No, no. Please come in.

MAYOR. I wanted to speak to you privately.

MRS STOCKMANN. We'll go into the living-room.

CAPTAIN HORSTER. And I'll come back later.

DR STOCKMANN. No, you go in too. I want to know more about that –

CAPTAIN HORSTER. Right, I'll wait, then.

    He goes with MRS STOCKMANN *and* PETRA *into the living-room. The* MAYOR *says nothing but glances at the windows.*

DR STOCKMANN. Do you find it draughty here today? Put your hat on.

MAYOR. Thank you, if I may. (*Does so.*) I think I caught a cold last night. [I stood there shivering –]

DR STOCKMANN. Really? I found it warm enough.

MAYOR. I regret that it didn't lie within my power to prevent those nocturnal extravagances.

DR STOCKMANN. Did you come out here to tell me that?

MAYOR (*takes out a large letter*). I have this document for you, from the Directors of the Baths.

DR STOCKMANN. Am I dismissed?

MAYOR. From the date of writing. (*Puts the letter on the table.*) It distresses us; but, frankly, we had no choice. Public opinion being what it is, we didn't dare –

DR STOCKMANN (*smiles*). [Didn't dare?] I've heard that word before today.

MAYOR. I beg you to realize your position. From now on you can't reckon on having any practice whatever in this town.

DR STOCKMANN. To hell with the practice! But what makes you so sure?

MAYOR. The Property Owners' Association has drawn up a round robin which it is sending from house to house. All respectable citizens are being urged not to employ you; and I'll guarantee that not a single householder will dare refuse to sign it. They just won't dare.

DR STOCKMANN. Yes, yes, I don't doubt that. But what then?

MAYOR. My advice would be that you should leave town for a while –

DR STOCKMANN. Yes, I'm thinking of doing that.

MAYOR. Good. Then, when you've had six months to think the matter over, you might, after mature consideration, possibly reconcile yourself to issuing a short statement admitting your error and expressing your regret –

DR STOCKMANN. And then, you mean, I might get my job back?

MAYOR. It's not unthinkable.

DR STOCKMANN. But what about public opinion? You daren't offend that.

MAYOR. Public opinion is very fickle. And, quite frankly, it's important to us that you should publish some such admission.

DR STOCKMANN. Yes, that'd make you smack your lips, wouldn't it? But, damn it, haven't I told you already what I think of that kind of chicanery?

MAYOR. Your position was somewhat stronger then. You had reason to suppose that the whole town was behind you –

DR STOCKMANN. And now they're rubbing my face in the dirt! (*Flares up.*) [I don't care if I've got the Devil himself and his great-grandmother on my back!] Never, I tell you, never!

MAYOR. A man with a family has no right to act as you're doing. You have no right, Thomas!

DR STOCKMANN. No right! There's only one thing in the world that a free man has no right to do! Do you know what that is?

MAYOR. No.

DR STOCKMANN. No, of course you don't. But I'll tell you. A free man has no right to befoul himself like a beast. He has no right to get himself into the position where he feels the need to spit in his own face!

MAYOR. That all sounds very plausible – if only there didn't happen to exist another explanation for your stubbornness. [But there does.]

DR STOCKMANN. What do you mean by that?

MAYOR. You know perfectly well. But as your brother, and as a man of the world, I would advise you not to put too much trust in expectations that might so easily not be fulfilled.

DR STOCKMANN. What on earth are you talking about?

MAYOR. Do you seriously expect me to believe that you don't know of the arrangements that Morten Kiil has made in his will?

DR STOCKMANN. I know that what little he has is to go to a home for retired artisans. But what's that got to do with me?

MAYOR. To begin with, it's not so little. Morten Kiil is a pretty wealthy man.

DR STOCKMANN. I had no idea –!

MAYOR. Hm – hadn't you really? Then I suppose you also have no idea that a considerable proportion of his money is earmarked for your children, and that you and your wife will be able to enjoy the interest for the rest of your lives. Hasn't he told you?

DR STOCKMANN. Indeed he has not! On the contrary, he's done nothing but complain about how disgracefully overtaxed he is. But are you quite sure of this, Peter?

MAYOR. I have it from an impeccable source.

DR STOCKMANN. But, good heavens – that means Catherine's future is secured – and the children's, too! I say, I must tell her! (*Shouts.*) Catherine, Catherine!

MAYOR (*holds him back*). Hush, don't say anything yet.

MRS STOCKMANN (*opens the door*). What is it?

DR STOCKMANN. Nothing, my dear. Go back in again.

MRS STOCKMANN *closes the door.*

DR STOCKMANN (*paces up and down the room*). Their future secured! [I can't believe it! All of them – and for life! Oh, it's a wonderful feeling to know that one's future is secured.] For ever!

MAYOR. But that's just what it isn't. Morten Kiil can revoke that will any day or hour that he chooses.

DR STOCKMANN. But he won't, my dear Peter. The Badger's

much too delighted at the embarrassment I've caused to you and your worthy friends.

MAYOR (*starts and looks searchingly at him*). Aha! So that's the explanation!

DR STOCKMANN. What do you mean?

MAYOR. This whole thing's been a conspiracy. These violent and unprincipled accusations which you've levelled against the authorities in the name of truth were simply your price for being remembered in that vindictive old idiot's will.

DR STOCKMANN (*almost speechless*). Peter – you are the lowest bastard I have ever met in all my life!

MAYOR. Things are finished between us now. Your dismissal is final. Now we have a weapon against you. (*He goes.*)

DR STOCKMANN. The filthy – damn, damn! (*Shouts.*) Catherine! Scrub the floors behind him! Tell her to bring in a bucket – that girl – what the devil's her name? – the one who's always got a dirty nose –!

MRS STOCKMANN (*in the doorway to the living-room*). Hush, hush, Thomas, please!

PETRA (*also in the doorway*). Father, Grandfather's here and says, can he speak to you privately?

DR STOCKMANN. Yes, of course. (*At the door.*) Come in, father.
    MORTEN KIIL *comes in.* DR STOCKMANN *closes the door behind him.*

DR STOCKMANN. Well, what is it? Sit down.

MORTEN KIIL. No, I won't sit. (*Looks around.*) Nice and cosy it looks here today, Stockmann.

DR STOCKMANN. Yes, doesn't it?

MORTEN KIIL. Very nice. And fresh air too! You've got enough of that oxygen you were talking about last night! Your conscience feels pretty good today, I suppose?

DR STOCKMANN. Yes, it does.

MORTEN KIIL. I thought it would. (*Thumps himself on the breast.*) But do you know what I've got here?

DR STOCKMANN. A good conscience too, I hope.

MORTEN KIIL (*snorts*). No, something better than that.

Takes out a thick pocket-book, opens it and shows a wad of papers.

DR STOCKMANN (*looks at him in amazement*). Shares in the Baths?

MORTEN KIIL. They weren't hard to come by today.

DR STOCKMANN. You mean you've been out and bought –?

MORTEN KIIL. As many as I could afford.

DR STOCKMANN. But, my dear Mr Kiil – the state those Baths are in now, you –!

MORTEN KIIL. If you act like a sensible man, you'll soon have them on their feet again.

DR STOCKMANN. You see for yourself I'm doing all I can, but –!
[The people of this town are quite mad!]

MORTEN KIIL. You said last night that the worst of the filth comes from my tannery. But if that were true, then my grandfather and my father before me, and I myself, have been polluting this town for generations like three angels of death. Do you think I'm going to let an imputation like that hang over my head?

DR STOCKMANN. I'm afraid it looks as though you'll have to.

MORTEN KIIL. No, thank you! I value my name and reputation. People call me 'the Badger,' I'm told. A badger's a dirty beast, isn't it? Well, I'll prove them wrong. I intend to live and die clean.

DR STOCKMANN. And how are you going to go about that?

MORTEN KIIL. You're going to make me clean, Stockmann.

DR STOCKMANN. I –!

MORTEN KIIL. Do you know what money I've used to buy these shares with? No, you can't; but I'll tell you. It's the money Catherine and Petra and the boys are going to inherit when I'm gone. I've managed to put a little aside, you see.

DR STOCKMANN (*flares up*). You mean you've spent Catherine's money on this?

MORTEN KIIL. Yes, now it's all invested in the Baths. So now we'll see if you're really as daft as you pretend, Stockmann. Every time you say there's vermin coming out of my tannery, it'll be as though you were cutting a pound of flesh from your wife's body, and Petra's and the children. But no self-respecting husband and father would do such a thing – unless he really was mad.

DR STOCKMANN (*walks up and down*). Yes, but I *am* mad! I *am* mad!

MORTEN KIIL. You can't be that mad when your wife and children are at stake.

DR STOCKMANN (*stops in front of him*). Why couldn't you have come and spoken to me before you went and bought all this waste paper?

MORTEN KIIL. Actions speak louder than words.

DR STOCKMANN (*wanders around restlessly*). If only I weren't so sure –! But I *know* I'm right!

MORTEN KIIL (*weighs the pocketbook in his hand*). If you persist in this lunacy, these shares won't be worth much, you know.
He puts the pocketbook back in his pocket.

DR STOCKMANN. But, damn it, science must be able to find some way. A preventative; or a purifier or something –

MORTEN KIIL. You mean something to kill these vermin?

DR STOCKMANN. Yes, or render them harmless.

MORTEN KIIL. Couldn't you try rat poison?

DR STOCKMANN. Oh, no, no! But everyone keeps saying it's just a fancy of mine. All right, then, let them have it that way. Those ignorant, narrow-minded curs denounced me as an enemy of the people, didn't they? And all but tore the clothes off my back!

MORTEN KIIL. And smashed your windows.

DR STOCKMANN. Yes. And then this question of my duty towards my family. I must talk to Catherine. She knows about these things.

MORTEN KIIL. That's a good idea. She's a sensible woman. Follow her advice.

DR STOCKMANN (*turns on him*). Why did you have to [do such a stupid thing? Hazard Catherine's money, and] put me in this frightful predicament! When I look at you, I feel as though I was looking at the Devil himself –

MORTEN KIIL. Then I'd best be off. But I want your answer by two o'clock. If it's no, I'm giving these shares to the Old Folks' Home – and I'll do it today.

DR STOCKMANN. And what will Catherine get then?

MORTEN KIIL. Not a farthing!

The door to the hall is opened. HOVSTAD *and* ASLAKSEN *are seen there.*

MORTEN KIIL. Well! Look whom we have here!

DR STOCKMANN (*stares at them*). What the devil –? Do you two still dare to visit me?

HOVSTAD. Indeed we do.

ASLAKSEN. We've something we want to talk to you about.

MORTEN KIIL (*whispers*). Yes or no – by two o'clock!

ASLAKSEN (*glances at* HOVSTAD). Aha!

MORTEN KIIL *goes.*

DR STOCKMANN. Well, what do you want? Make it short.

HOVSTAD. I dare say you don't feel too kindly towards us in view of the stand we took at last night's meeting –

DR STOCKMANN. Stand, you call it! A fine stand indeed! You just lay down like a couple of old women! Damn the pair of you!

HOVSTAD. Call it what you like; we *couldn't* do otherwise.

DR STOCKMANN. You *dared* not do otherwise! Isn't that what you mean?

HOVSTAD. If you wish.

ASLAKSEN. But why didn't you tip us off? You only needed to drop a hint to Mr Hovstad or me.

DR STOCKMANN. Hint? About what?

ASLAKSEN. Why you were doing it.

DR STOCKMANN. I don't understand.

ASLAKSEN (*nods conspiratorially*). Oh, yes you do, Dr Stockmann.

HOVSTAD. There's no need to keep it secret any longer.

DR STOCKMANN (*looks from one to the other*). What the devil –?

ASLAKSEN. Forgive the question, but isn't your father-in-law going round the town buying up all the shares in the Baths?

DR STOCKMANN. He has bought some today. But –

ASLAKSEN. You'd have done wiser to employ someone else. Someone not quite so close to you.

HOVSTAD. And you shouldn't have done all this under your own name. Nobody need have known that the attack on the Baths came from you. You ought to have taken me into your confidence, Dr Stockmann.

DR STOCKMANN (*stares straight in front of him. A light seems to dawn on him, and he says as though thunderstruck*). Is it conceivable? Could such a thing really be *done*?

ASLAKSEN (*smiles*). Apparently. But it ought to be done with a certain subtlety, you know.

HOVSTAD. And there ought to be more than one person in on it. A man doesn't have so much responsibility to bear if he's in partnership.

DR STOCKMANN (*composedly*). In brief, gentlemen, what do you want?

ASLAKSEN. Mr Hovstad can explain better than –

HOVSTAD. No, you tell him, Aslaksen.

ASLAKSEN. Well, it's just this really, that now we know how the land lies, we think we might venture to put the *People's Tribune* at your disposal.

DR STOCKMANN. You think you dare risk it? But what about public opinion? Aren't you afraid we might cause a storm?

HOVSTAD. We shall have to ride that storm.

ASLAKSEN. But you'll have to be quick on the trigger, Doctor. As soon as your campaign has done its job –

DR STOCKMANN. As soon as my father-in-law and I have got all the shares cheaply, you mean –?

HOVSTAD. It is of course principally in the cause of science that you are seeking to gain control of the Baths.

DR STOCKMANN. Of course. It was in the cause of science that I got the old Badger to come in with me on this. And then we'll tinker a bit with the water system and do a little digging on the beach and it won't cost the ratepayers half-a-crown. I think we'll get away with it, don't you! Eh?

HOVSTAD. I think so – if you have the *People's Tribune* behind you.

ASLAKSEN. In a free society the press is a power to be feared, Doctor.

DR STOCKMANN. Quite. And public opinion, too. Mr Aslaksen, you'll answer for the Property Owners' Association?

ASLAKSEN. The Property Owners' Association and the Temperance Society. Have no fear.

DR STOCKMANN. But, gentlemen – I blush to mention the matter, but – what consideration – er –

HOVSTAD. Well, of course we'd like to help you absolutely gratis. But the *People's Tribune* is going through an awkward period; we're having an uphill struggle, and I'm very reluctant to wind things up just now, when there are such splendid causes that need our support.

DR STOCKMANN. Of course. That'd be a bitter pill for a friend of the people like you to have to swallow. (*Flares up.*) But I – I am an enemy of the people! (*Strides around the room.*) Where's that stick of mine? Where the devil did I put my stick?

HOVSTAD. What do you mean?

ASLAKSEN. You surely aren't thinking of –?

DR STOCKMANN (*stops*). And suppose I don't give you a penny of my shares? We rich men are pretty close with our money, you must remember.

HOVSTAD. And *you* must remember that this little business of the shares would bear more than one interpretation.

DR STOCKMANN. Yes, that'd be right up your street, wouldn't it? If I don't come to the aid of the *People's Tribune*, you'll misrepresent my motives – you'll start a witch-hunt, drive me to ground, and throttle the life out of me as a hound throttles a hare!

HOVSTAD. That's the law of nature. Every animal has to fight for survival, you know.

ASLAKSEN. Bread doesn't grow on trees. You must take it where you can find it.

DR STOCKMANN. Then see if you can find any in the gutter! (*Strides around the room.*) Now, by heaven, we'll see which is the strongest animal of us three! (*Finds his umbrella.*) Aha! (*Swings it.*) Now –!

HOVSTAD. You wouldn't dare to assault us!

ASLAKSEN. Be careful with that umbrella!

DR STOCKMANN. Out of the window with you, Mr Hovstad!

HOVSTAD (*at the doorway to the hall*). Are you out of your mind?

DR STOCKMANN. Get through that window, Mr Aslaksen! Jump, I tell you! Don't dally!

ASLAKSEN (*runs round the desk*). Doctor, Doctor, restrain yourself! I'm a weak man – I can't stand excitement –! (*Screams.*) Help, help!

MRS STOCKMANN, PETRA *and* CAPTAIN HORSTER *enter from the living-room.*

MRS STOCKMANN. In heaven's name, Thomas, what's going on here?

DR STOCKMANN (*brandishes the umbrella*). Jump out, I tell you! Down into the gutter!

HOVSTAD. An unprovoked assault! I call you to witness, Captain Horster –! (*Runs out through the hall.*)

MRS STOCKMANN (*holds the* DOCTOR). Thomas, for mercy's sake control yourself!

ASLAKSEN (*desperate*). Restraint, Doctor! Restr – oh, dear! (*Scampers out through the living-room.*)

DR STOCKMANN (*throws away the umbrella*). Damn it, they got away after all!

MRS STOCKMANN. But what did they want?

DR STOCKMANN. I'll tell you later. I've other things to think about just now. (*Goes to the table and writes on a visiting card.*) Look at this, Catherine. What do you see here?

MRS STOCKMANN. 'No, no, no' – what does that mean?

DR STOCKMANN. I'll explain that later, too. (*Holds out the card.*) Here, Petra, tell that smutty-nosed girl to run up to the Badger with this as quickly as she can. Hurry!

    PETRA *goes out with the card through the hall.*

DR STOCKMANN. If I haven't had all the devil's messengers after me today, I really don't know who's left! But now I'll sharpen my pen against them until it's like a dagger! I'll dip it in gall and venom! I'll fling my inkstand against their stupid skulls!

MRS STOCKMANN. But Thomas, we're leaving!

    PETRA *returns.*

DR STOCKMANN. Well?

PETRA. She's taken it.

DR STOCKMANN. Good! Leaving, did you say? No, by God, we're not! We're staying here, Catherine!

PETRA. Staying?

MRS STOCKMANN. In this town?

DR STOCKMANN. Yes! This is the chosen battlefield, and it's here that the battle must be fought! And it's here that I shall win! As soon as you've sewn up those trousers of mine, I'll go into town and look for a house. We've got to have a roof over our heads [when winter comes].

CAPTAIN HORSTER. I can let you have my house.

DR STOCKMANN. Would you?

CAPTAIN HORSTER. Of course. I've plenty of rooms, and I'm hardly ever there.

MRS STOCKMANN. Oh, Captain Horster, how kind of you!

PETRA. Thank you!

DR STOCKMANN (*presses his hand*). Thank you, thank you! [Well, that problem's behind us! I'll start my campaign this very day!] Oh, [Catherine,] there's so much to be done! But luckily I'll be able to devote my whole time to it. Look at this. I've been sacked from the Baths –

MRS STOCKMANN (*sighs*). Ah, well, I was expecting that.

DR STOCKMANN. And they want to take away my practice too! All right, let them! At least I'll keep my poor patients – they're the ones who can't pay – well, heaven knows they're the ones who need me most. But, by God, they'll have to listen to me! I'll preach to them morning, noon and night.

MRS STOCKMANN. Oh, Thomas, Thomas! Surely you've seen what good preaching does!

DR STOCKMANN. You really are absurd, Catherine! Am I to allow myself to be chased from the field by public opinion, and the majority, and such fiddle-faddle? No, thank you! [What I want is so simple and straightforward and easy! I only want to knock it into the heads of these curs that the Liberals are the most insidious enemies of freedom – that party programmes strangle every new truth that deserves to live – and that expediency and self-interest turn morality and justice upside down, so that in the end life here becomes intolerable. Well, Captain Horster, don't you think I ought to be able to get people to grasp that?

CAPTAIN HORSTER. I dare say. I don't really understand these things.

DR STOCKMANN. Well, you see, the real point is this! It's the party bosses – they're the ones who've got to be rooted out! A party boss is like a hungry wolf – he needs a certain number of baby lambs to devour every year if he is to survive. Look at Hovstad and Aslaksen! How many innocent and vital young idealists have they knocked on the head! Or else they mangle and maul them till they're fit for nothing but to be property owners or subscribers to the *People's Tribune*!] (*Half-sits on the table.*) Come here, Catherine! Look how beautifully the sun's shining in through the windows today! And smell this glorious, fresh spring air which is being wafted in to us.

MRS STOCKMANN. Oh, my dear Thomas, if only we could live on sunshine and spring air!

DR STOCKMANN. Well, you may have to pinch and scrape a little, but we'll manage. That's the least of my worries. No, the worst is that I don't know of anyone sufficiently free and – *unplebeian* to carry on my work after me.

PETRA. Oh, never mind that, father. You'll find someone in time. Look, here are the boys!

EILIF *and* MORTEN *enter from the living-room.*

MRS STOCKMANN. Have you been given a holiday today?

MORTEN. No. But we had a fight with the other boys in the break, so –

EILIF. That's not true! It was the other boys who fought with us!

MORTEN. Yes. So I said to Dr Roerlund I thought it would be better if we stayed at home for a few days.

DR STOCKMANN (*snaps his fingers and jumps from the table*). I've got it! By heaven, I've got it! Neither of you shall ever set foot in that school again!

THE BOYS. Not go to school?

MRS STOCKMANN. But, Thomas –!

DR STOCKMANN. Never, I say! I'll teach you myself! You won't learn a damned thing –

MORTEN. Hurray!

DR STOCKMANN. But I'll make you free men! Aristocrats! Petra, you'll have to help me.

PETRA. Yes, father, of course.

DR STOCKMANN. And we'll hold the school in the room where they branded me as an enemy of the people. But we need more pupils. I must have at least twelve to begin with.

MRS STOCKMANN. You won't find them in this town.

DR STOCKMANN. We shall see. (*To the* BOYS.) Do you know any street urchins – real guttersnipes –?

EILIF. Oh yes, father, I know lots!

DR STOCKMANN. That's fine! Get hold of a few for me. I'm going to experiment with mongrels for once. They have good heads on them sometimes.

EILIF. But what shall we do when we've become [free men and] aristocrats?

DR STOCKMANN. Then, my boys, you'll chase all these damned politicians into the Atlantic Ocean!

    EILIF *looks somewhat doubtful.* MORTEN *jumps and cheers.*

MRS STOCKMANN. Let's hope it won't be the politicians who'll chase you out, Thomas.

DR STOCKMANN. Are you quite mad, Catherine? Chase me out? Now, when I am the strongest man in town?

MRS STOCKMANN. The strongest – now?

DR STOCKMANN. Yes! I'll go further! I am now one of the strongest men in the whole world.

MORTEN. Hurrah!

DR STOCKMANN (*lowers his voice*). Hush! You mustn't talk about it yet! But I've made a great discovery!

MRS STOCKMANN. Not again!

DR STOCKMANN. Yes – yes! (*Gathers them round him and whispers to them.*) The fact is, you see, that the strongest man in the world is he who stands most alone.

MRS STOCKMANN (*smiles and shakes her head*). Oh, Thomas –!

PETRA (*warmly, clasps his hands*). Father!

Note on the Translation

I have allowed myself a small amount of licence in translating one or two phrases. When Dr Stockmann likens aristocrats of the intellect to pedigree dogs, Ibsen makes him name the poodle as an example of refinement and intelligence; but poodles, at any rate in England today, have rather the wrong kind of associations, and I have altered this to 'greyhound'. And when he speaks of his hatred of *ledende mænd* (literally 'leading men' – in the political, not the theatrical sense, though Ibsen knew a thing or two about the latter kind too), I have translated the phrase as 'politicians'. Ibsen means by *ledende mænd* anyone who leads other men by the nose, which is a pretty accurate definition of a politician.

I have indicated, by square brackets in the text, suggested cuts for performance. *An Enemy of the People* is, with the single exception of *The Wild Duck*, the longest of Ibsen's mature prose plays and, even when cut as here, still runs for nearly three hours. Stockmann's address in the fourth act contains a certain amount of red herringry which it is no great loss to shed; and the opening of the final act, with its repetitious insistence on 'not daring', and the closing minutes, both profit, in my opinion, from judicious thinning. But any director who uses this translation is free to follow his own judgement in this matter.

Hedda Gabler

Introduction

Hedda Gabler occupies a curious, almost anachronistic position in the Ibsen cycle. He wrote it in 1890, between *The Lady from the Sea* and *The Master Builder*, but if one had to date it from internal evidence one would be tempted to place it ten years earlier, as a companion piece to *A Doll's House*, *Ghosts* and *An Enemy of the People*. Like them, it is written very simply and directly; we feel, as in those plays, that he is working within an illuminated circle and not, as in the plays of his final period from *The Lady from the Sea* onwards, that he is exploring the darkness outside that circle. At first sight, again, it appears to differ from these final plays in not being an exercise in self-analysis. This, however, is an illusion, for if we examine *Hedda Gabler* closely we find that it contains one of the most revealing self-portraits he ever painted. The play might, indeed, be subtitled 'Portrait of the Dramatist as a Young Woman'.

The circumstances under which he wrote *Hedda Gabler* were as follows. In the summer of 1889, while holidaying at Gossensass in the Tyrol, Ibsen, then aged sixty-one, had become violently infatuated with an eighteen-year-old Viennese girl named Emilie Bardach. After his return to Munich in September, they wrote to each other continuously for four months; then Ibsen broke off the correspondence, and apart from two brief letters towards the end of the year and a third, seven years later, in acknowledgement of a telegram of congratulations, he did not contact her again. Two years later he was to use this relationship of mutual infatuation as the basis for *The Master Builder*, but the change it wrought on Ibsen was immediate. For years he had deliberately suppressed his own emotional life, an undersized and ugly man resigned to a loveless marriage; but his encounter with Emilie had awoken him to the realization

that, as Graham Greene has remarked, fame is a powerful
aphrodisiac, and he now entered on a series of romantic
relationships with women thirty to forty years his junior.
(Indeed, the second of these, with the artist Helene Raff,
began while he was still corresponding with Emilie.)

It is unlikely, however, that any of these relationships ever
resulted in a physical affair, and this meant that, while im-
mensely enriching his work, they also introduced into it a
strong undertone of pessimism. In 1887, in a speech in Stockholm, he had startled his audience by describing himself as an
'optimist', and *The Lady from the Sea*, written in 1888, had
reflected this optimism. 'After so many tragedies,' Edmund
Gosse had written on its appearance, 'this is a comedy . . . the
tone is quite unusually sunny, and without a tinge of pessimism. It is in some respects the reverse of *Rosmersholm*, the
bitterness of restrained and balked individuality, which ends
in death, being contrasted with the sweetness of emancipated
and gratified individuality, which leads to health and peace.'
But none of his five subsequent plays could by any possible
stretch of the imagination be described as comedies. The mood
of *Hedda Gabler*, *The Master Builder*, *Little Eyolf*, *John Gabriel
Borkman* and *When We Dead Awaken* is, like that of *Rosmersholm*, 'restrained and balked individuality', and I do not
think there can be much doubt that this stems from the
realization that for various reasons (fear of scandal, sense of
duty towards his wife, consciousness of old age, perhaps the
consciousness or fear of physical impotence), he, who had
suppressed his emotional life for so long, now had the oppor-
tunities to fulfil it, but was unable to take advantage of them.
As a result of his meeting with Emilie Bardach a new glory,
but also a new darkness, entered into his work.

He began to plan a new play immediately on his return from
Gossensass. Only a week after arriving in Munich, on 7 October
1889, he wrote to Emilie: 'A new poem begins to dawn in me.
I want to work on it this winter, transmuting into it the glowing

inspiration of the summer. But the end may be disappointment. I feel it. It is my way.' A week later, on 15 October, he wrote to her: 'My imagination is ragingly at work, but always straying to where in working hours it should not. I cannot keep down the memories of the summer, neither do I want to. The things we have lived through I live again and again – and still again. To make of them a poem is for the time being impossible. For the time being? Shall I ever succeed in the future? And do I really wish that I could and would so succeed? For the moment, at any rate, I cannot.' However, on 19 November he wrote more cheerfully: 'I am greatly preoccupied with the preparations for my new play. Sit tight at my desk the whole day. Go out only towards evening. I dream and remember and write.'

Unfortunately, we do not know whether the play he was working on at this time was in fact *Hedda Gabler*. Ibsen left eight sets of rough notes dating from around this period; most of them obviously refer to *Hedda Gabler*, but some seem to point towards *The Master Builder* and others towards a third play which he never ultimately wrote, and since these notes are undated we cannot be sure to which of the three projects he was referring in his letters to Emilie. Some scholars think he did not begin to plan *Hedda* until April 1890; others believe he had already conceived it as early as February 1889. At any rate, by the spring of 1890 Ibsen's plans for *Hedda* were sufficiently advanced for him to express the hope that he would have his first draft ready by midsummer, so that he would be able to work on it during his summer holiday in (again) Gossensass. But on 29 June 1890 he wrote to Carl Snoilsky, the Swedish poet (generally assumed to be the original of Rosmer) that the play had not worked out and that he was staying in Munich until he could get the first draft finished. Perhaps he feared Gossensass might awake disturbing memories.

As things turned out, he did not complete the first draft of even Act 1 until 10 August. On 13 August he began Act 2, but early in September he scrapped this, and on 6 September he began a new draft of this act. Things now went better, for by 7 October he had completed the draft not only of Act 2 but also of Acts 3 and 4. The play was at this stage entitled simply *Hedda*, and the draft in which it exists bears all the appearance of having been made as a fair copy to send to the printer. But he was not satisfied, and rewrote the play thoroughly, introducing into it for the first time many of its most striking and famous features. This revisionary work occupied him until 18 November, and *Hedda Gabler*, as he now entitled it, to underline the fact that she was her father's daughter rather than her husband's wife, was published by Gyldendal of Copenhagen on 16 December 1890, only just in time for the Christmas sales – always an important consideration with Ibsen, who depended on book sales in Scandinavia for a large proportion of his income.[1]

As with every play he wrote after *A Doll's House* in 1879, excepting only the comparatively light and simple *Enemy of the People*, the public reaction was one of utter bewilderment. Halvdan Koht, in his introduction (1934) to the play in the centenary edition of Ibsen's works, has described how Norway received it. 'Its only message seemed to be despair. No meaning nor purpose, simply a suicide ending an absolutely pointless life. . . . In contemporary criticisms the most common word used to describe the main character is "puzzling", "improbable" or "incredible". Readers got the impression that in the concluding line of the play – "But, good God! People don't do such things!" – Ibsen was making fun of them; for it reminded them that too many of them had said just that about Nora's final action in *A Doll's House*. There were things in *Hedda Gabler* that seemed almost intended to parody *A Doll's*

---

[1] His plays, though widely staged, were usually put on for a few performances only. For example, it was not until 1925 that any English production of Ibsen achieved a run of fifty performances.

House – for example, Hedda's lie about having destroyed the manuscript to help her husband, or the curious form of "comradeship" between man and woman portrayed here.' Bredo Morgenstierna wrote in *Aftenposten* of 'the obscurity, the eccentric and abnormal psychology, the empty and desolate impression which the whole picture leaves', while Alfred Sinding-Larsen in *Morgenbladet* described Hedda herself as 'a horrid miscarriage of the imagination, a monster in female form to whom no parallel can be found in real life'.

Nor, as with some of his plays (e.g. *Ghosts*), were people much enlightened when *Hedda Gabler* was performed. At the première on 31 January 1891, at the Residenztheater, Munich, the public whistled. Ibsen was present and was much displeased at the declamatory manner of the actress who played Hedda. On 10 February there was a rather better performance at the Lessing Theatre in Berlin, but even here neither the public nor the critics seem to have understood the play. Nor was it a success in Stockholm or Gothenburg, while in Copenhagen on 25 February it was a complete fiasco, being greeted by hissing, whistling and laughter. The following evening it was given in Christiania, also inadequately. The first respectable performance of *Hedda Gabler* was, improbably, in London (20 April 1891), where, although it called forth the usual stream of abuse from the popular newspapers ('What a horrible story! What a hideous play!' wrote Clement Scott in the *Daily Telegraph*, and the *Pictorial World* commented: 'The play is simply a bad escape of moral sewage-gas . . . Hedda's soul is a-crawl with the foulest passions of humanity'), intelligent opinion was considerably impressed. Henry James, who had been puzzled by *Hedda Gabler* on reading it, found the performance gratifyingly illuminating. 'The play on perusal', he wrote (*On the Occasion of Hedda Gabler*, 1891), 'left one comparatively muddled and mystified, fascinated but – in one's intellectual sympathy – snubbed. Acted, it leads that sympathy over the straightest of roads with all the exhilaration of a superior pace.'

But he added a gentle rider. 'Much more, I confess, one doesn't get from it; but an hour of refreshing exercise is a reward in itself. . . . Ibsen is various, and *Hedda Gabler* is probably an ironical pleasantry, the artistic exercise of a mind saturated with the vision of human infirmities; saturated, above all, with a sense of the infinitude, for all its mortal savour, of *character*, finding that an endless romance and a perpetual challenge. Can there have been at the source of such a production a mere refinement of conscious power, an enjoyment of difficulty and a preconceived victory over it?'

There are many people who share James's view of *Hedda Gabler* as a brilliant but, for Ibsen, curiously detached, objective, almost brutal 'exercise' – a view which has been greatly fostered by the tendency of actresses to portray Hedda as an evil genius, a kind of suburban Lady Macbeth. The opposite view, that it is one of Ibsen's most 'committed' plays, has been brilliantly argued by Dr Arne Duve in his wayward but stimulating book *Symbolikken i Henrik Ibsens Skuespill* (Nasjonalforlaget, Oslo, 1945). Dr Duve suggests that Hedda represents Ibsen's repressed and crippled emotional life. As a young man, he reminds us, Ibsen had been wildly emotional; at eighteen he had fathered an illegitimate child, and at least once during those early years he became a near-alcoholic and is believed to have attempted suicide. Loevborg and Tesman, Dr Duve argues, are aspects of Ibsen's own self; Loevborg is an idealized portrait of himself as he had been in the wild years of his youth, Tesman a *reductio ad absurdum* of what he had chosen to become. Loevborg stands for Ibsen's emotional self, Tesman for his intellectual self. Ibsen was haunted throughout the latter half of his life by the feeling that he had stifled his emotional self and that only his bourgeois and slightly ludicrous intellectual self had lived on. He had persuaded himself to accept this state of affairs, but the encounter with Emilie Bardach seems to have brought all his old feelings of guilt rushing to the surface. Hedda longs to be like Loevborg, but lacks the courage; she is repelled by the reality of sex (as Ibsen himself was?) and prefers to experience it vicariously by encouraging Loevborg to describe his experiences to her. Two emotions are dominant in her, the fear of scandal and the fear of ridicule, and Ibsen himself, though always willing to trail his coat in print, seems also to have been privately dominated by these emotions.

But if *Hedda Gabler* is, in fact, a self-portrait, it is certainly an unconscious one – not that that makes it any the less truthful or valuable; rather the reverse. Ibsen's rough preliminary jottings referred to above make it clear that he *intended* the play as a tragedy of the purposelessness of life, and in particular of the purposelessness imposed on women of his time both by their upbringing and by the social conventions which limited their activities. The following extracts will serve as examples:

'(1) They aren't all created to be mothers.

(2) They all have a leaning towards sensuality, but are afraid of the scandal.

(3) They realize that life holds a purpose for them, but they cannot find that purpose.'

'Women have no influence on public affairs. So they want to influence individuals spiritually.'

'The great tragedy of life is that so many people have nothing to do but yearn for happiness without ever being able to find it.'

'Men and women don't belong to the same century.'

'There are very few true parents in the world. Most people are brought up by uncles or aunts – neglected or misunderstood or spoiled.'

'The play is to be about "the insuperable"—the longing and striving to defy convention, to defy what people accept (including Hedda).'

'Hedda is typical of women in her position and with her

character. One marries Tesman but one titillates one's imagination with Eilert Loevborg. One leans back in one's chair, closes
one's eyes and pictures to oneself his adventures. The enormous difference: Mrs Elvsted "works to improve him morally",
while for Hedda he is merely a subject for cowardly and tan-
talizing dreams. She lacks the courage to partake actively in
such going-on. Then her confession as to how she really feels.
Tied! Don't understand – But to be an object of ridicule!
Of ridicule!'

'The daemon in Hedda is that she wants to influence another
human being, but once that has happened, she despises him.'

'Loevborg has leanings towards Bohemianism. Hedda is also
attracted to it, but dares not take the jump.'

'It's really a man's life she wants to lead. In all respects. But
then scruples intervene. Some inherited – some implanted.'

'Remember I was born the child of an old man. And not
merely old. Played-out – or anyway, decrepit. Perhaps that has
left its mark.'

'It is a great delusion that one only loves one person.'

'Tesman represents propriety. Hedda represents *ennui*. Mrs
R. [i.e. Mrs Elvsted] modern nervousness and hysteria. Brack
the representative of bourgeois society.'

'H.L. [i.e. Loevborg]'s despair arises from the fact that he
wants to control the world but cannot control himself.'

'Life for Hedda is a farce which isn't worth seeing through
to the end.'

As usual with Ibsen's plays, certain elements in *Hedda Gabler*
can be traced to incidents in the lives of people whom he knew
personally or had heard or read about. For example, when he
visited Norway in 1885 he must have heard of the marriage
the previous winter between a famous beauty named Sophie
Magelssen and the philologist Peter Groth. Groth had married
her on a research grant which he had won in competition with
Hjalmar Falk, whom many thought the better scholar of the

two (and who gets a consolatory mention in the play as the dead Cabinet Minister who had previously owned the Tesmans' villa). Neither Tesman nor Loevborg, however, was modelled on either of these two. Ibsen told his son Sigurd that he had based Tesman on Julius Elias, a young German student of literature whom he had got to know in Munich. Elias's great passion was for 'putting other people's papers in order'; later he became a distinguished man of letters, and ironically enough it fell to him to put Ibsen's own papers in order when he shared with Halvdan Koht the task of editing the dramatist's literary remains.[1] Loevborg was closely modelled on a Dane named Julius Hoffory who was Professor of Scandinavian Philology and Phonetics in Berlin. Hoffory was a gifted but unbalanced man who mixed freely with women of low repute and had once lost the manuscript of a book during a nocturnal orgy. He recognized himself delightedly when *Hedda Gabler* appeared, and thereafter adopted Loevborg as his pseudonym.

Miss Tesman, George's aunt, was based on an old lady from Trondhjem named Elise Hokk. Ibsen had met her a number of times during the early seventies in Dresden, where she tended a sick sister for three years until the latter died. He wrote a charming poem in tribute to her in 1874. She is the only character in the play, as far as is known, who was based on a Norwegian original, and this may have influenced early critics who wrote that *Hedda Gabler* was the least Norwegian of Ibsen's plays and that the town (unnamed as usual) in which the action takes place was less suggestive of Christiania than of a Continental capital. William Archer, however, who knew Christiania well, felt sure that Ibsen had that city in mind, and

---

[1] In fairness to Elias, it should be stated that Tesman is a much less ridiculous character in the early draft of the play than Ibsen subsequently made him. His maddening repetition of nursery phrases such as 'Fancy that!' was added during revision.

added the interesting comment that Ibsen, although writing
in 1890, seemed to have set the play some thirty years earlier.
'The electric cars, telephones and other conspicuous factors
in the life of a modern capital', he wrote in his introduction
(1907) to the English translation by himself and Edmund
Gosse, 'are notably absent from the play. There is no electric
light in Secretary Falk's villa. It is still the habit for ladies to
return on foot from evening parties, with gallant swains escort-
ing them. This "suburbanism" which so distressed the London
critics of 1891, was characteristic of the Christiania Ibsen
himself had known in the eighteen-sixties – the Christiania of
Love's Comedy – rather than of the greatly extended and moder-
nised city of the end of the century.'

Three further incidents which came to Ibsen's notice found
their way into the play. While he was actually working on it, a
young married couple came to seek his advice; their happiness, they said, had been ruined because the husband had been
hypnotized by another woman. Then there was the unfortunate
case of the Norwegian composer Johan Svendsen, whose wife,
Sally, in a fit of rage at discovering a letter from another woman
hidden in a bouquet of flowers, had burned the score of a
symphony which he had just composed. Finally, he heard of
the even more unfortunate incident of the Norwegian lady
whose husband had cured himself of drink and had resolved
never to touch it again. To see how much power she had over
him, she rolled a keg of brandy into his room as a birthday
present, and before the day was over he was dead drunk. All
these episodes are reflected in *Hedda Gabler*.

The original of Hedda herself is not known. She has been
rather glibly assumed by some critics to be a portrait of Emilie,
on the grounds that both were beautiful and aristocratic and
did not know what to do with their lives, and that Ibsen's
description of Hedda (aristocratic face, fine complexion, veiled
expression in the eyes, etc.) corresponds to early photographs
of Emilie. The same characteristics could, however, be found

in the photograph of almost any well-born young lady of the period; the description would apply equally to Queen Alexandra; and few women of Ibsen's time, let alone girls of eighteen knew what to do with their lives. In any case, the idea of creating such a character had been at the back of Ibsen's mind long before he met Emilie, for his rough notes for *Rosmersholm* (1886) contain a sketch of a girl, intended as Rosmer's elder daughter, though he finally decided not to include her in the play, who 'is in danger of succumbing to inactivity and loneliness. She has rich talents which are lying unused.' On the other hand, Emilie must certainly have been at the back of his mind when he was writing *Hedda Gabler*, and it is possible that Hedda may be a portrait, conscious or unconscious, of what Emilie might become in ten years if she did not marry the right man or find a fixed purpose in life. If so, it was a prophecy that came uncomfortably near the truth, for Emilie, though she lived to be eighty-three – she died as late as 1 November 1955 – accomplished nothing and never married.

The differences between Ibsen's first draft and his final version as we know it are, as has already been remarked, numerous and revealing. Apart from changing Tesman from an ordinary bourgeois husband into a ninny spoiled (like Hjalmar Ekdal) by loving aunts, he improved him morally, for in the first draft it is Tesman who suggests hiding the manuscript to give Loevborg a fright, and so is partly responsible for the latter's death. Miss Tesman's important account to Bertha in Act 1 of Hedda's life with her father was an afterthought; so were Mademoiselle Danielle, Mrs Elvsted's abundant hair and Hedda's jealousy of it, the image of the vine-leaves, and Hedda's threat (before the play opens) to shoot Loevborg. Act 1 ends much less strongly in the draft, with no mention of the pistols; and Tesman and Mrs Elvsted both know of Hedda's former close relationship with Loevborg. Miss Tesman's role is less complex than in the final version; she does not realize in Act 1 that Hedda is going to have a baby, and has a far less effective scene with Hedda in Act 4. The conversation between Hedda, Loevborg and Tesman over the photograph album about the honeymoon contains a direct reference of Gossensass, subsequently deleted. And Brack, in a passage which one is rather sorry to lose, describes sadly to Hedda how three 'triangles' of which he was a part have been broken up during the past six months – not, as Hedda guesses, by other bachelors but by intruders far more destructive to extramarital relationships – children. Finally, one may note two remarks which Ibsen originally put into Hedda's mouth but subsequently deleted: (1) 'I can't understand how anyone could fall in love with a man who isn't married – or engaged – or at least in love with someone else.' (2) 'To take someone from someone else – I think that must be so wonderful!' He saved these thoughts for a character, already created in miniature in *The Lady from the Sea*, to whom he was to allot the principal female role in his next play two years later – Hilde Wangel in *The Master Builder*.

The repeated references to the 'vine-leaves' continue to puzzle critics, even though William Archer cleared the problem up fifty years ago. 'Surely', he wrote, 'this is a very obvious image or symbol of the beautiful, the ideal, aspect of bacchic elation and revelry. . . . Professor Dietrichson relates that among the young artists whose society Ibsen frequented during his first years in Rome it was customary, at their little festivals, for the revellers to deck themselves in this fashion. But the image is so obvious that there is no need to trace it to any personal experience. The attempt to place Hedda's vine-leaves among Ibsen's obscurities is an example of the firm resolution not to understand which animated the criticism of the nineties.' Not, alas, only of the nineties. The picture which the vine-leaves are intended to evoke is that of the young god, 'burning and unashamed', in Hedda's words; as Archer noted, it was an image which Ibsen had used previously in both *Peer Gynt* and *Emperor and Galilean*.

A point that is sometimes missed in production of *Hedda Gabler* is the importance of correct casting for Bertha, the Tesmans' maid. Ibsen never created a role, however tiny, that was not both integral to the play and rewarding to the player, and his servants are no exceptions – one thinks of the two butlers, the superior Pettersen and the inferior Jensen, in *The Wild Duck*, the housekeeper Mrs Helseth in *Rosmersholm*, and Malene, the sour maid in *John Gabriel Borkman*. Ibsen underlined Bertha's importance in a letter which he wrote to Kristine Steen on 14 January 1891 concerning the casting of the play for Christiania. 'Mrs Wolf', he wrote, 'wishes to be released from playing the maid Bertha in my new play, since she is of the opinion that this role could be adequately filled by any other member of the company. She is mistaken. There is no-one else at the theatre who can perform Bertha as I wish her to be performed. Only Mrs Wolf can do it. She has evidently not taken the trouble to read the play carefully, or she could hardly fail to appreciate this. George Tesman, his old aunts and Bertha together create a picture of completeness and unity. They have common thoughts, common memories, a common attitude towards life. To Hedda they represent a force foreign and hostile to her and to everything she stands for. The harmony that exists between them must be apparent on the stage. And this can be achieved if Mrs Wolf plays the part. But only if she does. My respect for Mrs Wolf's soundness of judgment is too great for me seriously to believe that she regards it as artistically beneath her to create a servant. I did not regard it as artistically beneath me to create this honest, artless old creature. Here in Munich this unpretentious character is to be created by one of the Hoftheater's leading actresses, and she has embraced the task with love and interest. Besides being an actress, she is also an artist. By this I mean that she regards it as a matter of honour not merely to "give a performance" but to turn a created character into a thing of flesh and blood.' Ibsen's plea fell, however, on deaf ears, for Mrs Wolf still refused to play the part.

Despite its early failures on the stages of Europe, *Hedda Gabler* has come to be accepted as one of the most popular of Ibsen's plays. London has seen no less than twenty-seven separate productions, a number exceeded only, among Ibsen's other plays, by *A Doll's House* and *Ghosts*. Among the actresses who have played it there are Elizabeth Robins (1891 and 1893), Eleonora Duse (in Italian, 1903), Mrs Patrick Campbell (1907 and 1922), Lydia Yavorska (in Russian, 1909, and in English, 1911), Jean Forbes-Robertson (1931, 1936 and 1951), Peggy Ashcroft (1954), Maggie Smith (1970) and Janet Suzman (1977). Probably the finest English Hedda, however, was Pamela Brown, who in 1941, at the age of twenty-two, gave a performance at the Oxford Playhouse which caused James Agate seriously to compare her with the young Sarah Bernhardt. 'The moment that unquiet spirit appeared in the curtain'd doorway, drew a long breath, and paused to survey the Tesmanesque scene in marble, cold disfavour', he wrote, 'why, then we knew that Hedda was going to be present. . . . I was not playgoing in 1867, when She Who Must Not Be Named was 22, which is the age of Miss Pamela Brown. But as that great player must have been in her experimental years, so is this young actress now'. Another admired and acclaimed performance in the role was that of Catherine Lacey at the Bristol Old Vic in 1948. America first saw the play on 30 March 1898, when Elizabeth Robins presented a single performance at the Fifth Avenue Theatre in New York. *The Critic* wrote of this production that 'it was, on the whole, the most satisfactory representation of an Ibsen play ever given in this city', and described Miss Robins's performance as 'in every way a remarkable achievement'. Unfortunately, according to Norman Hapgood in *The Stage in America, 1897–1900*, 'it failed to interest the public enough to continue contemplated Ibsen experiments'. Blanche Bates played it for a single matinée in Washington in 1900; then in 1903 Minnie Fiske presented it in New York for a whole week to crowded houses, and brought it back to the Manhattan Theatre in November 1904, when it achieved the, by the standard of those days, considerable number of twenty-six performances. The cast included George Arliss as Judge Brack. In 1905 Alla Nazimova played it at the Russian Theatre, New York, in Russian, and the following year she performed it in English, créating a tremendous impression. Subsequent Heddas in New York have included Emily Stevens, Eva le Gallienne, Tallulah Bankhead (on television), Anne Meacham and Claire Bloom.

MICHAEL MEYER

This translation of Hedda Gabler *was first performed on 9 November 1960 at the 4th Street Theatre, New York, in a production by David Ross with Anne Meacham as Hedda. The first London performance was on 29 June 1970 at the Cambridge Theatre, under the auspices of the National Theatre. The cast was:*

GEORGE TESMAN, *research graduate in cultural history*	Jeremy Brett
HEDDA TESMAN, *his wife*	Maggie Smith
MISS JULIANA TESMAN, *his aunt*	Jeanne Watts
MRS ELVSTED	Sheila Reid
JUDGE BRACK	John Moffat
EILERT LOEVBORG	Robert Stephens
BERTHA, *a maid*	Julia McCarthy

Directed by Ingmar Bergman

The action takes place in TESMAN's villa in the fashionable quarter of town.

Act One

*A large drawing-room, handsomely and tastefully furnished;
decorated in dark colours. In the rear wall is a broad open doorway, with curtains drawn back to either side. It leads to a smaller
room, decorated in the same style as the drawing-room. In the
right-hand wall of the drawing-room a folding door leads out to
the hall. The opposite wall, on the left, contains french windows,
also with curtains drawn back on either side. Through the glass
we can see part of a veranda, and trees in autumn colours.
Downstage stands an oval table, covered by a cloth and surrounded
by chairs. Downstage right, against the wall, is a broad stove tiled
with dark porcelain; in front of it stand a high-backed armchair,
a cushioned footrest and two footstools. Upstage right, in an
alcove, is a corner sofa, with a small, round table. Downstage left,
a little away from the wall, is another sofa. Upstage of the french
windows, a piano. On either side of the open doorway in the rear
wall stand what-nots holding ornaments of terra-cotta and
majolica. Against the rear wall of the smaller room can be seen a
sofa, a table and a couple of chairs. Above this sofa hangs the
portrait of a handsome old man in general's uniform. Above the
table a lamp hangs from the ceiling, with a shade of opalescent,
milky glass. All round the drawing-room bunches of flowers stand
in vases and glasses. More bunches lie on the tables. The floors of
both rooms are covered with thick carpets. Morning light. The
sun shines in through the french windows.*

MISS JULIANA TESMAN, *wearing a hat and carrying a parasol, enters from the hall, followed by* BERTHA, *who is carrying
a bunch of flowers wrapped in paper.* MISS TESMAN *is about
sixty-five, of pleasant and kindly appearance. She is neatly
but simply dressed in grey outdoor clothes.* BERTHA, *the maid,
is rather simple and rustic-looking. She is getting on in years.*

MISS TESMAN (*stops just inside the door, listens, and says in a hushed voice*). Well, fancy that! They're not up yet!

BERTHA (*also in hushed tones*). What did I tell you, miss? The boat didn't get in till midnight. And when they did turn up – Jesus, miss, you should have seen all the things madam made me unpack before she'd go to bed!

MISS TESMAN. Ah, well. Let them have a good lie in. But let's have some nice fresh air waiting for them when they do come down. (*Goes to the french windows and throws them wide open.*)

BERTHA (*bewildered at the table, the bunch of flowers in her hand*). I'm blessed if there's a square inch left to put anything. I'll have to let it lie here, miss. (*Puts it on the piano.*)

MISS TESMAN. Well, Bertha dear, so now you have a new mistress. Heaven knows it nearly broke my heart to have to part with you.

BERTHA (*snivels*). What about me, Miss Juju? How do you suppose I felt? After all the happy years I've spent with you and Miss Rena?

MISS TESMAN. We must accept it bravely, Bertha. It was the only way. George needs you to take care of him. He could never manage without you. You've looked after him ever since he was a tiny boy.

BERTHA. Oh, but, Miss Juju, I can't help thinking about Miss Rena, lying there all helpless, poor dear. And that new girl! She'll never learn the proper way to handle an invalid.

MISS TESMAN. Oh, I'll manage to train her. I'll do most of the work myself, you know. You needn't worry about my poor sister, Bertha dear.

BERTHA. But, Miss Juju, there's another thing. I'm frightened madam may not find me suitable.

MISS TESMAN. Oh, nonsense, Bertha. There may be one or two little things to begin with –

BERTHA. She's a real lady. Wants everything just so.

MISS TESMAN. But of course she does! General Gabler's
daughter! Think of what she was accustomed to when the
general was alive. You remember how we used to see her
out riding with her father? In that long black skirt? With
the feather in her hat?

BERTHA. Oh, yes, miss. As if I could forget! But, Lord! I
never dreamed I'd live to see a match between her and Master Georgie.

MISS TESMAN. Neither did I. By the way, Bertha, from now
on you must stop calling him Master Georgie. You must
say Dr Tesman.

BERTHA. Yes, madam said something about that too. Last
night – the moment they'd set foot inside the door. Is it true,
then, miss?

MISS TESMAN. Indeed it is. Just fancy, Bertha, some foreigners
have made him a doctor. It happened while they were away.
I had no idea till he told me when they got off the boat.

BERTHA. Well, I suppose there's no limit to what he won't
become. He's that clever. I never thought he'd go in for
hospital work, though.

MISS TESMAN. No, he's not that kind of doctor. (*Nods im-
pressively.*) In any case, you may soon have to address him
by an even grander title.

BERTHA. You don't say! What might that be, miss?

MISS TESMAN (*smiles*). Ah! If you only knew! (*Moved.*) Dear
God, if only poor Joachim could rise out of his grave and
see what his little son has grown into! (*Looks round.*) But,
Bertha, why have you done this? Taken the chintz covers
off all the furniture!

BERTHA. Madam said I was to. Can't stand chintz covers on
chairs, she said.

MISS TESMAN. But surely they're not going to use this room
as a parlour?

BERTHA. So I gathered, miss. From what madam said. He
didn't say anything. The Doctor.

GEORGE TESMAN *comes into the rear room from the right, humming, with an open, empty travelling-bag in his hand. He is about thirty-three, of medium height and youthful appearance, rather plump, with an open, round, contented face, and fair hair and beard. He wears spectacles, and is dressed in comfortable indoor clothes.*

MISS TESMAN. Good morning! Good morning, George!

TESMAN (*in open doorway*). Auntie Juju! Dear Auntie Juju! (*Comes forward and shakes her hand.*) You've come all the way out here! And so early! What?

MISS TESMAN. Well, I had to make sure you'd settled in comfortably.

TESMAN. But you can't have had a proper night's sleep.

MISS TESMAN. Oh, never mind that.

TESMAN. But you got home safely?

MISS TESMAN. Oh, yes. Judge Brack kindly saw me home.

TESMAN. We were so sorry we couldn't give you a lift. But you saw how it was – Hedda had so much luggage – and she insisted on having it all with her.

MISS TESMAN. Yes, I've never seen so much luggage.

BERTHA (*to* TESMAN). Shall I go and ask madam if there's anything I can lend her a hand with?

TESMAN. Er – thank you, Bertha, no, you needn't bother. She says if she wants you for anything she'll ring.

BERTHA (*over to right*). Oh. Very good.

TESMAN. Oh, Bertha – take this bag, will you?

BERTHA (*takes it*). I'll put it in the attic. (*Goes.*)

TESMAN. Just fancy, Auntie Juju, I filled that whole bag with notes for my book. You know, it's really incredible what I've managed to find rooting through those archives. By Jove! Wonderful old things no one even knew existed –

MISS TESMAN. I'm sure you didn't waste a single moment of your honeymoon, George dear.

TESMAN. No, I think I can truthfully claim that. But, Auntie

Juju, do take your hat off. Here. Let me untie it for you. What?

MISS TESMAN (*as he does so*). Oh dear, oh dear! It's just as if you were still living at home with us.

TESMAN (*turns the hat in his hand and looks at it*). I say! What a splendid new hat!

MISS TESMAN. I bought it for Hedda's sake.

TESMAN. For Hedda's sake? What?

MISS TESMAN. So that Hedda needn't be ashamed of me, in case we ever go for a walk together.

TESMAN (*pats her cheek*). You still think of everything, don't you, Auntie Juju? (*Puts the hat down on a chair by the table.*) Come on, let's sit down here on the sofa. And have a little chat while we wait for Hedda.

They sit. She puts her parasol in the corner of the sofa.

MISS TESMAN (*clasps both his hands and looks at him*). Oh, George, it's so wonderful to have you back, and be able to see you with my own eyes again! Poor dear Joachim's own son!

TESMAN. What about me? It's wonderful for me to see you again, Auntie Juju. You've been a mother to me. And a father, too.

MISS TESMAN. You'll always keep a soft spot in your heart for your old aunties, won't you, George dear?

TESMAN. I suppose Auntie Rena's no better? What?

MISS TESMAN. Alas, no. I'm afraid she'll never get better, poor dear. She's lying there just as she has for all these years. Please God I may be allowed to keep her for a little longer. If I lost her I don't know what I'd do. Especially now I haven't you to look after.

TESMAN (*pats her on the back*). There, there, there!

MISS TESMAN (*with a sudden change of mood*). Oh, but, George, fancy you being a married man! And to think it's you who've

won Hedda Gabler! The beautiful Hedda Gabler! Fancy!
She was always so surrounded by admirers.

TESMAN (*hums a little and smiles contentedly*). Yes, I suppose
there are quite a few people in this town who wouldn't mind
being in my shoes. What?

MISS TESMAN. And what a honeymoon! Five months! Nearly
six.

TESMAN. Well, I've done a lot of work, you know. All those
archives to go through. And I've had to read lots of
books.

MISS TESMAN. Yes, dear, of course. (*Lowers her voice con-
fidentially.*) But tell me, George – haven't you any – any extra
little piece of news to give me?

TESMAN. You mean, arising out of the honeymoon?

MISS TESMAN. Yes.

TESMAN. No, I don't think there's anything I didn't tell you
in my letters. My doctorate, of course – but I told you about
that last night, didn't I?

MISS TESMAN. Yes, yes, I didn't mean that kind of thing. I
was just wondering – are you – are you expecting–?

TESMAN. Expecting what?

MISS TESMAN. Oh, come on, George, I'm your old aunt!

TESMAN. Well, actually – yes, I am expecting something.

MISS TESMAN. I knew it!

TESMAN. You'll be happy to learn that before very long I
expect to become a – professor.

MISS TESMAN. Professor?

TESMAN. I think I may say that the matter has been decided.
But, Auntie Juju, you know about this.

MISS TESMAN (*gives a little laugh*). Yes, of course. I'd forgotten. (*Changes her tone.*) But we were talking about your
honeymoon. It must have cost a dreadful amount of money,
George?

TESMAN. Oh well, you know, that big research grant I got
helped a good deal.

MISS TESMAN. But how on earth did you manage to make it do for two?

TESMAN. Well, to tell the truth it was a bit tricky. What?

MISS TESMAN. Especially when one's travelling with a lady. A little bird tells me that makes things very much more expensive.

TESMAN. Well, yes, of course it does make things a little more expensive. But Hedda has to do things in style, Auntie Juju. I mean, she has to. Anything less grand wouldn't have suited her.

MISS TESMAN. No, no, I suppose not. A honeymoon abroad seems to be the vogue nowadays. But tell me, have you had time to look round the house?

TESMAN. You bet. I've been up since the crack of dawn.

MISS TESMAN. Well, what do you think of it?

TESMAN. Splendid. Absolutely splendid. I'm only wondering what we're going to do with those two empty rooms between that little one and Hedda's bedroom.

MISS TESMAN (*laughs slyly*). Ah, George dear, I'm sure you'll manage to find some use for them – in time.

TESMAN. Yes, of course, Auntie Juju, how stupid of me. You're thinking of my books? What?

MISS TESMAN. Yes, yes, dear boy. I was thinking of your books.

TESMAN. You know, I'm so happy for Hedda's sake that we've managed to get this house. Before we became engaged she often used to say this was the only house in town she felt she could really bear to live in. It used to belong to Mrs Falk – you know, the Prime Minister's widow.

MISS TESMAN. Fancy that! And what a stroke of luck it happened to come into the market. Just as you'd left on your honeymoon.

TESMAN. Yes, Auntie Juju, we've certainly had all the luck with us. What?

MISS TESMAN. But, George dear, the expense! It's going to make a dreadful hole in your pocket, all this.

TESMAN (*a little downcast*). Yes, I – I suppose it will, won't it?

MISS TESMAN. Oh, George, really!

TESMAN. How much do you think it'll cost? Roughly, I mean? What?

MISS TESMAN. I can't possibly say till I see the bills.

TESMAN. Well, luckily Judge Brack's managed to get it on very favourable terms. He wrote and told Hedda so.

MISS TESMAN. Don't you worry, George dear. Anyway, I've stood security for all the furniture and carpets.

TESMAN. Security? But dear, sweet Auntie Juju, how could you possibly stand security?

MISS TESMAN. I've arranged a mortgage on our annuity.

TESMAN (*jumps up*). What? On your annuity? And – Auntie Rena's?

MISS TESMAN. Yes. Well, I couldn't think of any other way.

TESMAN (*stands in front of her*). Auntie Juju, have you gone completely out of your mind? That annuity's all you and Auntie Rena have.

MISS TESMAN. All right, there's no need to get so excited about it. It's a pure formality, you know. Judge Brack told me so. He was so kind as to arrange it all for me. A pure formality; those were his very words.

TESMAN. I dare say. All the same –

MISS TESMAN. Anyway, you'll have a salary of your own now. And, good heavens, even if we did have to fork out a little – tighten our belts for a week or two – why, we'd be happy to do so for your sake.

TESMAN. Oh, Auntie Juju! Will you never stop sacrificing yourself for me?

MISS TESMAN (*gets up and puts her hands on his shoulders*). What else have I to live for but to smooth your road a little, my dear boy? You've never had any mother or father to turn to. And now at last we've achieved our goal. I won't deny we've had our little difficulties now and then. But now, thank the good Lord, George dear, all your worries are past.

TESMAN. Yes, it's wonderful really how everything's gone just right for me.

MISS TESMAN. Yes! And the enemies who tried to bar your way have been struck down. They have been made to bite the dust. The man who was your most dangerous rival has had the mightiest fall. And now he's lying there in the pit he dug for himself, poor misguided creature.

TESMAN. Have you heard any news of Eilert? Since I went away?

MISS TESMAN. Only that he's said to have published a new book.

TESMAN. What! Eilert Loevborg? You mean – just recently? What?

MISS TESMAN. So they say. I don't imagine it can be of any value, do you? When your new book comes out, that'll be another story. What's it going to be about?

TESMAN. The domestic industries of Brabant in the Middle Ages.

MISS TESMAN. Oh, George! The things you know about!

TESMAN. Mind you, it may be some time before I actually get down to writing it. I've made these very extensive notes, and I've got to file and index them first.

MISS TESMAN. Ah, yes! Making notes; filing and indexing; you've always been wonderful at that. Poor dear Joachim was just the same.

TESMAN. I'm looking forward so much to getting down to that. Especially now I've a home of my own to work in.

MISS TESMAN. And above all, now that you have the girl you set your heart on, George dear.

TESMAN (embraces her). Oh, yes, Auntie Juju, yes! Hedda's the loveliest thing of all! (Looks towards the doorway.) I think I hear her coming. What?

HEDDA enters the rear room from the left, and comes into the drawing-room. She is a woman of twenty-nine. Distinguished, *aristocratic face and figure. Her complexion is pale and opalescent. Her eyes are steel-grey, with an expression of cold, calm serenity. Her hair is of a handsome auburn colour, but is not especially abundant. She is dressed in an elegant, somewhat loose-fitting morning gown.*

MISS TESMAN (*goes to greet her*). Good morning, Hedda dear! Good morning!

HEDDA (*holds out her hand*). Good morning, dear Miss Tesman. What an early hour to call. So kind of you.

MISS TESMAN (*seems somewhat embarrassed*). And has the young bride slept well in her new home?

HEDDA. Oh – thank you, yes. Passably well.

TESMAN (*laughs*). Passably? I say. Hedda, that's good! When I jumped out of bed, you were sleeping like a top.

HEDDA. Yes. Fortunately. One has to accustom oneself to anything new, Miss Tesman. It takes time. (*Looks left.*) Oh, that maid's left the french windows open. This room's flooded with sun.

MISS TESMAN (*goes towards the windows*). Oh – let me close them.

HEDDA. No, no, don't do that. Tesman dear, draw the curtains. This light's blinding me.

TESMAN (*at the windows*). Yes, yes, dear. There, Hedda, now you've got shade and fresh air.

HEDDA. This room needs fresh air. All these flowers –! But my dear Miss Tesman, won't you take a seat?

MISS TESMAN. No, really not, thank you. I just wanted to make sure you have everything you need. I must see about getting back home. My poor dear sister will be waiting for me.

TESMAN. Be sure to give her my love, won't you? Tell her I'll run over and see her later today.

MISS TESMAN. Oh yes, I'll tell her that. Oh, George – (*Fumbles in the pocket of her skirt.*) I almost forgot. I've brought something for you.

TESMAN. What's that, Auntie Juju? What?

MISS TESMAN (*pulls out a flat package wrapped in newspaper and gives it to him*). Open and see, dear boy.

TESMAN (*opens the package*). Good heavens! Auntie Juju, you've kept them! Hedda, this is really very touching. What?

HEDDA (*by the what-nots, on the right*). What is it, Tesman?

TESMAN. My old shoes! My slippers, Hedda!

HEDDA. Oh, them. I remember you kept talking about them on our honeymoon.

TESMAN. Yes, I missed them dreadfully. (*Goes over to her.*) Here, Hedda, take a look.

HEDDA (*goes away towards the stove*). Thanks, I won't bother.

TESMAN (*follows her*). Fancy, Hedda, Auntie Rena's embroidered them for me. Despite her being so ill. Oh, you can't imagine what memories they have for me.

HEDDA (*by the table*). Not for me.

MISS TESMAN. No, Hedda's right there, George.

TESMAN. Yes, but I thought since she's one of the family now –

HEDDA (*interrupts*). Tesman, we really can't go on keeping this maid.

MISS TESMAN. Not keep Bertha?

TESMAN. What makes you say that, dear? What?

HEDDA (*points*). Look at that! She's left her old hat lying on the chair.

TESMAN (*appalled, drops his slippers on the floor*). But, Hedda –!

HEDDA. Suppose someone came in and saw it?

TESMAN. But, Hedda – that's Auntie Juju's hat.

HEDDA. Oh?

MISS TESMAN (*picks up the hat*). Indeed it's mine. And it doesn't happen to be old, Hedda dear.

HEDDA. I didn't look at it very closely, Miss Tesman.

MISS TESMAN (*tying on the hat*). As a matter of fact, it's the first time I've worn it. As the good Lord is my witness.

TESMAN. It's very pretty, too. Really smart.

MISS TESMAN. Oh, I'm afraid it's nothing much really. (*Looks round.*) My parasol. Ah, there it is. (*Takes it.*) This is mine, too. (*Murmurs.*) Not Bertha's.

TESMAN. A new hat and a new parasol! I say, Hedda, fancy that!

HEDDA. Very pretty and charming.

TESMAN. Yes, isn't it? What? But, Auntie Juju, take a good look at Hedda before you go. Isn't she pretty and charming?

MISS TESMAN. Dear boy, there's nothing new in that. Hedda's been a beauty ever since the day she was born. (*Nods and goes right.*)

TESMAN (*follows her*). Yes, but have you noticed how strong and healthy she's looking? And how she's filled out since we went away?

MISS TESMAN (*stops and turns*). Filled out?

HEDDA (*walks across the room*). Oh, can't we forget it?

TESMAN. Yes, Auntie Juju – you can't see it so clearly with that dress on. But I've good reason to know –

HEDDA (*by the french windows, impatiently*). You haven't good reason to know anything.

TESMAN. It must have been the mountain air up there in the Tyrol –

HEDDA (*curtly, interrupts him*). I'm exactly the same as when I went away.

TESMAN. You keep on saying so. But you're not. I'm right, aren't I, Auntie Juju?

MISS TESMAN (*has folded her hands and is gazing at her*). She's beautiful – beautiful. Hedda is beautiful. (*Goes over to* HEDDA, *takes her head between her hands, draws it down and kisses her hair.*) God bless and keep you, Hedda Tesman. For George's sake.

HEDDA (*frees herself politely*). Oh – let me go, please.

MISS TESMAN (*quietly, emotionally*). I shall come and see you both every day.

TESMAN. Yes, Auntie Juju, please do. What?

MISS TESMAN. Good-bye! Good-bye!

She goes out into the hall. TESMAN *follows her. The door remains open.* TESMAN *is heard sending his love to* AUNT RENA *and thanking* MISS TESMAN *for his slippers. Meanwhile* HEDDA *walks up and down the room, raising her arms and clenching her fists as though in desperation. Then she throws aside the curtains from the french windows and stands there, looking out. A few moments later* TESMAN *returns and closes the door behind him.*

TESMAN (*picks up his slippers from the floor*). What are you looking at, Hedda?

HEDDA (*calm and controlled again*). Only the leaves. They're so golden and withered.

TESMAN (*wraps up the slippers and lays them on the table*). Well, we're in September now.

HEDDA (*restless again*). Yes. We're already into September.

TESMAN. Auntie Juju was behaving rather oddly, I thought, didn't you? Almost as though she was in church or something. I wonder what came over her. Any idea?

HEDDA. I hardly know her. Does she often act like that?

TESMAN. Not to the extent she did today.

HEDDA (*goes away from the french windows*). Do you think she was hurt by what I said about the hat?

TESMAN. Oh, I don't think so. A little at first, perhaps –

HEDDA. But what a thing to do, throw her hat down in some-one's drawing-room. People don't do such things.

TESMAN. I'm sure Auntie Juju doesn't do it very often.

HEDDA. Oh well, I'll make it up with her.

TESMAN. Oh Hedda, would you?

HEDDA. When you see them this afternoon invite her to come out here this evening.

TESMAN. You bet I will! I say, there's another thing which would please her enormously.

HEDDA. Oh?

TESMAN. If you could bring yourself to call her Auntie Juju. For my sake, Hedda? What?

HEDDA. Oh no, really, Tesman, you mustn't ask me to do that. I've told you so once before. I'll try to call her Aunt Juliana. That's as far as I'll go.

TESMAN (*after a moment*). I say, Hedda, is anything wrong? What?

HEDDA. I'm just looking at my old piano. It doesn't really go with all this.

TESMAN. As soon as I start getting my salary we'll see about changing it.

HEDDA. No, no, don't let's change it. I don't want to part with it. We can move it into that little room and get another one to put in here.

TESMAN (*a little downcast*). Yes, we – might do that.

HEDDA (*picks up the bunch of flowers from the piano*). These flowers weren't here when we arrived last night.

TESMAN. I expect Auntie Juju brought them.

HEDDA. Here's a card. (*Takes it out and reads.*) 'Will come back later today.' Guess who it's from?

TESMAN. No idea. Who? What?

HEDDA. It says: 'Mrs Elvsted.'

TESMAN. No, really? Mrs Elvsted! She used to be Miss Rysing, didn't she?

HEDDA. Yes. She was the one with that irritating hair she was always showing off. I hear she used to be an old flame of yours.

TESMAN (*laughs*). That didn't last long. Anyway, that was before I got to know you, Hedda. By Jove, fancy her being in town!

HEDDA. Strange she should call. I only knew her at school.

TESMAN. Yes, I haven't seen her for – oh, heaven knows how long. I don't know how she manages to stick it out up there in the north. What?

HEDDA (*thinks for a moment, then says suddenly*). Tell me, Tesman, doesn't he live somewhere up in those parts? You know – Eilert Loevborg?

TESMAN. Yes, that's right. So he does.

BERTHA *enters from the hall.*

BERTHA. She's here again, madam. The lady who came and left the flowers. (*Points.*) The ones you're holding.

HEDDA. Oh, is she? Well, show her in.

BERTHA *opens the door for* MRS ELVSTED *and goes out.* MRS ELVSTED *is a delicately built woman with gentle, attractive features. Her eyes are light blue, large, and somewhat prominent, with a frightened, questioning expression. Her hair is extremely fair, almost flaxen, and is exceptionally wavy and abundant. She is two or three years younger than* HEDDA. *She is wearing a dark visiting dress, in good taste but not quite in the latest fashion.*

(*Goes cordially to greet her.*) Dear Mrs Elvsted, good morning! How delightful to see you again after all this time!

MRS ELVSTED (*nervously, trying to control herself*). Yes, it's many years since we met.

TESMAN. And since *we* met. What?

HEDDA. Thank you for your lovely flowers.

MRS ELVSTED. I wanted to come yesterday afternoon. But they told me you were away –

TESMAN. You've only just arrived in town, then? What?

MRS ELVSTED. I got here yesterday, around midday. Oh, I became almost desperate when I heard you weren't here.

HEDDA. Desperate? Why?

TESMAN. My dear Mrs Rysing – Elvsted –

HEDDA. There's nothing wrong, I hope?

MRS ELVSTED. Yes, there is. And I don't know anyone else here whom I can turn to.

HEDDA (*puts the flowers down on the table*). Come and sit with me on the sofa –

MRS ELVSTED. Oh, I feel too restless to sit down.

HEDDA. You must. Come along, now.

She pulls MRS ELVSTED *down on to the sofa and sits beside her.*

TESMAN. Well? Tell us, Mrs – er –

HEDDA. Has something happened at home?

MRS ELVSTED. Yes – that is, yes and no. Oh, I do hope you won't misunderstand me –

HEDDA. Then you'd better tell us the whole story, Mrs Elvsted.

TESMAN. That's why you've come. What?

MRS ELVSTED. Yes – yes, it is. Well, then – in case you don't already know – Eilert Loevborg is in town.

HEDDA. Loevborg here?

TESMAN. Eilert back in town? Fancy, Hedda, did you hear that?

HEDDA. Yes, of course I heard.

MRS ELVSTED. He's been here a week. A whole week! In this city. Alone. With all those dreadful people –

HEDDA. But, my dear Mrs Elvsted, what concern is he of yours?

MRS ELVSTED (*gives her a frightened look and says quickly*). He's been tutoring the children.

HEDDA. Your children?

MRS ELVSTED. My husband's. I have none.

HEDDA. Oh, you mean your stepchildren.

MRS ELVSTED. Yes.

TESMAN (*gropingly*). But was he sufficiently – I don't know how to put it – sufficiently regular in his habits to be suited to such a post? What?

MRS ELVSTED. For the past two to three years he has been living irreproachably.

TESMAN. You don't say! Hedda, do you hear that?

HEDDA. I hear.

MRS ELVSTED. Quite irreproachably, I assure you. In every

respect. All the same – in this big city – with money in his pockets – I'm so dreadfully frightened something may happen to him.

TESMAN. But why didn't he stay up there with you and your husband?

MRS ELVSTED. Once his book had come out, he became restless.

TESMAN. Oh, yes – Auntie Juju said he's brought out a new book.

MRS ELVSTED. Yes, a big new book about the history of civilization. A kind of general survey. It came out a fortnight ago. Everyone's been buying it and reading it – it's created a tremendous stir –

TESMAN. Has it really? It must be something he's dug up, then.

MRS ELVSTED. You mean from the old days?

TESMAN. Yes.

MRS ELVSTED. No, he's written it all since he came to live with us.

TESMAN. Well, that's splendid news, Hedda. Fancy that!

MRS ELVSTED. Oh, yes! If only he can go on like this!

HEDDA. Have you met him since you came here?

MRS ELVSTED. No, not yet. I had such dreadful difficulty finding his address. But this morning I managed to track him down at last.

HEDDA (*looks searchingly at her*). I must say I find it a little strange that your husband – hm –

MRS ELVSTED (*starts nervously*). My husband! What do you mean?

HEDDA. That he should send you all the way here on an errand of this kind. I'm surprised he didn't come himself to keep an eye on his friend.

MRS ELVSTED. Oh, no, no – my husband hasn't the time. Besides, I – er – wanted to do some shopping here.

HEDDA (*with a slight smile*). Ah. Well, that's different.

MRS ELVSTED (*gets up quickly, restlessly*). Please, Mr Tesman, I beg you – be kind to Eilert Loevborg if he comes here. I'm sure he will. I mean, you used to be such good friends in the old days. And you're both studying the same subject, as far as I can understand. You're in the same field, aren't you?

TESMAN. Well, we used to be, anyway.

MRS ELVSTED. Yes – so I beg you earnestly, do please, please, keep an eye on him. Oh, Mr Tesman, do promise me you will.

TESMAN. I shall be only too happy to do so, Mrs Rysing.

HEDDA. Elvsted.

TESMAN. I'll do everything for Eilert that lies in my power. You can rely on that.

MRS ELVSTED. Oh, how good and kind you are! (*Presses his hands.*) Thank you, thank you, thank you. (*Frightened.*) My husband's so fond of him, you see.

HEDDA (*gets up*). You'd better send him a note, Tesman. He may not come to you of his own accord.

TESMAN. Yes, that'd probably be the best plan, Hedda. What?

HEDDA. The sooner the better. Why not do it now?

MRS ELVSTED (*pleadingly*). Oh yes, if only you would!

TESMAN. I'll do it this very moment. Do you have his address, Mrs – er – Elvsted?

MRS ELVSTED. Yes. (*Takes a small piece of paper from her pocket and gives it to him.*)

TESMAN. Good, good. Right, well, I'll go inside and – (*Looks round.*) Where are my slippers? Oh yes, here. (*Picks up the package and is about to go.*)

HEDDA. Try to sound friendly. Make it a nice long letter.

TESMAN. Right, I will.

MRS ELVSTED. Please don't say anything about my having seen you.

TESMAN. Good heavens, no, of course not. What?

He goes out through the rear room to the right.

HEDDA (*goes over to* MRS ELVSTED, *smiles, and says softly*). Well! Now we've killed two birds with one stone.

MRS ELVSTED. What do you mean?

HEDDA. Didn't you realize I wanted to get him out of the room?

MRS ELVSTED. So that he could write the letter?

HEDDA. And so that I could talk to you alone.

MRS ELVSTED (*confused*). About this?

HEDDA. Yes, about this.

MRS ELVSTED (*in alarm*). But there's nothing more to tell, Mrs Tesman. Really there isn't.

HEDDA. Oh, yes, there is. There's a lot more. I can see that. Come along, let's sit down and have a little chat.

She pushes MRS ELVSTED *down into the armchair by the stove and seats herself on one of the footstools.*

MRS ELVSTED (*looks anxiously at her watch*). Really, Mrs Tesman, I think I ought to be going now.

HEDDA. There's no hurry. Well? How are things at home?

MRS ELVSTED. I'd rather not speak about that.

HEDDA. But, my dear, you can tell me. Good heavens, we were at school together.

MRS ELVSTED. Yes, but you were a year senior to me. Oh, I used to be terribly frightened of you in those days.

HEDDA. Frightened of me?

MRS ELVSTED. Yes, terribly frightened. Whenever you met me on the staircase you used to pull my hair.

HEDDA. No, did I?

MRS ELVSTED. Yes. And once you said you'd burn it all off.

HEDDA. Oh, that was only in fun.

MRS ELVSTED. Yes, but I was so silly in those days. And then afterwards – I mean, we've drifted so far apart. Our backgrounds were so different.

HEDDA. Well, now we must try to drift together again. Now listen. When we were at school we used to call each other by our Christian names –

MRS ELVSTED. No, I'm sure you're mistaken.

HEDDA. I'm sure I'm not. I remember it quite clearly. Let's tell each other our secrets, as we used to in the old days. (*Moves closer on her footstool.*) There, now. (*Kisses her on the cheek.*) You must call me Hedda.

MRS ELVSTED (*squeezes her hands and pats them*). Oh, you're so kind. I'm not used to people being so nice to me.

HEDDA. Now, now, now. And I shall call you Tora, the way I used to.

MRS ELVSTED. My name is Thea.

HEDDA. Yes, of course. Of course. I meant Thea. (*Looks at her sympathetically.*) So you're not used to kindness, Thea? In your own home?

MRS ELVSTED. Oh, if only I had a home! But I haven't. I've never had one.

HEDDA (*looks at her for a moment*). I thought that was it.

MRS ELVSTED (*stares blankly and helplessly*). Yes – yes – yes.

HEDDA. I can't remember exactly, but didn't you first go to Mr Elvsted as a housekeeper?

MRS ELVSTED. Governess, actually. But his wife – at the time, I mean – she was an invalid, and had to spend most of her time in bed. So I had to look after the house, too.

HEDDA. But in the end, you became mistress of the house.

MRS ELVSTED (*sadly*). Yes, I did.

HEDDA. Let me see. Roughly how long ago was that?

MRS ELVSTED. When I got married, you mean?

HEDDA. Yes.

MRS ELVSTED. About five years.

HEDDA. Yes; it must be about that.

MRS ELVSTED. Oh, those five years! Especially the last two or three. Oh, Mrs Tesman, if you only knew – !

HEDDA (*slaps her hand gently*). Mrs Tesman? Oh, Thea!

MRS ELVSTED. I'm sorry, I'll try to remember. Yes – if you had any idea –

HEDDA (*casually*). Eilert Loevborg's been up there, too, for about three years, hasn't he?

MRS ELVSTED (*looks at her uncertainly*). Eilert Loevborg? Yes, he has.

HEDDA. Did you know him before? When you were here?

MRS ELVSTED. No, not really. That is – I knew him by name, of course.

HEDDA. But up there, he used to visit you?

MRS ELVSTED. Yes, he used to come and see us every day. To give the children lessons. I found I couldn't do that as well as manage the house.

HEDDA. I'm sure you couldn't. And your husband – ? I suppose being a magistrate he has to be away from home a good deal?

MRS ELVSTED. Yes. You see, Mrs – you see, Hedda, he has to cover the whole district.

HEDDA (*leans against the arm of* MRS ELVSTED'S *chair*). Poor, pretty little Thea! Now you must tell me the whole story. From beginning to end.

MRS ELVSTED. Well – what do you want to know?

HEDDA. What kind of a man is your husband, Thea? I mean, as a person. Is he kind to you?

MRS ELVSTED (*evasively*). I'm sure he does his best to be.

HEDDA. I only wonder if he isn't too old for you. There's more than twenty years between you, isn't there?

MRS ELVSTED (*irritably*). Yes, there's that, too. Oh, there are so many things. We're different in every way. We've nothing in common. Nothing whatever.

HEDDA. But he loves you, surely? In his own way?

MRS ELVSTED. Oh, I don't know. I think he just finds me useful. And then I don't cost much to keep. I'm cheap.

HEDDA. Now you're being stupid.

MRS ELVSTED (*shakes her head*). It can't be any different. With him. He doesn't love anyone except himself. And perhaps the children – a little.

HEDDA. He must be fond of Eilert Loevborg, Thea.

MRS ELVSTED (*looks at her*). Eilert Loevborg? What makes you think that?

HEDDA. Well, if he sends you all the way down here to look for him – (*Smiles almost imperceptibly.*) Besides, you said so yourself to Tesman.

MRS ELVSTED (*with a nervous twitch*). Did I? Oh yes, I suppose I did. (*Impulsively, but keeping her voice low.*) Well, I might as well tell you the whole story. It's bound to come out sooner or later.

HEDDA. But, my dear Thea—?

MRS ELVSTED. My husband had no idea I was coming here.

HEDDA. What? Your husband didn't know?

MRS ELVSTED. No, of course not. As a matter of fact, he wasn't even there. He was away at the assizes. Oh, I couldn't stand it any longer, Hedda! I just couldn't. I'd be so dreadfully lonely up there now.

HEDDA. Go on.

MRS ELVSTED. So I packed a few things. Secretly. And went.

HEDDA. Without telling anyone?

MRS ELVSTED. Yes. I caught the train and came straight here.

HEDDA. But, my dear Thea! How brave of you!

MRS ELVSTED (*gets up and walks across the room*). Well, what else could I do?

HEDDA. But what do you suppose your husband will say when you get back?

MRS ELVSTED (*by the table, looks at her*). Back there? To him?

HEDDA. Yes. Surely – ?

MRS ELVSTED. I shall never go back to him.

HEDDA (*gets up and goes closer*). You mean you've left your home for good?

MRS ELVSTED. Yes. I didn't see what else I could do.

HEDDA. But to do it so openly!

MRS ELVSTED. Oh, it's no use trying to keep a thing like that secret.

HEDDA. But what do you suppose people will say?

MRS ELVSTED. They can say what they like. (*Sits sadly, wearily on the sofa.*) I had to do it.

HEDDA (*after a short silence*). What do you intend to do now? How are you going to live?

MRS ELVSTED. I don't know. I only know that I must live wherever Eilert Loevborg is. If I am to go on living.

HEDDA (*moves a chair from the table, sits on it near MRS ELVSTED and strokes her hands*). Tell me, Thea, how did this – friendship between you and Eilert Loevborg begin?

MRS ELVSTED. Oh, it came about gradually. I developed a kind of – power over him.

HEDDA. Oh?

MRS ELVSTED. He gave up his old habits. Not because I asked him to. I'd never have dared to do that. I suppose he just noticed I didn't like that kind of thing. So he gave it up.

HEDDA (*hides a smile*). So you've made a new man of him! Clever little Thea!

MRS ELVSTED. Yes – anyway, he says I have. And he's made a – sort of – real person of me. Taught me to think – and to understand all kinds of things.

HEDDA. Did he give you lessons, too?

MRS ELVSTED. Not exactly lessons. But he talked to me. About – oh, you've no idea – so many things! And then he let me work with him. Oh, it was wonderful. I was so happy to be allowed to help him.

HEDDA. Did he allow you to help him?

MRS ELVSTED. Yes. Whenever he wrote anything we always – did it together.

HEDDA. Like good friends?

MRS ELVSTED (*eagerly*). Friends! Yes – why, Hedda that's exactly the word he used! Oh, I ought to feel so happy. But I can't. I don't know if it will last.

HEDDA. You don't seem very sure of him.

MRS ELVSTED (*sadly*). Something stands between Eilert Loevborg and me. The shadow of another woman.

HEDDA. Who can that be?

MRS ELVSTED. I don't know. Someone he used to be friendly with in – in the old days. Someone he's never been able to forget.

HEDDA. What has he told you about her?

MRS ELVSTED. Oh, he only mentioned her once, casually.

HEDDA. Well! What did he say?

MRS ELVSTED. He said when he left her she tried to shoot him with a pistol.

HEDDA (*cold, controlled*). What nonsense. People don't do such things. The kind of people we know.

MRS ELVSTED. No. I think it must have been that red-haired singer he used to –

HEDDA. Ah yes, very probably.

MRS ELVSTED. I remember they used to say she always carried a loaded pistol.

HEDDA. Well then, it must be her.

MRS ELVSTED. But, Hedda, I hear she's come back, and is living here. Oh, I'm so desperate – !

HEDDA (*glances towards the rear room*). Ssh! Tesman's coming. (*Gets up and whispers.*) Thea, we mustn't breathe a word about this to anyone.

MRS ELVSTED (*jumps up*). Oh, no, no! Please don't!

GEORGE TESMAN *appears from the right in the rear room with a letter in his hand, and comes into the drawing-room.*

TESMAN. Well, here's my little epistle all signed and sealed.

HEDDA. Good. I think Mrs Elvsted wants to go now. Wait a moment – I'll see you as far as the garden gate.

TESMAN. Er – Hedda, do you think Bertha could deal with this?

HEDDA (*takes the letter*). I'll give her instructions.

BERTHA *enters from the hall.*

BERTHA. Judge Brack is here and asks if he may pay his respects to madam and the Doctor.

HEDDA. Yes, ask him to be so good as to come in. And – wait a moment – drop this letter in the post box.

BERTHA (*takes the letter*). Very good, madam.

> *She opens the door for* JUDGE BRACK, *and goes out.* JUDGE BRACK *is forty-five; rather short, but well built, and elastic in his movements. He has a roundish face with an aristocratic profile. His hair, cut short, is still almost black, and is carefully barbered. Eyes lively and humorous. Thick eyebrows. His moustache is also thick, and is trimmed square at the ends. He is wearing outdoor clothes which are elegant but a little too youthful for him. He has a monocle in one eye; now and then he lets it drop.*

BRACK (*hat in hand, bows*). May one presume to call so early?

HEDDA. One may presume.

TESMAN (*shakes his hand*). You're welcome here any time. Judge Brack – Mrs Rysing.

HEDDA *sighs.*

BRACK (*bows*). Ah – charmed –

HEDDA (*looks at him and laughs*). What fun to be able to see you by daylight for once, Judge.

BRACK. Do I look – different?

HEDDA. Yes. A little younger, I think.

BRACK. Too kind.

TESMAN. Well, what do you think of Hedda? What? Doesn't she look well? Hasn't she filled out – ?

HEDDA. Oh, do stop it. You ought to be thanking Judge Brack for all the inconvenience he's put himself to –

BRACK. Nonsense, it was a pleasure –

HEDDA. You're a loyal friend. But my other friend is pining to get away. Au revoir, Judge. I won't be a minute.

Mutual salutations. MRS ELVSTED *and* HEDDA *go out through the hall.*

BRACK. Well, is your wife satisfied with everything?

TESMAN. Yes, we can't thank you enough. That is – we may have to shift one or two things around, she tells me. And we're short of one or two little items we'll have to purchase.

BRACK. Oh? Really?

TESMAN. But you mustn't worry your head about that. Hedda says she'll get what's needed. I say, why don't we sit down? What?

BRACK. Thanks, just for a moment. (*Sits at the table.*) There's something I'd like to talk to you about, my dear Tesman.

TESMAN. Oh? Ah yes, of course. (*Sits.*) After the feast comes the reckoning. What?

BRACK. Oh, never mind about the financial side – there's no hurry about that. Though I could wish we'd arranged things a little less palatially.

TESMAN. Good heavens, that'd never have done. Think of Hedda, my dear chap. You know her. I couldn't possibly ask her to live like a petty bourgeois.

BRACK. No, no – that's just the problem.

TESMAN. Anyway, it can't be long now before my nomination comes through.

BRACK. Well, you know, these things often take time.

TESMAN. Have you heard any more news? What?

BRACK. Nothing definite. (*Changing the subject.*) Oh, by the way, I have one piece of news for you.

TESMAN. What?

BRACK. Your old friend Eilert Loevborg is back in town.

TESMAN. I know that already.

BRACK. Oh? How did you hear that?

TESMAN. She told me. That lady who went out with Hedda.

BRACK. I see. What was her name? I didn't catch it.

TESMAN. Mrs Elvsted.

BRACK. Oh, the magistrate's wife. Yes, Loevborg's been living up near them, hasn't he?

TESMAN. I'm delighted to hear he's become a decent human being again.

BRACK. Yes, so they say.

TESMAN. I gather he's published a new book, too. What?

BRACK. Indeed he has.

TESMAN. I hear it's created rather a stir.

BRACK. Quite an unusual stir.

TESMAN. I say, isn't that splendid news! He's such a gifted chap – and I was afraid he'd gone to the dogs for good.

BRACK. Most people thought he had.

TESMAN. But I can't think what he'll do now. How on earth will he manage to make ends meet? What?

As he speaks his last words HEDDA *enters from the hall.*

HEDDA (*to* BRACK, *laughs slightly scornfully*). Tesman is always worrying about making ends meet.

TESMAN. We were talking about poor Eilert Loevborg, Hedda dear.

HEDDA (*gives him a quick look*). Oh, were you? (*Sits in the armchair by the stove and asks casually.*) Is he in trouble?

TESMAN. Well, he must have run through his inheritance long ago by now. And he can't write a new book every year. What? So I'm wondering what's going to become of him.

BRACK. I may be able to enlighten you there.

TESMAN. Oh?

BRACK. You mustn't forget he has relatives who wield a good deal of influence.

TESMAN. Relatives? Oh, they've quite washed their hands of him, I'm afraid.

BRACK. They used to regard him as the hope of the family.

TESMAN. Used to, yes. But he's put an end to that.

HEDDA. Who knows? (*With a little smile.*) I hear the Elvsteds have made a new man of him.

BRACK. And then this book he's just published –

TESMAN. Well, let's hope they find something for him. I've just written him a note. Oh, by the way, Hedda, I asked him to come over and see us this evening.

BRACK. But, my dear chap, you're coming to me this evening. My bachelor party. You promised me last night when I met you at the boat.

HEDDA. Had you forgotten, Tesman?

TESMAN. Good heavens, yes, I'd quite forgotten.

BRACK. Anyway, you can be quite sure he won't turn up here.

TESMAN. Why do you think that? What?

BRACK (*a little unwillingly, gets up and rests his hands on th. back of his chair*). My dear Tesman – and you, too, Mrs Tesman – there's something I feel you ought to know.

TESMAN. Concerning Eilert?

BRACK. Concerning him and you.

TESMAN Well, my dear Judge, tell us, please!

BRACK. You must be prepared for your nomination not to come through quite as quickly as you hope and expect.

TESMAN (*jumps up uneasily*). Is anything wrong? What?

BRACK. There's a possibility that the appointment may be decided by competition –

TESMAN. Competition! Hedda, fancy that!

HEDDA (*leans further back in her chair*). Ah! How interesting!

TESMAN. But who else – ? I say, you don't mean – ?

BRACK. Exactly. By competition with Eilert Loevborg.

TESMAN (*clasps his hands in alarm*). No, no, but this is inconceivable! It's absolutely impossible! What?

BRACK. Hm. We may find it'll happen, all the same.

TESMAN. No, but – Judge Brack, they couldn't be so inconsiderate towards me! (*Waves his arms.*) I mean, by Jove, I – I'm a married man! It was on the strength of this that Hedda and I *got* married! We've run up some pretty hefty debts. And borrowed money from Auntie Juju! I mean, good heavens, they practically promised me the appointment. What?

BRACK. Well, well, I'm sure you'll get it. But you'll have to go through a competition.

HEDDA (*motionless in her armchair*). How exciting, Tesman. It'll be a kind of duel, by Jove.

TESMAN. My dear Hedda, how can you take it so lightly?

HEDDA (*as before*). I'm not. I can't wait to see who's going to win.

BRACK. In any case, Mrs Tesman, it's best you should know how things stand. I mean before you commit yourself to these little items I hear you're threatening to purchase.

HEDDA. I can't allow this to alter my plans.

BRACK. Indeed? Well, that's your business. Good-bye. (*To* TESMAN.) I'll come and collect you on the way home from my afternoon walk.

TESMAN. Oh, yes, yes. I'm sorry, I'm all upside down just now.

HEDDA (*lying in her chair, holds out her hand*). Good-bye, Judge. See you this afternoon.

BRACK. Thank you. Good-bye, good-bye.

TESMAN (*sees him to the door*): Good-bye, my dear Judge. You will excuse me, won't you?

JUDGE BRACK *goes out through the hall.*

(*Pacing up and down*). Oh, Hedda! One oughtn't to go plunging off on wild adventures. What?

HEDDA (*looks at him and smiles*). Like you're doing?

TESMAN. Yes. I mean, there's no denying it, it was a pretty big adventure to go off and get married and set up house merely on expectation.

HEDDA. Perhaps you're right.

TESMAN. Well, anyway, we have our home, Hedda. My word, yes! The home we dreamed of. And set our hearts on. What?

HEDDA (*gets up slowly, wearily*). You agreed that we should enter society. And keep open house. That was the bargain.

TESMAN. Yes. Good heavens, I was looking forward to it all so much. To seeing you play hostess to a select circle! By Jove! What? Ah, well, for the time being we shall have to make do with each other's company, Hedda. Perhaps have Auntie Juju in now and then. Oh dear, this wasn't at all what you had in mind –

HEDDA. I won't be able to have a liveried footman. For a start.

TESMAN. Oh no, we couldn't possibly afford a footman.

HEDDA. And the bay mare you promised me –

TESMAN (*fearfully*). Bay mare!

HEDDA. I mustn't even think of that now.

TESMAN. Heaven forbid!

HEDDA (*walks across the room*). Ah, well. I still have one thing left to amuse myself with.

TESMAN (*joyfully*). Thank goodness for that. What's that, Hedda? What?

HEDDA (*in the open doorway, looks at him with concealed scorn*). My pistols, George darling.

TESMAN (*alarmed*). Pistols!

HEDDA (*her eyes cold*). General Gabler's pistols.

She goes into the rear room and disappears.

TESMAN (*runs to the doorway and calls after her*). For heaven's sake, Hedda dear, don't touch those things. They're dangerous. Hedda – please – for my sake! What?

Act Two

The same as in Act One, except that the piano has been removed and an elegant little writing-table, with a bookcase, stands in its place. By the sofa on the left a smaller table has been placed. Most of the flowers have been removed. MRS ELVSTED'S *bouquet stands on the larger table, downstage. It is afternoon.*

HEDDA, *dressed to receive callers, is alone in the room. She is standing by the open french windows, loading a revolver. The pair to it is lying in an open pistol-case on the writing-table.*

HEDDA (*looks down into the garden and calls*). Good afternoon, Judge.

BRACK (*in the distance, below*). Afternoon, Mrs Tesman.

HEDDA (*raises the pistol and takes aim*). I'm going to shoot you, Judge Brack.

BRACK (*shouts from below*). No, no, no! Don't aim that thing at me!

HEDDA. This'll teach you to enter houses by the back door.

She fires.

BRACK (*below*). Have you gone completely out of your mind?

HEDDA. Oh dear! Did I hit you?

BRACK (*still outside*). Stop playing these silly tricks.

HEDDA. All right, Judge. Come along in.

JUDGE BRACK, *dressed for a bachelor party, enters through the french windows. He has a light overcoat on his arm.*

BRACK. For God's sake, haven't you stopped fooling around with those things yet? What are you trying to hit?

HEDDA. Oh, I was just shooting at the sky.

BRACK (*takes the pistol gently from her hand*). By your leave, ma'am. (*Looks at it.*) Ah, yes – I know this old friend well.

(*Looks around.*) Where's the case? Oh, yes. (*Puts the pistol in the case and closes it.*) That's enough of that little game for today.

HEDDA. Well, what on earth *am* I to do?

BRACK. You haven't had any visitors?

HEDDA (*closes the french windows*). Not one. I suppose the best people are all still in the country.

BRACK. Your husband isn't home yet?

HEDDA (*locks the pistol-case away in a drawer of the writing-table*). No. The moment he'd finished eating he ran off to his aunties. He wasn't expecting you so early.

BRACK. Ah, why didn't I think of that? How stupid of me.

HEDDA (*turns her head and looks at him*). Why stupid?

BRACK. I'd have come a little sooner.

HEDDA (*walks across the room*). There'd have been no one to receive you. I've been in my room since lunch, dressing.

BRACK. You haven't a tiny crack in the door through which we might have negotiated?

HEDDA. You forgot to arrange one.

BRACK. Another stupidity.

HEDDA. Well, we'll have to sit down here. And wait. Tesman won't be back for some time.

BRACK. Sad. Well, I'll be patient.

> HEDDA *sits on the corner of the sofa.* BRACK *puts his coat over the back of the nearest chair and seats himself, keeping his hat in his hand. Short pause. They look at each other.*

HEDDA. Well?

BRACK (*in the same tone of voice*). Well?

HEDDA. I asked first.

BRACK (*leans forward slightly*). Yes, well, now we can enjoy a nice, cosy little chat – Mrs Hedda.

HEDDA (*leans further back in her chair*). It seems ages since we had a talk. I don't count last night or this morning.

BRACK. You mean: *à deux?*

HEDDA. Mm – yes. That's roughly what I meant.

BRACK. I've been longing so much for you to come home.

HEDDA. So have I.

BRACK. You? Really, Mrs Hedda? And I thought you were having such a wonderful honeymoon.

HEDDA. Oh, yes. Wonderful!

BRACK. But your husband wrote such ecstatic letters.

HEDDA. He! Oh, yes! He thinks life has nothing better to offer than rooting around in libraries and copying old pieces of parchment, or whatever it is he does.

BRACK (*a little maliciously*). Well, that *is* his life. Most of it, anyway.

HEDDA. Yes, I know. Well, it's all right for him. But for me! Oh no, my dear Judge. I've been bored to death.

BRACK (*sympathetically*). Do you mean that? Seriously?

HEDDA. Yes. Can you imagine? Six whole months without ever meeting a single person who was one of us, and to whom I could talk about the kind of things we talk about.

BRACK. Yes, I can understand. I'd miss that, too.

HEDDA. That wasn't the worst, though.

BRACK. What was?

HEDDA. Having to spend every minute of one's life with – with the same person.

BRACK. (*nods*). Yes. What a thought! Morning; noon; *and* –

HEDDA (*coldly*). As I said: every minute of one's life.

BRACK. I stand corrected. But dear Tesman is such a clever fellow, I should have thought one ought to be able –

HEDDA. Tesman is only interested in one thing, my dear Judge. His special subject.

BRACK. True.

HEDDA. And people who are only interested in one thing don't make the most amusing company. Not for long, anyway.

BRACK. Not even when they happen to be the person one loves?

HEDDA. Oh, don't use that sickly, stupid word.

BRACK (*starts*). But, Mrs Hedda – !

HEDDA (*half laughing, half annoyed*). You just try it, Judge. Listening to the history of civilization morning, noon and –

BRACK (*corrects her*). Every minute of one's life.

HEDDA. All right. Oh, and those domestic industries of Brabant in the Middle Ages! That really is beyond the limit.

BRACK (*looks at her searchingly*). But, tell me – if you feel like this why on earth did you – ? Hm –

HEDDA. Why on earth did I marry George Tesman?

BRACK. If you like to put it that way.

HEDDA. Do you think it so very strange?

BRACK. Yes – and no, Mrs Hedda.

HEDDA. I'd danced myself tired, Judge. I felt my time was up – (*Gives a slight shudder.*) No, I mustn't say that. Or even think it.

BRACK. You've no rational cause to think it.

HEDDA. Oh – cause, cause – (*Looks searchingly at him.*) After all, George Tesman – well, I mean, he's a very respectable man.

BRACK. Very respectable, sound as a rock. No denying that.

HEDDA. And there's nothing exactly ridiculous about him. Is there?

BRACK. Ridiculous? N-no, I wouldn't say that.

HEDDA. Mm. He's very clever at collecting material and all that, isn't he? I mean, he may go quite far in time.

BRACK (*looks at her a little uncertainly*). I thought you believed, like everyone else, that he would become a very prominent man.

HEDDA (*looks tired*). Yes, I did. And when he came and begged me on his bended knees to be allowed to love and to cherish me, I didn't see why I shouldn't let him.

BRACK. No, well – if one looks at it like that –

HEDDA. It was more than my other admirers were prepared to do, Judge dear.

BRACK (*laughs*). Well, I can't answer for the others. As far as I myself am concerned, you know I've always had a considerable respect for the institution of marriage. As an institution.

HEDDA (*lightly*). Oh, I've never entertained any hopes of you.

BRACK. All I want is to have a circle of friends whom I can trust, whom I can help with advice or – or by any other means, and into whose houses I may come and go as a – trusted friend.

HEDDA. Of the husband?

BRACK (*bows*). Preferably, to be frank, of the wife. And of the husband too, of course. Yes, you know, this kind of triangle is a delightful arrangement for all parties concerned.

HEDDA. Yes, I often longed for a third person while I was away. Oh, those hours we spent alone in railway compartments –

BRACK. Fortunately your honeymoon is now over.

HEDDA (*shakes her head*). There's a long, long way still to go. I've only reached a stop on the line.

BRACK. Why not jump out and stretch your legs a little, Mrs Hedda?

HEDDA. I'm not the jumping sort.

BRACK. Aren't you?

HEDDA. No. There's always someone around who –

BRACK (*laughs*). Who looks at one's legs?

HEDDA. Yes. Exactly.

BRACK. Well, but surely –

HEDDA (*with a gesture of rejection*). I don't like it. I'd rather stay where I am. Sitting in the compartment. *À deux.*

BRACK. But suppose a third person were to step into the compartment?

HEDDA. That would be different.

BRACK. A trusted friend – someone who understood –

HEDDA. And was lively and amusing –

BRACK. And interested in – more subjects than one –

HEDDA (*sighs audibly*). Yes, that'd be a relief.

BRACK (*hears the front door open and shut*). The triangle is completed.

HEDDA (*half under her breath*). And the train goes on.

> GEORGE TESMAN, *in grey walking dress with a soft felt hat, enters from the hall. He has a number of paper-covered books under his arm and in his pockets.*

TESMAN (*goes over to the table by the corner sofa*). Phew! It's too hot to be lugging all this around. (*Puts the books down.*) I'm positively sweating, Hedda. Why, hullo, hullo! You here already, Judge? What? Bertha didn't tell me.

BRACK (*gets up*). I came in through the garden.

HEDDA. What are all those books you've got there?

TESMAN (*stands glancing through them*). Oh, some new publications dealing with my special subject. I had to buy them.

HEDDA. Your special subject?

BRACK. His special subject, Mrs Tesman.

> BRACK *and* HEDDA *exchange a smile.*

HEDDA. Haven't you collected enough material on your special subject?

TESMAN. My dear Hedda, one can never have too much. One must keep abreast of what other people are writing.

HEDDA. Yes. Of course.

TESMAN (*rooting among the books*). Look – I bought a copy of Eilert Loevborg's new book, too. (*Holds it out to her.*) Perhaps you'd like to have a look at it, Hedda? What?

HEDDA. No, thank you. Er – yes, perhaps I will, later.

TESMAN. I glanced through it on my way home.

BRACK. What's your opinion – as a specialist on the subject?

TESMAN. I'm amazed how sound and balanced it is. He never used to write like that. (*Gathers his books together.*) Well, I must get down to these at once. I can hardly wait to cut the pages. Oh, I've got to change, too. (*To* BRACK.) We don't have to be off just yet, do we? What?

BRACK. Heavens, no. We've plenty of time yet.

TESMAN. Good, I needn't hurry, then. (*Goes with his books, but stops and turns in the doorway.*) Oh, by the way, Hedda, Auntie Juju won't be coming to see you this evening.

HEDDA. Won't she? Oh – the hat, I suppose.

TESMAN. Good heavens, no. How could you think such a thing of Auntie Juju? Fancy –! No, Auntie Rena's very ill.

HEDDA. She always is.

TESMAN. Yes, but today she's been taken really bad.

HEDDA. Oh, then it's quite understandable that the other one should want to stay with her. Well, I shall have to swallow my disappointment.

TESMAN. You can't imagine how happy Auntie Juju was in spite of everything. At your looking so well after the honeymoon!

HEDDA (*half beneath her breath, as she rises*). Oh, these everlasting aunts!

TESMAN. What?

HEDDA (*goes over to the french windows*). Nothing.

TESMAN. Oh. All right. (*Goes into the rear room and out of sight.*)

BRACK. What was that about the hat?

HEDDA. Oh, something that happened with Miss Tesman this morning. She'd put her hat down on a chair. (*Looks at him and smiles.*) And I pretended to think it was the servant's.

BRACK (*shakes his head*). But, my dear Mrs Hedda, how could you do such a thing? To that poor old lady?

HEDDA (*nervously, walking across the room*). Sometimes a mood like that hits me. And I can't stop myself. (*Throws herself down in the armchair by the stove.*) Oh, I don't know how to explain it.

BRACK (*behind her chair*). You're not really happy. That's the answer.

HEDDA (*stares ahead of her*). Why on earth should I be happy? Can you give me a reason?

BRACK. Yes. For one thing you've got the home you always wanted.

HEDDA (*looks at him*). You really believe that story?

BRACK. You mean it isn't true?

HEDDA. Oh, yes, it's partly true.

BRACK. Well?

HEDDA. It's true I got Tesman to see me home from parties last summer –

BRACK. It was a pity my home lay in another direction.

HEDDA. Yes. Your interests lay in another direction, too.

BRACK (*laughs*). That's naughty of you, Mrs Hedda. But to return to you and George –

HEDDA. Well, we walked past this house one evening. And poor Tesman was fidgeting in his boots trying to find something to talk about. I felt sorry for the great scholar –

BRACK (*smiles incredulously*). Did you? Hm.

HEDDA. Yes, honestly I did. Well, to help him out of his misery, I happened to say quite frivolously how much I'd love to live in this house.

BRACK. Was that all?

HEDDA. That evening, yes.

BRACK. But – afterwards?

HEDDA. Yes. My little frivolity had its consequences, my dear Judge.

BRACK. Our little frivolities do. Much too often, unfortunately.

HEDDA. Thank you. Well, it was our mutual admiration for the late Prime Minister's house that brought George Tesman and me together on common ground. So we got engaged, and we got married, and we went on our honeymoon, and – Ah well, Judge, I've – made my bed and I must lie in it, I was about to say.

BRACK. How utterly fantastic! And you didn't really care in the least about the house?

HEDDA. God knows I didn't.

BRACK. Yes, but now that we've furnished it so beautifully for you?

HEDDA. Ugh – all the rooms smell of lavender and dried roses. But perhaps Auntie Juju brought that in.

BRACK (*laughs*). More likely the Prime Minister's widow, rest her soul.

HEDDA. Yes, it's got the odour of death about it. It reminds me of the flowers one has worn at a ball – the morning after. (*Clasps her hands behind her neck, leans back in the chair and looks up at him.*) Oh, my dear Judge, you've no idea how hideously bored I'm going to be out here.

BRACK. Couldn't you find some – occupation, Mrs Hedda? Like your husband?

HEDDA. Occupation? That'd interest me?

BRACK. Well – preferably.

HEDDA. God knows what. I've often thought – (*Breaks off.*) No, that wouldn't work either.

BRACK. Who knows? Tell me about it.

HEDDA. I was thinking – if I could persuade Tesman to go into politics, for example.

BRACK (*laughs*). Tesman! No, honestly, I don't think he's quite cut out to be a politician.

HEDDA. Perhaps not. But if I could persuade him to have a go at it?

BRACK. What satisfaction would that give you? If he turned out to be no good? Why do you want to make him do that?

HEDDA. Because I'm bored. (*After a moment.*) You feel there's absolutely no possibility of Tesman becoming Prime Minister, then?

BRACK. Well, you know, Mrs Hedda, for one thing he'd have to be pretty well off before he could become that.

HEDDA (*gets up impatiently*). There you are! (*Walks across the room.*) It's this wretched poverty that makes life so hateful. And ludicrous. Well, it is!

BRACK. I don't think that's the real cause.

HEDDA. What is, then?

BRACK. Nothing really exciting has ever happened to you.

HEDDA. Nothing serious, you mean?

BRACK. Call it that if you like. But now perhaps it may.

HEDDA (*tosses her head*). Oh, you're thinking of this competition for that wretched professorship? That's Tesman's affair. I'm not going to waste my time worrying about that.

BRACK. Very well, let's forget about that, then. But suppose you were to find yourself faced with what people call – to use the conventional phrase – the most solemn of human responsibilities? (*Smiles.*) A new responsibility, little Mrs Hedda.

HEDDA (*angrily*). Be quiet! Nothing like that's going to happen.

BRACK (*warily*). We'll talk about it again in a year's time. If not earlier.

HEDDA (*curtly*). I've no leanings in that direction, Judge. I don't want any – responsibilities.

BRACK. But surely you must feel some inclination to make use of that – natural talent which every woman –

HEDDA (*over by the french windows*). Oh, be quiet, I say! I often think there's only one thing for which I have any natural talent.

BRACK (*goes closer*). And what is that, if I may be so bold as to ask?

HEDDA (*stands looking out*). For boring myself to death. Now you know. (*Turns, looks towards the rear room and laughs.*) Talking of boring, here comes the professor.

BRACK (*quietly, warningly*). Now, now, now, Mrs Hedda!

GEORGE TESMAN, *in evening dress, with gloves and hat in his hand, enters through the rear room from the right.*

TESMAN. Hedda, hasn't any message come from Eilert? What?

HEDDA. No.

TESMAN. Ah, then we'll have him here presently. You wait and see.

BRACK. You really think he'll come?

TESMAN. Yes, I'm almost sure he will. What you were saying about him this morning is just gossip.

BRACK. Oh?

TESMAN. Yes. Auntie Juju said she didn't believe he'd ever dare to stand in my way again. Fancy that!

BRACK. Then everything in the garden's lovely.

TESMAN (*puts his hat, with his gloves in it, on a chair, right*). Yes, but you really must let me wait for him as long as possible.

BRACK. We've plenty of time. No one'll be turning up at my place before seven or half past.

TESMAN. Ah, then we can keep Hedda company a little longer. And see if he turns up. What?

HEDDA (*picks up* BRACK'S *coat and hat and carries them over to the corner sofa*). And if the worst comes to the worst, Mr Loevborg can sit here and talk to me.

BRACK (*offering to take his things from her*). No, please. What do you mean by 'if the worst comes to the worst'?

HEDDA. If he doesn't want to go with you and Tesman.

TESMAN (*looks doubtfully at her*). I say, Hedda, do you think it'll be all right for him to stay here with you? What? Remember Auntie Juju isn't coming.

HEDDA. Yes, but Mrs Elvsted is. The three of us can have a cup of tea together.

TESMAN. Ah, that'll be all right.

BRACK (*smiles*). It's probably the safest solution as far as he's concerned.

HEDDA. Why?

BRACK. My dear Mrs Tesman, you always say of my little bachelor parties that they should only be attended by men of the strongest principles.

HEDDA. But Mr Loevborg is a man of principle now. You know what they say about a reformed sinner –

BERTHA *enters from the hall.*

BERTHA. Madam, there's a gentleman here who wants to see you –

HEDDA. Ask him to come in.

TESMAN (*quietly*). I'm sure it's him. By Jove. Fancy that!

EILERT LOEVBORG *enters from the hall. He is slim and lean, of the same age as* TESMAN, *but looks older and somewhat haggard. His hair and beard are of a blackish-brown; his face is long and pale, but with a couple of reddish patches on his cheekbones. He is dressed in an elegant and fairly new black suit, and carries black gloves and a top-hat in his hand. He stops just inside the door and bows abruptly. He seems somewhat embarrassed.*

(*Goes over and shakes his hand.*) My dear Eilert! How grand to see you again after all these years!

EILERT LOEVBORG (*speaks softly*). It was good of you to write, George. (*Goes nearer to* HEDDA.) May I shake hands with you, too, Mrs Tesman?

HEDDA (*accepts his hand*). Delighted to see you, Mr Loevborg. (*With a gesture.*) I don't know if you two gentlemen –

LOEVBORG (*bows slightly*). Judge Brack, I believe.

BRACK (*also with a slight bow*). Correct. We – met some years ago –

TESMAN (*puts his hands on* LOEVBORG'S *shoulders*). Now, you're to treat this house just as though it were your own home, Eilert. Isn't that right, Hedda? I hear you've decided to settle here again. What?

LOEVBORG. Yes, I have.

TESMAN. Quite understandable. Oh, by the by – I've just bought your new book. Though to tell the truth I haven't found time to read it yet.

LOEVBORG. You needn't bother.

TESMAN. Oh? Why?

LOEVBORG. There's nothing much in it.

TESMAN. By Jove, fancy hearing that from you!

BRACK. But everyone's praising it.

LOEVBORG. That was exactly what I wanted to happen. So I only wrote what I knew everyone would agree with.

BRACK. Very sensible.

TESMAN. Yes, but my dear Eilert –

LOEVBORG. I want to try to re-establish myself. To begin again – from the beginning.

TESMAN (*a little embarrassed*). Yes, I – er – suppose you do. What?

LOEVBORG (*smiles, puts down his hat and takes a package wrapped in paper from his coat pocket*). But when this gets published – George Tesman – read it. This is my real book. The one in which I have spoken with my own voice.

TESMAN. Oh, really? What's it about?

LOEVBORG. It's the sequel.

TESMAN. Sequel? To what?

LOEVBORG. To the other book.

TESMAN. The one that's just come out?

LOEVBORG. Yes.

TESMAN. But my dear Eilert, that covers the subject right up to the present day.

LOEVBORG. It does. But this is about the future.

TESMAN. The future! But, I say, we don't know anything about that.

LOEVBORG. No. But there are one or two things that need to be said about it. (*Opens the package.*) Here, have a look.

TESMAN. Surely that's not your handwriting?

LOEVBORG. I dictated it. (*Turns the pages.*) It's in two parts. The first deals with the forces that will shape our civilization. (*Turns further on towards the end.*) And the second indicates the direction in which that civilization may develop.

TESMAN. Amazing! I'd never think of writing about anything like that.

HEDDA (*by the french windows, drumming on the pane*). No. You wouldn't.

LOEVBORG (*puts the pages back into their cover and lays the package on the table*). I brought it because I thought I might possibly read you a few pages this evening.

TESMAN. I say, what a kind idea! Oh, but this evening – ? (*Glances at* BRACK) I'm not quite sure whether –

LOEVBORG. Well, some other time, then. There's no hurry.

BRACK. The truth is, Mr Loevborg, I'm giving a little dinner this evening. In Tesman's honour, you know.

LOEVBORG (*looks round for his hat*). Oh – then I mustn't –

BRACK. No, wait a minute. Won't you do me the honour of joining us?

LOEVBORG (*curtly, with decision*). No, I can't. Thank you so much.

BRACK. Oh, nonsense. Do – please. There'll only be a few of us. And I can promise you we shall have some good sport, as Hed – as Mrs Tesman puts it.

LOEVBORG. I've no doubt. Nevertheless

BRACK. You could bring your manuscript along and read it to Tesman at my place. I could lend you a room.

TESMAN. Well, yes, that's an idea. What?

HEDDA (*interposes*). But, Tesman, Mr Loevborg doesn't want to go. I'm sure Mr Loevborg would much rather sit here and have supper with me.

LOEVBORG (*looks at her*). With you, Mrs Tesman?

HEDDA. And Mrs Elvsted.

LOEVBORG. Oh. (*Casually.*) I ran into her this afternoon.

HEDDA. Did you? Well, she's coming here this evening. So you really must stay, Mr Loevborg. Otherwise she'll have no one to see her home.

LOEVBORG. That's true. Well – thank you, Mrs Tesman, I'll stay then.

HEDDA. I'll just tell the servant.

She goes to the door which leads into the hall, and rings.
BERTHA *enters.* HEDDA *talks softly to her and points towards
the rear room.* BERTHA *nods and goes out.*

TESMAN (*to* LOEVBORG, *as* HEDDA *does this*). I say, Eilert.
This new subject of yours – the – er – future – is that the one
you're going to lecture about?

LOEVBORG. Yes.

TESMAN. They told me down at the bookshop that you're
going to hold a series of lectures here during the autumn.

LOEVBORG. Yes, I am. I – hope you don't mind, Tesman.

TESMAN. Good heavens, no! But – ?

LOEVBORG. I can quite understand it might queer your pitch
a little.

TESMAN (*dejectedly*). Oh well, I can't expect you to put them
off for my sake.

LOEVBORG. I'll wait till your appointment's been announced.

TESMAN. You'll wait! But – but – aren't you going to compete
with me for the post? What?

LOEVBORG. No. I only want to defeat you in the eyes of the
world.

TESMAN. Good heavens! Then Auntie Juju was right after all!
Oh, I knew it, I knew it! Hear that, Hedda? Fancy! Eilert
doesn't want to stand in our way.

HEDDA (*curtly*): Our? Leave me out of it, please.

She goes towards the rear room, where BERTHA *is setting a
tray with decanters and glasses on the table.* HEDDA *nods
approval, and comes back into the drawing-room.* BERTHA
goes out.

TESMAN (*while this is happening*). Judge Brack, what do you
think about all this? What?

BRACK. Oh, I think honour and victory can be very splendid
things –

TESMAN. Of course they can. Still –

HEDDA (*looks at* TESMAN, *with a cold smile*). You look as if you'd been hit by a thunderbolt.

TESMAN. Yes, I feel rather like it.

BRACK. There was a black cloud looming up, Mrs Tesman. But it seems to have passed over.

HEDDA (*points towards the rear room*). Well, gentlemen, won't you go in and take a glass of cold punch?

BRACK (*glances at his watch*). One for the road? Yes, why not?

TESMAN. An admirable suggestion, Hedda. Admirable! Oh, I feel so relieved!

HEDDA. Won't you have one, too, Mr Loevborg?

LOEVBORG. No, thank you. I'd rather not.

BRACK. Great heavens, man, cold punch isn't poison. Take my word for it.

LOEVBORG. Not for everyone, perhaps.

HEDDA. I'll keep Mr Loevborg company while you drink.

TESMAN. Yes, Hedda dear, would you?

He and BRACK *go into the rear room, sit down, drink punch, smoke cigarettes and talk cheerfully during the following scene.* EILERT LOEVBORG *remains standing by the stove.* HEDDA *goes to the writing-table.*

HEDDA (*raising her voice slightly*). I've some photographs I'd like to show you, if you'd care to see them. Tesman and I visited the Tyrol on our way home.

She comes back with an album, places it on the table by the sofa and sits in the upstage corner of the sofa. EILERT LOEVBORG *comes towards her, stops, and looks at her. Then he takes a chair and sits down on her left, with his back towards the rear room.*

(*Opens the album.*) You see these mountains, Mr Loevborg? That's the Ortler group. Tesman has written the name underneath. You see: 'The Ortler Group near Meran.'

LOEVBORG (*has not taken his eyes from her; says softly, slowly*).
Hedda – Gabler!

HEDDA (*gives him a quick glance*). Ssh!

LOEVBORG (*repeats softly*). Hedda Gabler!

HEDDA (*looks at the album*). Yes, that used to be my name.
When we first knew each other.

LOEVBORG. And from now on – for the rest of my life – I must
teach myself never to say: Hedda Gabler.

HEDDA (*still turning the pages*). Yes, you must. You'd better
start getting into practice. The sooner the better.

LOEVBORG (*bitterly*). Hedda Gabler married? And to George
Tesman!

HEDDA. Yes. Well – that's life.

LOEVBORG. Oh, Hedda, Hedda! How could you throw yourself away like that?

HEDDA (*looks sharply at him*). Stop it.

LOEVBORG. What do you mean?

TESMAN *comes in and goes towards the sofa.*

HEDDA (*hears him coming and says casually*). And this, Mr
Loevborg, is the view from the Ampezzo valley. Look at
those mountains. (*Glances affectionately up at* TESMAN.)
What did you say those curious mountains were called, dear?

TESMAN. Let me have a look. Oh, those are the Dolomites.

HEDDA. Of course. Those are the Dolomites, Mr Loevborg.

TESMAN. Hedda, I just wanted to ask you, can't we bring
some punch in here? A glass for you, anyway. What?

HEDDA. Thank you, yes. And a biscuit or two, perhaps.

TESMAN. You wouldn't like a cigarette?

HEDDA. No.

TESMAN. Right.

He goes into the rear room and over to the right. BRACK *is
seated there, glancing occasionally at* HEDDA *and* LOEV-
BORG.

LOEVBORG (*softly, as before*). Answer me, Hedda. How could you do it?

HEDDA (*apparently absorbed in the album*). If you go on calling me Hedda I won't talk to you any more.

LOEVBORG. Mayn't I even when we're alone?

HEDDA. No. You can think it. But you mustn't say it.

LOEVBORG. Oh, I see. Because you love George Tesman.

HEDDA (*glances at him and smiles*). Love? Don't be funny.

LOEVBORG. You don't love him?

HEDDA. I don't intend to be unfaithful to him. That's not what I want.

LOEVBORG. Hedda – just tell me one thing –

HEDDA. Ssh!

TESMAN *enters from the rear room, carrying a tray.*

TESMAN. Here we are! Here come the refreshments.

He puts the tray down on the table.

HEDDA. Why didn't you ask the servant to bring it in?

TESMAN (*fills the glasses*). I like waiting on you, Hedda.

HEDDA. But you've filled both glasses. Mr Loevborg doesn't want to drink.

TESMAN. Yes, but Mrs Elvsted'll be here soon.

HEDDA. Oh yes, that's true. Mrs Elvsted –

TESMAN. Had you forgotten her? What?

HEDDA. We're so absorbed with these photographs. (*Shows him one.*) You remember this little village?

TESMAN. Oh, that one down by the Brenner Pass. We spent a night there –

HEDDA. Yes, and met all those amusing people.

TESMAN. Oh yes, it was there, wasn't it? By Jove, if only we could have had you with us, Eilert! Ah, well.

He goes back into the other room and sits down with BRACK.

LOEVBORG. Tell me one thing, Hedda.

HEDDA. Yes?

LOEVBORG. Didn't you love me either? Not – just a little?

HEDDA. Well now, I wonder? No, I think we were just good friends. (*Smiles.*) You certainly poured your heart out to me.

LOEVBORG. You begged me to.

HEDDA. Looking back on it, there was something beautiful and fascinating – and brave – about the way we told each other everything. That secret friendship no one else knew about.

LOEVBORG. Yes, Hedda, yes! Do you remember? How I used to come up to your father's house in the afternoon – and the General sat by the window and read his newspapers – with his back towards us –

HEDDA. And we sat on the sofa in the corner –

LOEVBORG. Always reading the same illustrated magazine –

HEDDA. We hadn't any photograph album.

LOEVBORG. Yes, Hedda. I regarded you as a kind of confessor. Told you things about myself which no one else knew about – then. Those days and nights of drinking and – oh, Hedda, what power did you have to make me confess such things?

HEDDA. Power? You think I had some power over you?

LOEVBORG. Yes – I don't know how else to explain it. And all those – oblique questions you asked me –

HEDDA. You knew what they meant.

LOEVBORG. But that you could sit there and ask me such questions! So unashamedly –

HEDDA. I thought you said they were oblique.

LOEVBORG. Yes, but you asked them so unashamedly. That you could question me about – about that kind of thing!

HEDDA. You answered willingly enough.

LOEVBORG. Yes – that's what I can't understand – looking back on it. But tell me, Hedda – what you felt for me – wasn't that – love? When you asked me those questions and made me confess my sins to you, wasn't it because you wanted to wash me clean?

HEDDA. No, not exactly.

LOEVBORG. Why did you do it, then?

HEDDA. Do you find it so incredible that a young girl, given the chance in secret, should want to be allowed a glimpse into a forbidden world of whose existence she is supposed to be ignorant?

LOEVBORG. So that was it?

HEDDA. One reason. One reason – I think.

LOEVBORG. You didn't love me, then. You just wanted – knowledge. But if that was so, why did you break it off?

HEDDA. That was your fault.

LOEVBORG. It was you who put an end to it.

HEDDA. Yes, when I realized that our friendship was threatening to develop into something – something else. Shame on you, Eilert Loevborg! How could you abuse the trust of your dearest friend?

LOEVBORG (*clenches his fist*). Oh, why didn't you do it? Why didn't you shoot me dead? As you threatened to!

HEDDA. I was afraid. Of the scandal.

LOEVBORG. Yes, Hedda. You're a coward at heart.

HEDDA. A dreadful coward. (*Changes her tone.*) Luckily for you. Well, now you've found consolation with the Elvsteds.

LOEVBORG. I know what Thea's been telling you.

HEDDA. I dare say you told her about us.

LOEVBORG. Not a word. She's too silly to understand that kind of thing.

HEDDA. Silly?

LOEVBORG. She's silly about that kind of thing.

HEDDA. And I'm a coward. (*Leans closer to him, without looking him in the eyes, and says quietly.*) But let me tell you something. Something you don't know.

LOEVBORG (*tensely*). Yes?

HEDDA. My failure to shoot you wasn't my worst act of cowardice that evening.

LOEVBORG (*looks at her for a moment, realizes her meaning, and whispers passionately*). Oh, Hedda! Hedda Gabler! Now I see what was behind those questions. Yes! It wasn't knowledge you wanted! It was life!

HEDDA (*flashes a look at him and says quietly*). Take care! Don't you delude yourself!

> *It has begun to grow dark.* BERTHA, *from outside, opens the door leading into the hall.*

HEDDA (*closes the album with a snap and cries, smiling*). Ah, at last! Come in, Thea dear!

> MRS ELVSTED *enters from the hall, in evening dress. The door is closed behind her.*

HEDDA (*on the sofa, stretches out her arms towards her*). Thea darling, I thought you were never coming!

> MRS ELVSTED *makes a slight bow to the gentlemen in the rear room as she passes the open doorway, and they to her. Then she goes to the table and holds out her hand to* HEDDA. EILERT LOEVBORG *has risen from his chair. He and* MRS ELVSTED *nod silently to each other.*

MRS ELVSTED. Perhaps I ought to go in and say a few words to your husband?

HEDDA. Oh, there's no need. They're happy by themselves. They'll be going soon.

MRS ELVSTED. Going?

HEDDA. Yes, they're off on a spree this evening.

MRS ELVSTED (*quickly, to* LOEVBORG). You're not going with them?

LOEVBORG. No.

HEDDA. Mr Loevborg is staying here with us.

MRS ELVSTED (*takes a chair and is about to sit down beside him*). Oh, how nice it is to be here!

HEDDA. No, Thea darling, not there. Come over here and sit beside me. I want to be in the middle.

MRS ELVSTED. Yes, just as you wish.

She goes round the table and sits on the sofa, on HEDDA'S *right.* LOEVBORG *sits down again in his chair.*

LOEVBORG (*after a short pause, to* HEDDA). Isn't she lovely to look at?

HEDDA (*strokes her hair gently*). Only to look at?

LOEVBORG. Yes. We're just good friends. We trust each other implicitly. We can talk to each other quite unashamedly.

HEDDA. No need to be oblique?

MRS ELVSTED (*nestles close to* HEDDA *and says quietly*). Oh, Hedda, I'm so happy. Imagine – he says I've inspired him!

HEDDA (*looks at her with a smile*). Dear Thea! Does he really?

LOEVBORG. She has the courage of her convictions, Mrs Tesman.

MRS ELVSTED. I? Courage?

LOEVBORG. Absolute courage. Where friendship is concerned.

HEDDA. Yes. Courage. Yes. If only one had that –

LOEVBORG. Yes?

HEDDA. One might be able to live. In spite of everything. (*Changes her tone suddenly.*) Well, Thea darling, now you're going to drink a nice glass of cold punch.

MRS ELVSTED. No thank you. I never drink anything like that.

HEDDA. Oh. You, Mr Loevborg?

LOEVBORG. Thank you, I don't either.

MRS ELVSTED. No, he doesn't, either.

HEDDA (*looks into his eyes*). But if I want you to.

LOEVBORG. That doesn't make any difference.

HEDDA (*laughs*). Have I no power over you at all? Poor me!

LOEVBORG. Not where this is concerned.

HEDDA. Seriously, I think you should. For your own sake.

MRS ELVSTED. Hedda!

LOEVBORG. Why?

HEDDA. Or perhaps I should say for other people's sake.

LOEVBORG. What do you mean?

HEDDA. People might think you didn't feel absolutely and unashamedly sure of yourself. In your heart of hearts.

MRS ELVSTED (*quietly*). Oh, Hedda, no!

LOEVBORG. People can think what they like. For the present.

MRS ELVSTED (*happily*). Yes, that's true.

HEDDA. I saw it so clearly in Judge Brack a few minutes ago.

LOEVBORG. Oh. What did you see?

HEDDA. He smiled so scornfully when he saw you were afraid to go in there and drink with them.

LOEVBORG. Afraid! I wanted to stay here and talk to you.

MRS ELVSTED. That was only natural, Hedda.

HEDDA. But the Judge wasn't to know that. I saw him wink at Tesman when you showed you didn't dare to join their wretched little party.

LOEVBORG. Didn't dare! Are you saying I didn't dare?

HEDDA. I'm not saying so. But that was what Judge Brack thought.

LOEVBORG. Well, let him.

HEDDA. You're not going, then?

LOEVBORG. I'm staying here with you and Thea.

MRS ELVSTED. Yes, Hedda, of course he is.

HEDDA (*smiles, and nods approvingly to* LOEVBORG). Firm as a rock! A man of principle! That's how a man should be! (*Turns to* MRS ELVSTED *and strokes her cheek.*) Didn't I tell you so this morning when you came here in such a panic – ?

LOEVBORG (*starts*). Panic?

MRS ELVSTED (*frightened*). Hedda! But – Hedda!

HEDDA. Well, now you can see for yourself. There's no earthly need for you to get scared to death just because – (*Stops.*) Well! Let's all three cheer up and enjoy ourselves.

LOEVBORG. Mrs Tesman, would you mind explaining to me what this is all about?

MRS ELVSTED. Oh, my God, my God, Hedda, what are you saying? What are you doing?

HEDDA. Keep calm. That horrid Judge has his eye on you.

LOEVBORG. Scared to death, were you? For my sake?

MRS ELVSTED (*quietly, trembling*). Oh, Hedda! You've made me so unhappy!

LOEVBORG (*looks coldly at her for a moment. His face is distorted*). So that was how much you trusted me.

MRS ELVSTED. Eilert dear, please listen to me –

LOEVBORG (*takes one of the glasses of punch, raises it and says quietly, hoarsely*). Skoal, Thea!

> *He empties the glass, puts it down and picks up one of the others.*

MRS ELVSTED (*quietly*). Hedda, Hedda! Why did you want this to happen?

HEDDA. *I* – want it? Are you mad?

LOEVBORG. Skoal to you, too, Mrs Tesman. Thanks for telling me the truth. Here's to the truth!

> *He empties his glass and refills it.*

HEDDA (*puts her hand on his arm*). Steady. That's enough for now. Don't forget the party.

MRS ELVSTED. No, no, no!

HEDDA. Ssh! They're looking at you.

LOEVBORG (*puts down his glass*). Thea, tell me the truth –

MRS ELVSTED. Yes!

LOEVBORG. Did your husband know you were following me?

MRS ELVSTED. Oh, Hedda!

LOEVBORG. Did you and he have an agreement that you should come here and keep an eye on me? Perhaps he gave you the idea? After all, he's a magistrate. I suppose he needed me back in his office. Or did he miss my companionship at the card-table?

MRS ELVSTED (*quietly, sobbing*). Eilert, Eilert!

LOEVBORG (*seizes a glass and is about to fill it*). Let's drink to him, too.

HEDDA. No more now. Remember you're going to read your book to Tesman.

LOEVBORG (*calm again, puts down his glass*). That was silly of me, Thea. To take it like that, I mean. Don't be angry with me, my dear. You'll see – yes, and they'll see, too – that though I fell, I – I have raised myself up again. With your help, Thea.

MRS ELVSTED (*happily*). Oh, thank God!

> BRACK *has meanwhile glanced at his watch. He and* TESMAN *get up and come into the drawing-room.*

BRACK (*takes his hat and overcoat*). Well, Mrs Tesman, it's time for us to go.

HEDDA. Yes, I suppose it must be.

LOEVBORG (*gets up*). Time for me, too, Judge.

MRS ELVSTED (*quietly, pleadingly*). Eilert, please don't!

HEDDA (*pinches her arm*). They can hear you.

MRS ELVSTED (*gives a little cry*). Oh!

LOEVBORG (*to* BRACK). You were kind enough to ask me to join you.

BRACK. Are you coming?

LOEVBORG. If I may.

BRACK. Delighted.

LOEVBORG (*puts the paper package in his pocket and says to* TESMAN). I'd like to show you one or two things before I send it off to the printer.

TESMAN. I say, that'll be fun. Fancy – ! Oh, but, Hedda, how'll Mrs Elvsted get home? What?

HEDDA. Oh, we'll manage somehow.

LOEVBORG (*glances over towards the ladies*). Mrs Elvsted? I shall come back and collect her, naturally. (*Goes closer.*) About ten o'clock, Mrs Tesman? Will that suit you?

HEDDA. Yes. That'll suit me admirably.

TESMAN. Good, that's settled. But you mustn't expect me back so early, Hedda.

HEDDA. Stay as long as you c – as long as you like, dear.

MRS ELVSTED (*trying to hide her anxiety*). Well then, Mr Loevborg, I'll wait here till you come.

LOEVBORG (*his hat in his hand*). Pray do, Mrs Elvsted.

BRACK. Well, gentlemen, now the party begins. I trust that, in the words of a certain fair lady, we shall enjoy good sport.

HEDDA. What a pity the fair lady can't be there, invisible.

BRACK. Why invisible?

HEDDA. So as to be able to hear some of your uncensored witticisms, your honour.

BRACK (*laughs*). Oh, I shouldn't advise the fair lady to do that.

TESMAN (*laughs, too*). I say, Hedda, that's good. What!

BRACK. Well, good night, ladies, good night!

LOEVBORG (*bows farewell*). About ten o'clock then.

> BRACK, LOEVBORG *and* TESMAN *go out through the hall. As they do so,* BERTHA *enters from the rear room with a lighted lamp. She puts it on the drawing-room table, then goes out the way she came.*

MRS ELVSTED (*has got up and is walking uneasily to and fro*). Oh, Hedda, Hedda! How is all this going to end?

HEDDA. At ten o'clock, then. He'll be here. I can see him. With a crown of vine leaves in his hair. Burning and unashamed!

MRS ELVSTED. Oh, I do hope so!

HEDDA. Can't you see? Then he'll be himself again! He'll be a free man for the rest of his days!

MRS ELVSTED. Please God you're right.

HEDDA. That's how he'll come! (*Gets up and goes closer.*) You can doubt him as much as you like. I believe in him! Now we'll see which of us –

MRS ELVSTED. You're after something, Hedda.

HEDDA. Yes, I am. For once in my life I want to have the power to shape a man's destiny.

MRS ELVSTED. Haven't you that power already?

HEDDA. No, I haven't. I've never had it.

MRS ELVSTED. What about your husband?

HEDDA. Him! Oh, if you could only understand how poor I am. And you're allowed to be so rich, so rich! (*Clasps her passionately.*) I think I'll burn your hair off after all!

MRS ELVSTED. Let me go! Let me go! You frighten me, Hedda!

BERTHA (*in the open doorway*). I've laid tea in the dining-room, madam.

HEDDA. Good, we're coming.

MRS ELVSTED. No, no, no! I'd rather go home alone! Now – at once!

HEDDA. Rubbish! First you're going to have some tea, you little idiot. And then – at ten o'clock – Eilert Loevborg will come. With a crown of vine leaves in his hair!

She drags MRS ELVSTED *almost forcibly towards the open doorway.*

Act Three

The same. The curtains are drawn across the open doorway, and also across the french windows. The lamp, half turned down, with a shade over it, is burning on the table. In the stove, the door of which is open, a fire has been burning, but it is now almost out. MRS ELVSTED, *wrapped in a large shawl and with her feet resting on a footstool, is sitting near the stove, huddled in the armchair.* HEDDA *is lying asleep on the sofa, fully dressed, with a blanket over her.*

MRS ELVSTED (*after a pause, suddenly sits up in her chair and listens tensely. Then she sinks wearily back again and sighs.*) Not back yet! Oh, God! Oh, God! Not back yet!

> BERTHA *tiptoes cautiously in from the hall. She has a letter in her hand.*

(*Turns and whispers.*) What is it? Has someone come?

BERTHA (*quietly*). Yes, a servant's just called with this letter.

MRS ELVSTED (*quickly, holding out her hand*). A letter! Give it to me!

BERTHA. But it's for the Doctor, madam.

MRS ELVSTED. Oh, I see.

BERTHA. Miss Tesman's maid brought it. I'll leave it here on the table.

MRS ELVSTED. Yes, do.

BERTHA (*puts down the letter*). I'd better put the lamp out. It's starting to smoke.

MRS ELVSTED. Yes, put it out. It'll soon be daylight.

BERTHA (*puts out the lamp*). It's daylight already, madam.

MRS ELVSTED. Yes. Broad day. And not home yet.

BERTHA. Oh dear, I was afraid this would happen.

MRS ELVSTED. Were you?

BERTHA. Yes. When I heard that a certain gentleman had returned to town, and saw him go off with them. I've heard all about him.

MRS ELVSTED. Don't talk so loud. You'll wake your mistress.

BERTHA (*looks at the sofa and sighs*). Yes. Let her go on sleeping, poor dear. Shall I put some more wood on the fire?

MRS ELVSTED. Thank you, don't bother on my account.

BERTHA. Very good.

She goes quietly out through the hall.

HEDDA (*wakes as the door closes and looks up*). What's that?

MRS ELVSTED. It was only the maid.

HEDDA (*looks round*). What am I doing here? Oh, now I remember. (*Sits up on the sofa, stretches herself and rubs her eyes.*) What time is it, Thea?

MRS ELVSTED. It's gone seven.

HEDDA. When did Tesman get back?

MRS ELVSTED. He's not back yet.

HEDDA. Not home yet?

MRS ELVSTED (*gets up*). No one's come.

HEDDA. And we sat up waiting for them till four o'clock.

MRS ELVSTED. God! How I waited for him!

HEDDA (*yawns and says with her hand in front of her mouth*). Oh, dear. We might have saved ourselves the trouble.

MRS ELVSTED. Did you manage to sleep?

HEDDA. Oh, yes. Quite well, I think. Didn't you get any?

MRS ELVSTED. Not a wink. I couldn't, Hedda. I just couldn't.

HEDDA (*gets up and comes over to her*). Now, now, now. There's nothing to worry about. I know what's happened.

MRS ELVSTED. What? Please tell me.

HEDDA. Well, obviously the party went on very late –

MRS ELVSTED. Oh dear, I suppose it must have. But –

HEDDA. And Tesman didn't want to come home and wake us all up in the middle of the night. (*Laughs.*) Probably wasn't too keen to show his face either, after a spree like that.

MRS ELVSTED. But where could he have gone?

HEDDA. I should think he's probably slept at his aunts'. They keep his old room for him.

MRS ELVSTED. No, he can't be with them. A letter came for him just now from Miss Tesman. It's over there.

HEDDA. Oh? (*Looks at the envelope.*) Yes, it's Auntie Juju's handwriting. Well, he must still be at Judge Brack's, then. And Eilert Loevborg is sitting there, reading to him. With a crown of vine leaves in his hair.

MRS ELVSTED. Hedda, you're only saying that. You don't believe it.

HEDDA. Thea, you really are a little fool.

MRS ELVSTED. Perhaps I am.

HEDDA. You look tired to death.

MRS ELVSTED. Yes. I am tired to death.

HEDDA. Go to my room and lie down for a little. Do as I say, now; don't argue.

MRS ELVSTED. No, no. I couldn't possibly sleep.

HEDDA. Of course you can.

MRS ELVSTED. But your husband'll be home soon. And I must know at once –

HEDDA. I'll tell you when he comes.

MRS ELVSTED. Promise me, Hedda?

HEDDA. Yes, don't worry. Go and get some sleep.

MRS ELVSTED. Thank you. All right, I'll try.

> *She goes out through the rear room.* HEDDA *goes to the french windows and draws the curtains. Broad daylight floods into the room. She goes to the writing-table, takes a small hand-mirror from it and arranges her hair. Then she goes to the door leading into the hall and presses the bell. After a few moments,* BERTHA *enters.*

BERTHA. Did you want anything, madam?

HEDDA. Yes, put some more wood on the fire. I'm freezing.

BERTHA. Bless you, I'll soon have this room warmed up. (*She rakes the embers together and puts a fresh piece of wood on them. Suddenly she stops and listens.*) There's someone at the front door, madam.

HEDDA. Well, go and open it. I'll see to the fire.

BERTHA. It'll burn up in a moment.

> *She goes out through the hall.* HEDDA *kneels on the footstool and puts more wood in the stove. After a few seconds,* GEORGE TESMAN *enters from the hall. He looks tired, and rather worried. He tiptoes towards the open doorway and is about to slip through the curtains.*

HEDDA (*at the stove, without looking up*). Good morning.

TESMAN (*turns*). Hedda! (*Comes nearer.*) Good heavens, are you up already? What?

HEDDA. Yes I got up very early this morning.

TESMAN. I was sure you'd still be sleeping. Fancy that!

HEDDA. Don't talk so loud. Mrs Elvsted's asleep in my room.

TESMAN. Mrs Elvsted? Has she stayed the night here?

HEDDA. Yes. No one came to escort her home.

TESMAN. Oh. No, I suppose not.

HEDDA (*closes the door of the stove and gets up*). Well. Was it fun?

TESMAN. Have you been anxious about me? What?

HEDDA. Not in the least. I asked if you'd had fun.

TESMAN. Oh yes, rather! Well, I thought, for once in a while –! The first part was the best; when Eilert read his book to me. We arrived over an hour too early – what about that, eh? Fancy – ! Brack had a lot of things to see to, so Eilert read to me.

HEDDA (*sits at the right-hand side of the table*). Well? Tell me about it.

TESMAN (*sits on a footstool by the stove*). Honestly, Hedda, you've no idea what a book that's going to be. It's really one of the most remarkable things that's ever been written. By Jove!

HEDDA. Oh, never mind about the book –

TESMAN. I'm going to make a confession to you, Hedda. When he'd finished reading a sort of beastly feeling came over me.

HEDDA. Beastly feeling?

TESMAN. I found myself envying Eilert for being able to write like that. Imagine that, Hedda!

HEDDA. Yes. I can imagine.

TESMAN. What a tragedy that with all those gifts he should be so incorrigible.

HEDDA. You mean he's less afraid of life than most men?

TESMAN. Good heavens, no. He just doesn't know the meaning of the word moderation.

HEDDA. What happened afterwards?

TESMAN. Well, looking back on it, I suppose you might almost call it an orgy, Hedda.

HEDDA. Had he vine leaves in his hair?

TESMAN. Vine leaves? No, I didn't see any of them. He made a long, rambling oration in honour of the woman who'd inspired him to write this book. Yes, those were the words he used.

HEDDA. Did he name her?

TESMAN. No. But I suppose it must be Mrs Elvsted. You wait and see!

HEDDA. Where did you leave him?

TESMAN. On the way home. We left in a bunch – the last of us, that is – and Brack came with us to get a little fresh air. Well, then, you see, we agreed we ought to see Eilert home. He'd had a drop too much.

HEDDA. You don't say?

TESMAN. But now comes the funny part, Hedda. Or I should really say the tragic part. Oh, I'm almost ashamed to tell you. For Eilert's sake, I mean –

HEDDA. Why, what happened?

TESMAN. Well, you see, as we were walking towards town I

happened to drop behind for a minute. Only for a minute –
er – you understand –

HEDDA. Yes, yes – ?

TESMAN. Well then, when I ran on to catch them up, what do
you think I found by the roadside. What?

HEDDA. How on earth should I know?

TESMAN. You mustn't tell anyone, Hedda. What? Promise me
that – for Eilert's sake. (*Takes a package wrapped in paper
from his coat pocket.*) Just fancy! I found this.

HEDDA. Isn't this the one he brought here yesterday?

TESMAN. Yes! The whole of that precious, irreplaceable manuscript! And he went and lost it! Didn't even notice! What
about that? Tragic.

HEDDA. But why didn't you give it back to him?

TESMAN. I didn't dare to, in the state he was in.

HEDDA. Didn't you tell any of the others?

TESMAN. Good heavens, no. I didn't want to do that. For
Eilert's sake, you understand.

HEDDA. Then no one else knows you have his manuscript?

TESMAN. No. And no one must be allowed to know.

HEDDA. Didn't it come up in the conversation later?

TESMAN. I didn't get a chance to talk to him any more. As
soon as we got into the outskirts of town, he and one or two
of the others gave us the slip. Disappeared, by Jove!

HEDDA. Oh? I suppose they took him home.

TESMAN. Yes, I imagine that was the idea. Brack left us, too.

HEDDA. And what have you been up to since then?

TESMAN. Well, I and one or two of the others – awfully jolly
chaps, they were – went back to where one of them lived
and had a cup of morning coffee. Morning-after coffee –
what? Ah, well. I'll just lie down for a bit and give Eilert
time to sleep it off, poor chap, then I'll run over and give
this back to him.

HEDDA (*holds out her hand for the package*). No, don't do that.
Not just yet. Let me read it first.

TESMAN. Oh no, really, Hedda dear, honestly, I daren't do that.

HEDDA. Daren't?

TESMAN. No – imagine how desperate he'll be when he wakes up and finds his manuscript's missing. He hasn't any copy, you see. He told me so himself.

HEDDA. Can't a thing like that be rewritten?

TESMAN. Oh no, not possibly, I shouldn't think. I mean, the inspiration, you know –

HEDDA. Oh, yes, I'd forgotten that. (*Casually.*) By the way, there's a letter for you.

TESMAN. Is there? Fancy that!

HEDDA (*holds it out to him*). It came early this morning.

TESMAN. I say, it's from Auntie Juju! What on earth can it be? (*Puts the package on the other footstool, opens the letter, reads it and jumps up.*) Oh, Hedda! She says poor Auntie Rena's dying.

HEDDA. Well, we've been expecting that.

TESMAN. She says if I want to see her I must go quickly. I'll run over at once.

HEDDA (*hides a smile*). Run?

TESMAN. Hedda dear, I suppose you wouldn't like to come with me? What about that, eh?

HEDDA (*gets up and says wearily and with repulsion*). No, no, don't ask me to do anything like that. I can't bear illness or death. I loathe anything ugly.

TESMAN. Yes, yes. Of course. (*In a dither.*) My hat? My over-coat? Oh yes, in the hall. I do hope I won't get there too late, Hedda! What?

HEDDA. You'll be all right if you run.

BERTHA *enters from the hall.*

BERTHA. Judge Brack's outside and wants to know if he can come in.

TESMAN. At this hour? No, I can't possibly receive him now.

HEDDA. I can. (*To* BERTHA.) Ask his honour to come in.

BERTHA goes.

(*Whispers quickly.*) The manuscript, Tesman.

She snatches it from the footstool.

TESMAN. Yes, give it to me.

HEDDA. No, I'll look after it for now.

She goes over to the writing-table and puts it in the bookcase. TESMAN *stands dithering, unable to get his gloves on.* JUDGE BRACK *enters from the hall.*

(*Nods to him.*) Well, you're an early bird.

BRACK. Yes, aren't I? (*To* TESMAN.) Are you up and about, too?

TESMAN. Yes, I've got to go and see my aunts. Poor Auntie Rena's dying.

BRACK. Oh dear, is she? Then you mustn't let me detain you. At so tragic a –

TESMAN. Yes, I really must run. Good-bye! Good-bye!

He runs out through the hall.

HEDDA (*goes nearer*). You seem to have had excellent sport last night – Judge.

BRACK. Indeed yes, Mrs Hedda. I haven't even had time to take my clothes off.

HEDDA. *You* haven't either?

BRACK. As you see. What's Tesman told you about last night's escapades?

HEDDA. Oh, only some boring story about having gone and drunk coffee somewhere.

BRACK. Yes, I've heard about that coffee-party. Eilert Loevborg wasn't with them, I gather?

HEDDA. No, they took him home first.

BRACK. Did Tesman go with him?

HEDDA. No, one or two of the others, he said.

BRACK (*smiles*). George Tesman is a credulous man, Mrs Hedda.

HEDDA. God knows. But – has something happened?

BRACK. Well, yes, I'm afraid it has.

HEDDA. I see. Sit down and tell me.

She sits on the left of the table, BRACK *at the long side of it, near her.*

Well?

BRACK. I had a special reason for keeping track of my guests last night. Or perhaps I should say some of my guests.

HEDDA. Including Eilert Loevborg?

BRACK. I must confess – yes.

HEDDA. You're beginning to make me curious.

BRACK. Do you know where he and some of my other guests spent the latter half of last night, Mrs Hedda?

HEDDA. Tell me. If it won't shock me.

BRACK. Oh, I don't think it'll shock you. They found themselves participating in an exceedingly animated *soirée*.

HEDDA. Of a sporting character?

BRACK. Of a highly sporting character.

HEDDA. Tell me more.

BRACK. Loevborg had received an invitation in advance – as had the others. I knew all about that. But he had refused. As you know, he's become a new man.

HEDDA. Up at the Elvsteds', yes. But he went?

BRACK. Well, you see, Mrs Hedda, last night at my house, unhappily, the spirit moved him.

HEDDA. Yes, I hear he became inspired.

BRACK. Somewhat violently inspired. And as a result, I suppose, his thoughts strayed. We men, alas, don't always stick to our principles as firmly as we should.

HEDDA. I'm sure you're an exception, Judge Brack. But go on about Loevborg.

BRACK. Well, to cut a long story short, he ended up in the establishment of a certain Mademoiselle Danielle.

HEDDA. Mademoiselle Danielle?

BRACK. She was holding the *soirée*. For a selected circle of friends and admirers.

HEDDA. Has she got red hair?

BRACK. She has.

HEDDA. A singer of some kind?

BRACK. Yes – among other accomplishments. She's also a celebrated huntress – of men, Mrs Hedda. I'm sure you've heard about her. Eilert Loevborg used to be one of her most ardent patrons. In his salad days.

HEDDA. And how did all this end?

BRACK. Not entirely amicably, from all accounts. Mademoiselle Danielle began by receiving him with the utmost tenderness and ended by resorting to her fists.

HEDDA. Against Loevborg?

BRACK. Yes. He accused her, or her friends, of having robbed him. He claimed his pocket-book had been stolen. Among other things. In short, he seems to have made a blood-thirsty scene.

HEDDA. And what did this lead to?

BRACK. It led to a general free-for-all, in which both sexes participated. Fortunately, in the end the police arrived.

HEDDA. The police, too?

BRACK. Yes. I'm afraid it may turn out to be rather an expensive joke for Master Eilert. Crazy fool!

HEDDA. Oh?

BRACK. Apparently he put up a very violent resistance. Hit one of the constables on the ear and tore his uniform. He had to accompany them to the police station.

HEDDA. Where did you learn all this?

BRACK. From the police.

HEDDA (*to herself*). So that's what happened. He didn't have a crown of vine leaves in his hair.

BRACK. Vine leaves, Mrs Hedda?

HEDDA (*in her normal voice again*). But, tell me, Judge, why do you take such a close interest in Eilert Loevborg?

BRACK. For one thing it'll hardly be a matter of complete indifference to me if it's revealed in court that he came there straight from my house.

HEDDA. Will it come to court?

BRACK. Of course. Well, I don't regard that as particularly serious. Still, I thought it my duty, as a friend of the family, to give you and your husband a full account of his nocturnal adventures.

HEDDA. Why?

BRACK. Because I've a shrewd suspicion that he's hoping to use you as a kind of screen.

HEDDA. What makes you think that?

BRACK. Oh, for heaven's sake, Mrs Hedda, we're not blind. You wait and see. This Mrs Elvsted won't be going back to her husband just yet.

HEDDA. Well, if there were anything between those two there are plenty of other places where they could meet.

BRACK. Not in anyone's home. From now on every respectable house will once again be closed to Eilert Loevborg.

HEDDA. And mine should be, too, you mean?

BRACK. Yes. I confess I should find it more than irksome if this gentleman were to be granted unrestricted access to this house. If he were superfluously to intrude into –

HEDDA. The triangle?

BRACK. Precisely. For me it would be like losing a home.

HEDDA (*looks at him and smiles*). I see. You want to be the cock of the walk.

BRACK (*nods slowly and lowers his voice*). Yes, that is my aim. And I shall fight for it with – every weapon at my disposal.

HEDDA (*as her smile fades*). You're a dangerous man, aren't you? When you really want something.

BRACK. You think so?

HEDDA. Yes, I'm beginning to think so. I'm deeply thankful
you haven't any kind of hold over me.

BRACK (*laughs equivocally*). Well, well, Mrs Hedda – perhaps
you're right. If I had, who knows what I might not think up?

HEDDA. Come, Judge Brack. That sounds almost like a threat.

BRACK (*gets up*). Heaven forbid! In the creation of a triangle –
and its continuance – the question of compulsion should
never arise.

HEDDA. Exactly what I was thinking.

BRACK. Well, I've said what I came to say. I must be getting
back. Good-bye, Mrs Hedda. (*Goes towards the french windows.*)

HEDDA (*gets up*). Are you going out through the garden?

BRACK. Yes, it's shorter.

HEDDA. Yes. And it's the back door, isn't it?

BRACK. I've nothing against back doors. They can be quite
intriguing – sometimes.

HEDDA. When people fire pistols out of them, for example?

BRACK (*in the doorway, laughs*). Oh, people don't shoot tame
cocks.

HEDDA (*laughs, too*). I suppose not. When they've only got one.

*They nod good-bye, laughing. He goes. She closes the french
windows behind him, and stands for a moment, looking out
pensively. Then she walks across the room and glances through
the curtains in the open doorway. Goes to the writing-table,
takes* LOEVBORG'S *package from the bookcase and is about to
turn through the pages when* BERTHA *is heard remonstrating
loudly in the hall.* HEDDA *turns and listens. She hastily puts
the package back in the drawer, locks it and puts the key
on the inkstand.* EILERT LOEVBORG, *with his overcoat on
and his hat in his hand, throws the door open. He looks somewhat confused and excited.*

LOEVBORG (*shouts as he enters*). I must come in, I tell you! Let
me pass!

He closes the door, turns, sees HEDDA, *controls himself immediately and bows.*

HEDDA (*at the writing-table*). Well, Mr Loevborg, this is rather a late hour to be collecting Thea.

LOEVBORG. And an early hour to call on you. Please forgive me.

HEDDA. How do you know she's still here?

LOEVBORG. They told me at her lodgings that she has been out all night.

HEDDA (*goes to the table*). Did you notice anything about their behaviour when they told you?

LOEVBORG (*looks at her, puzzled*). Notice anything?

HEDDA. Did they sound as if they thought it – strange?

LOEVBORG (*suddenly understands*). Oh, I see what you mean. I'm dragging her down with me. No, as a matter of fact I didn't notice anything. I suppose Tesman isn't up yet?

HEDDA. No, I don't think so.

LOEVBORG. When did he get home?

HEDDA. Very late.

LOEVBORG. Did he tell you anything?

HEDDA. Yes. I gather you had a merry party at Judge Brack's last night.

LOEVBORG. He didn't tell you anything else?

HEDDA. I don't think so. I was so terribly sleepy –

MRS ELVSTED *comes through the curtains in the open doorway.*

MRS ELVSTED (*runs towards him*). Oh, Eilert! At last!

LOEVBORG. Yes – at last. And too late.

MRS ELVSTED. What is too late?

LOEVBORG. Everything – now. I'm finished, Thea.

MRS ELVSTED. Oh, no, no! Don't say that!

LOEVBORG. You'll say it yourself, when you've heard what I –

MRS ELVSTED. I don't want to hear anything!

HEDDA. Perhaps you'd rather speak to her alone? I'd better go.

LOEVBORG. No, stay.

MRS ELVSTED. But I don't want to hear anything, I tell you!

LOEVBORG. It's not about last night.

MRS ELVSTED. Then what – ?

LOEVBORG. I want to tell you that from now on we must stop seeing each other.

MRS ELVSTED. Stop seeing each other!

HEDDA (*involuntarily*). I knew it!

LOEVBORG. I have no further use for you, Thea.

MRS ELVSTED. You can stand there and say that! No further use for me! Surely I can go on helping you? We'll go on working together, won't we?

LOEVBORG. I don't intend to do any more work from now on.

MRS ELVSTED (*desperately*). Then what use have I for my life?

LOEVBORG. You must try to live as if you had never known me.

MRS ELVSTED. But I can't!

LOEVBORG. Try to, Thea. Go back home –

MRS ELVSTED. Never! I want to be wherever you are! I won't let myself be driven away like this! I want to stay here – and be with you when the book comes out.

HEDDA (*whispers*). Ah, yes! The book!

LOEVBORG (*looks at her*). Our book; Thea's and mine. It belongs to both of us.

MRS ELVSTED. Oh, yes! I feel that, too! And I've a right to be with you when it comes into the world. I want to see people respect and honour you again. And the joy! The joy! I want to share it with you!

LOEVBORG. Thea – our book will never come into the world.

HEDDA. Ah!

MRS ELVSTED. Not – ?

LOEVBORG. It cannot. Ever.

MRS ELVSTED. Eilert – what have you done with the manuscript?

HEDDA. Yes – the manuscript?

MRS ELVSTED. Where is it?

LOEVBORG. Oh, Thea, please don't ask me that!

MRS ELVSTED. Yes, yes – I must know. I've a right to know. Now!

LOEVBORG. The manuscript. Yes. I've torn it up.

MRS ELVSTED (*screams*). No, no!

HEDDA (*involuntarily*). But that's not – !

LOEVBORG (*looks at her*). Not true, you think.

HEDDA (*controls herself*). Why – yes, of course it is, if you say so. It sounded so incredible –

LOEVBORG. It's true, nevertheless.

MRS ELVSTED. Oh, my God, my God, Hedda – he's destroyed his own book!

LOEVBORG. I have destroyed my life. Why not my life's work, too?

MRS ELVSTED. And you – did this last night?

LOEVBORG. Yes, Thea. I tore it into a thousand pieces. And scattered them out across the fjord. It's good, clean, salt water. Let it carry them away; let them drift in the current and the wind. And in a little while, they will sink. Deeper and deeper. As I shall, Thea.

MRS ELVSTED. Do you know, Eilert – this book – all my life I shall feel as though you'd killed a little child?

LOEVBORG. You're right. It is like killing a child.

MRS ELVSTED. But how could you? It was my child, too!

HEDDA (*almost inaudibly*). Oh – the child – !

MRS ELVSTED (*breathes heavily*). It's all over, then. Well – I'll go now, Hedda.

HEDDA. You're not leaving town?

MRS ELVSTED. I don't know what I'm going to do. I can't see anything except – darkness.

She goes out through the hall.

HEDDA (*waits a moment*). Aren't you going to escort her home, Mr Loevborg?

LOEVBORG. I? Through the streets? Do you want me to let people see her with me?

HEDDA. Of course, I don't know what else may have happened last night. But is it so utterly beyond redress?

LOEVBORG. It isn't just last night. It'll go on happening. I know it. But the curse of it is, I don't want to live that kind of life. I don't want to start all that again. She's broken my courage. I can't spit in the eyes of the world any longer.

HEDDA (*as though to herself*). That pretty little fool's been trying to shape a man's destiny. (*Looks at him.*) But how could you be so heartless towards her?

LOEVBORG. Don't call me heartless!

HEDDA. To go and destroy the one thing that's made her life worth living? You don't call that heartless?

LOEVBORG. Do you want to know the truth, Hedda?

HEDDA. The truth?

LOEVBORG. Promise me first – give me your word – that you'll never let Thea know about this.

HEDDA. I give you my word.

LOEVBORG. Good. Well; what I told her just now was a lie.

HEDDA. About the manuscript?

LOEVBORG. Yes. I didn't tear it up. Or throw it in the fjord.

HEDDA. You didn't? But where is it, then?

LOEVBORG. I destroyed it, all the same. I destroyed it, Hedda!

HEDDA. I don't understand.

LOEVBORG. Thea said that what I had done was like killing a child.

HEDDA. Yes. That's what she said.

LOEVBORG. But to kill a child isn't the worst thing a father can do to it.

HEDDA. What could be worse than that?

LOEVBORG. Hedda – suppose a man came home one morning, after a night of debauchery, and said to the mother of his child: 'Look here. I've been wandering round all night. I've been to – such-and-such a place and such-and-such a

place. And I had our child with me. I took him to – these
places. And I've lost him. Just – lost him. God knows
where he is or whose hands he's fallen into.'

HEDDA. I see. But when all's said and done, this was only a
book –

LOEVBORG. Thea's heart and soul were in that book. It was her
whole life.

HEDDA. Yes, I understand.

LOEVBORG. Well, then you must also understand that she and
I cannot possibly ever see each other again.

HEDDA. Where will you go?

LOEVBORG. Nowhere. I just want to put an end to it all. As
soon as possible.

HEDDA (*takes a step towards him*). Eilert Loevborg, listen to
me. Do it – beautifully!

LOEVBORG. Beautifully? (*Smiles.*) With a crown of vine leaves
in my hair? The way you used to dream of me – in the old
days?

HEDDA. No. I don't believe in that crown any longer. But –
do it beautifully, all the same. Just this once. Good-bye.
You must go now. And don't come back.

LOEVBORG. Adieu, madame. Give my love to George Tesman.
(*Turns to go.*)

HEDDA. Wait. I want to give you a souvenir to take with you.

*She goes over to the writing-table, opens the drawer and the
pistol-case, and comes back to* LOEVBORG *with one of the
pistols.*

LOEVBORG (*looks at her*). This? Is this the souvenir?

HEDDA (*nods slowly*). You recognize it? You looked down its
barrel once.

LOEVBORG. You should have used it then.

HEDDA. Here! Use it now!

LOEVBORG (*puts the pistol in his breast pocket*). Thank you.

HEDDA. Do it beautifully, Eilert Loevborg. Only promise me
that!

LOEVBORG. Good-bye, Hedda Gabler.

He goes out through the hall. HEDDA *stands by the door for a
moment, listening. Then she goes over to the writing-table,
takes out the package containing the manuscript, glances
inside it, pulls some of the pages half out and looks at them.
Then she takes it to the armchair by the stove and sits down
with the package in her lap. After a moment, she opens the
door of the stove; then she opens the packet.*

HEDDA (*throws one of the pages into the stove and whispers to
herself*). I'm burning your child, Thea! You with your
beautiful, wavy hair! (*She throws a few more pages into the
stove.*) The child Eilert Loevborg gave you. (*Throws the rest
of the manuscript in.*) I'm burning it! I'm burning your
child!

Act Four

The same. It is evening. The drawing-room is in darkness. The small room is illuminated by the hanging lamp over the table. The curtains are drawn across the french windows. HEDDA, *dressed in black, is walking up and down in the darkened room. Then she goes into the small room and crosses to the left. A few chords are heard from the piano. She comes back into the drawing-room.*

BERTHA *comes through the small room from the right with a lighted lamp, which she places on the table in front of the corner sofa in the drawing-room. Her eyes are red with crying, and she has black ribbons on her cap. She goes quietly out, right.* HEDDA *goes over to the french windows, draws the curtains slightly to one side and looks out into the darkness.*

A few moments later, MISS TESMAN *enters from the hall. She is dressed in mourning, with a black hat and veil.* HEDDA *goes to meet her and holds out her hand.*

MISS TESMAN. Well, Hedda, here I am in the weeds of sorrow. My poor sister has ended her struggles at last.

HEDDA. I've already heard. Tesman sent me a card.

MISS TESMAN. Yes, he promised me he would. But I thought, no, I must go and break the news of death to Hedda myself – here, in the house of life.

HEDDA. It's very kind of you.

MISS TESMAN. Ah, Rena shouldn't have chosen a time like this to pass away. This is no moment for Hedda's house to be a place of mourning.

HEDDA (*changing the subject*). She died peacefully, Miss Tesman?

MISS TESMAN. Oh, it was quite beautiful! The end came so

calmly. And she was so happy at being able to see George once again. And say good-bye to him. Hasn't he come home yet?

HEDDA. No. He wrote that I mustn't expect him too soon. But please sit down.

MISS TESMAN. No, thank you, Hedda dear – bless you. I'd like to. But I've so little time. I must dress her and lay her out as well as I can. She shall go to her grave looking really beautiful.

HEDDA. Can't I help with anything?

MISS TESMAN. Why, you mustn't think of such a thing! Hedda Tesman mustn't let her hands be soiled by contact with death. Or her thoughts. Not at this time.

HEDDA. One can't always control one's thoughts.

MISS TESMAN (*continues*). Ah, well, that's life. Now we must start to sew poor Rena's shroud. There'll be sewing to be done in this house, too, before long, I shouldn't wonder. But not for a shroud, praise God.

GEORGE TESMAN *enters from the hall.*

HEDDA. You've come at least! Thank heavens!

TESMAN. Are you here, Auntie Juju? With Hedda? Fancy that!

MISS TESMAN. I was just on the point of leaving, dear boy. Well, have you done everything you promised me?

TESMAN. No, I'm afraid I forgot half of it. I'll have to run over again tomorrow. My head's in a complete whirl today. I can't collect my thoughts.

MISS TESMAN. But, George dear, you mustn't take it like this.

TESMAN. Oh? Well – er – how should I?

MISS TESMAN. You must be happy in your grief. Happy for what's happened. As I am.

TESMAN. Oh, yes, yes. You're thinking of Aunt Rena.

HEDDA. It'll be lonely for you now, Miss Tesman.

MISS TESMAN. For the first few days, yes. But it won't last

long, I hope. Poor dear Rena's little room isn't going to stay empty.

TESMAN. Oh? Whom are you going to move in there? What?

MISS TESMAN. Oh, there's always some poor invalid who needs care and attention.

HEDDA. Do you really want another cross like that to bear?

MISS TESMAN. Cross! God forgive you, child. It's been no cross for me.

HEDDA. But now – if a complete stranger comes to live with you – ?

MISS TESMAN. Oh, one soon makes friends with invalids. And I need so much to have someone to live for. Like you, my dear. Well, I expect there'll soon be work in this house too for an old aunt, praise God!

HEDDA. Oh – please!

TESMAN. My word, yes! What a splendid time the three of us could have together if –

HEDDA. If?

TESMAN (*uneasily*). Oh, never mind. It'll all work out. Let's hope so – what?

MISS TESMAN. Yes, yes. Well, I'm sure you two would like to be alone. (*Smiles.*) Perhaps Hedda may have something to tell you, George. Good-bye. I must go home to Rena. (*Turns to the door.*) Dear God, how strange! Now Rena is with me and with poor dear Joachim.

TESMAN. Why, yes, Auntie Juju! What?

MISS TESMAN *goes out through the hall.*

HEDDA (*follows* TESMAN *coldly and searchingly with her eyes*). I really believe this death distresses you more than it does her.

TESMAN. Oh, it isn't just Auntie Rena. It's Eilert I'm so worried about.

HEDDA (*quickly*). Is there any news of him?

TESMAN. I ran over to see him this afternoon. I wanted to tell him his manuscript was in safe hands.

HEDDA. Oh? You didn't find him?

TESMAN. No. He wasn't at home. But later I met Mrs Elvsted and she told me he'd been here early this morning.

HEDDA. Yes, just after you'd left.

TESMAN. It seems he said he'd torn the manuscript up. What?

HEDDA. Yes, he claimed to have done so.

TESMAN. You told him we had it, of course?

HEDDA. No. (*Quickly.*) Did you tell Mrs Elvsted?

TESMAN. No, I didn't like to. But you ought to have told him. Think if he should go home and do something desperate! Give me the manuscript, Hedda. I'll run over to him with it right away. Where did you put it?

HEDDA (*cold and motionless, leaning against the armchair*). I haven't got it any longer.

TESMAN. Haven't got it? What on earth do you mean?

HEDDA. I've burned it.

TESMAN (*starts, terrified*). Burned it! Burned Eilert's manuscript.

HEDDA. Don't shout. The servant will hear you.

TESMAN. Burned it! But in heaven's name – ! Oh, no, no, no! This is impossible!

HEDDA. Well, it's true.

TESMAN. But, Hedda, do you realize what you've done? That's appropriating lost property! It's against the law! By God! You ask Judge Brack and see if I'm not right.

HEDDA. You'd be well advised not to talk about it to Judge Brack or anyone else.

TESMAN. But how could you go and do such a dreadul thing? What on earth put the idea into your head? What came over you? Answer me! What?

HEDDA (*represses an almost imperceptible smile*). I did it for your sake, George.

TESMAN. For my sake?

HEDDA. When you came home this morning and described how he'd read his book to you –

TESMAN. Yes, yes?

HEDDA. You admitted you were jealous of him.

TESMAN. But, good heavens, I didn't mean it literally!

HEDDA. No matter. I couldn't bear the thought that anyone else should push you into the background.

TESMAN (*torn between doubt and joy*). Hedda – is this true? But – but – but I never realized you loved me like that! Fancy that!

HEDDA. Well, I suppose you'd better know. I'm going to have – (*Breaks off and says violently.*) No, no – you'd better ask your Auntie Juju. She'll tell you.

TESMAN. Hedda! I think I understand what you mean. (*Clasps his hands.*) Good heavens, can it really be true? What?

HEDDA. Don't shout. The servant will hear you.

TESMAN (*laughing with joy*). The servant! I say, that's good! The servant! Why, that's Bertha! I'll run out and tell her at once!

HEDDA (*clenches her hands in despair*). Oh, it's destroying me, all this – it's destroying me!

TESMAN. I say, Hedda, what's up? What?

HEDDA (*cold, controlled*). Oh, it's all so – absurd – George.

TESMAN. Absurd? That I'm so happy? But surely – ? Ah, well – perhaps I won't say anything to Bertha.

HEDDA. No, do. She might as well know, too.

TESMAN. No, no, I won't tell her yet. But Auntie Juju – I must let her know! And you – you called me George! For the first time! Fancy that! Oh, it'll make Auntie Juju so happy, all this! So very happy!

HEDDA. Will she be happy when she heard I've burned Eilert Loevborg's manuscript – for your sake?

TESMAN. No, I'd forgotten about that. Of course, no one must be allowed to know about the manuscript. But that you're burning with love for me, Hedda, I must certainly let Auntie Juju know that. I say, I wonder if young wives often feel like that towards their husbands? What?

HEDDA. You might ask Auntie Juju about that, too.

TESMAN. I will, as soon as I get the chance. (*Looks uneasy and thoughtful again.*) But I say, you know, that manuscript. Dreadful business. Poor Eilert!

MRS ELVSTED, *dressed as on her first visit, with hat and overcoat, enters from the hall.*

MRS ELVSTED (*greets them hastily and tremulously*). Oh, Hedda dear, do please forgive me for coming here again.

HEDDA. Why, Thea, what's happened?

TESMAN. Is it anything to do with Eilert Loevborg? What?

MRS ELVSTED. Yes – I'm so dreadfully afraid he may have met with an accident.

HEDDA (*grips her arm*). You think so?

TESMAN. But, good heavens, Mrs Elvsted, what makes you think that?

MRS ELVSTED. I heard them talking about him at the boarding-house, as I went in. Oh, there are the most terrible rumours being spread about him in town today.

TESMAN. Er – yes, I heard about them, too. But I can testify that he went straight home to bed. Fancy –!

HEDDA. Well – what did they say in the boarding-house?

MRS ELVSTED. Oh, I couldn't find out anything. Either they didn't know, or else – They stopped talking when they saw me. And I didn't dare to ask.

TESMAN (*fidgets uneasily*). We must hope – we must hope you misheard them, Mrs Elvsted.

MRS ELVSTED. No, no, I'm sure it was him they were talking about. I heard them say something about a hospital –

TESMAN. Hospital!

HEDDA. Oh no, surely that's impossible!

MRS ELVSTED. Oh, I became so afraid. So I went up to his rooms and asked to see him.

HEDDA. Do you think that was wise, Thea?

MRS ELVSTED. Well, what else could I do? I couldn't bear the uncertainty any longer.

TESMAN. But *you* didn't manage to find him either? What?

MRS ELVSTED. No. And they had no idea where he was. They said he hadn't been home since yesterday afternoon.

TESMAN. Since yesterday? Fancy that!

MRS ELVSTED. I'm sure he must have met with an accident.

TESMAN. Hedda, I wonder if I ought to go into town and make one or two enquiries?

HEDDA. No, no, don't you get mixed up in this.

JUDGE BRACK *enters from the hall, hat in hand.* BERTHA, *who has opened the door for him, closes it. He looks serious and greets them silently.*

TESMAN. Hullo, my dear Judge. Fancy seeing you!

BRACK. I had to come and talk to you.

TESMAN. I can see Auntie Juju's told you the news.

BRACK. Yes, I've heard about that, too.

TESMAN. Tragic, isn't it?

BRACK. Well, my dear chap, that depends how you look at it.

TESMAN (*looks uncertainly at him*). Has something else happened?

BRACK. Yes.

HEDDA. Another tragedy?

BRACK. That also depends on how you look at it, Mrs Tesman.

MRS ELVSTED. Oh, it's something to do with Eilert Loevborg!

BRACK (*looks at her for a moment*). How did you guess? Perhaps you've heard already – ?

MRS ELVSTED (*confused*). No, no, not at all – I –

TESMAN. For heaven's sake, tell us!

BRACK (*shrugs his shoulders*). Well, I'm afraid they've taken him to the hospital. He's dying.

MRS ELVSTED (*screams*). Oh God, God!

TESMAN. The hospital! Dying!

HEDDA (*involuntarily*). So quickly!

MRS ELVSTED (*weeping*). Oh, Hedda! And we parted enemies!

HEDDA (*whispers*). Thea – Thea!

MRS ELVSTED (*ignoring her*). I must see him! I must see him before he dies!

BRACK. It's no use, Mrs Elvsted. No one's allowed to see him now.

MRS ELVSTED. But what's happened to him? You must tell me!

TESMAN. He hasn't tried to do anything to himself? What?

HEDDA. Yes, he has. I'm sure of it.

TESMAN. Hedda, how can you – ?

BRACK (*who has not taken his eyes from her*). I'm afraid you've guessed correctly, Mrs Tesman.

MRS ELVSTED. How dreadful!

TESMAN. Attempted suicide! Fancy that!

HEDDA. Shot himself!

BRACK. Right again, Mrs Tesman.

MRS ELVSTED (*tries to compose herself*). When did this happen, Judge Brack?

BRACK. This afternoon. Between three and four.

TESMAN. But, good heavens – where? What?

BRACK (*a little hesitantly*). Where? Why, my dear chap, in his rooms, of course.

MRS ELVSTED. No, that's impossible. I was there soon after six.

BRACK. Well, it must have been somewhere else, then. I don't know exactly. I only know that they found him. He's shot himself – through the breast.

MRS ELVSTED. Oh, how horrible! That he should end like that!

HEDDA (*to* BRACK). Through the breast, you said?

BRACK. That is what I said.

HEDDA. Not through the head?

BRACK. Through the breast, Mrs Tesman.

HEDDA. The breast. Yes; yes. That's good, too.

BRACK. Why, Mrs Tesman?

HEDDA. Oh – no, I didn't mean anything.

TESMAN. And the wound's dangerous, you say? What?

BRACK. Mortal. He's probably already dead.

MRS ELVSTED. Yes, yes – I feel it! It's all over. All over. Oh
Hedda – !

TESMAN. But, tell me, how did you manage to learn all this?

BRACK (curtly). From the police. I spoke to one of them.

HEDDA (loudly, clearly). Thank God! At last!

TESMAN (appalled). For God's sake, Hedda, what are you
saying?

HEDDA. I am saying there's beauty in what he has done.

BRACK. Hm – Mrs Tesman –

TESMAN. Beauty! Oh, but I say!

MRS ELVSTED. Hedda, how can you talk of beauty in con-
nexion with a thing like this?

HEDDA. Eilert Loevborg has settled his account with life. He's
had the courage to do what – what he had to do.

MRS ELVSTED. No, that's not why it happened. He did it
because he was mad.

TESMAN. He did it because he was desperate.

HEDDA. You're wrong! I know!

MRS ELVSTED. He must have been mad. The same as when he
tore up the manuscript.

BRACK (starts). Manuscript? Did he tear it up?

MRS ELVSTED. Yes. Last night.

TESMAN (whispers). Oh, Hedda, we shall never be able to
escape from this.

BRACK. Hm. Strange.

TESMAN (wanders round the room). To think of Eilert dying
like that. And not leaving behind him the thing that would
have made his name endure.

MRS ELVSTED. If only it could be pieced together again!

TESMAN. Yes, yes, yes! If only it could! I'd give anything –

MRS ELVSTED. Perhaps it can, Mr Tesman.

TESMAN. What do you mean?

MRS ELVSTED (*searches in the pocket of her dress*). Look. I kept the notes he dictated it from.

HEDDA (*takes a step nearer*). Ah!

TESMAN. You kept them, Mrs Elvsted! What?

MRS ELVSTED. Yes, here they are. I brought them with me when I left home. They've been in my pocket ever since.

TESMAN. Let me have a look.

MRS ELVSTED (*hands him a wad of small sheets of paper*). They're in a terrible muddle. All mixed up.

TESMAN. I say, just fancy if we could sort them out! Perhaps if we work on them together – ?

MRS ELVSTED. Oh, yes! Let's try, anyway!

TESMAN. We'll manage it. We must! I shall dedicate my life to this.

HEDDA. *You*, George? Your life?

TESMAN. Yes – well, all the time I can spare. My book'll have to wait. Hedda, you do understand? What? I owe it to Eilert's memory.

HEDDA. Perhaps.

TESMAN. Well, my dear Mrs Elvsted, you and I'll have to pool our brains. No use crying over spilt milk, what? We must try to approach this matter calmly.

MRS ELVSTED. Yes, yes, Mr Tesman. I'll do my best.

TESMAN. Well, come over here and let's start looking at these notes right away. Where shall we sit? Here? No, the other room. You'll excuse us, won't you, Judge? Come along with me, Mrs Elvsted.

MRS ELVSTED. Oh, God! If only we can manage to do it!

TESMAN *and* MRS ELVSTED *go into the rear room. He takes off his hat and overcoat. They sit at the table beneath the hanging lamp and absorb themselves in the notes.* HEDDA *walks across to the stove and sits in the armchair. After a moment,* BRACK *goes over to her.*

HEDDA (*half aloud*). Oh, Judge! This act of Eilert Loevborg's – doesn't it give one a sense of release!

BRACK. Release, Mrs Hedda? Well, it's a release for him, of course –

HEDDA. Oh, I don't mean him – I mean me! The release of knowing that someone can do something really brave! Something beautiful!

BRACK (*smiles*). Hm – my dear Mrs Hedda –

HEDDA. Oh, I know what you're going to say. You're a *bourgeois* at heart, too, just like – ah, well!

BRACK (*looks at her*). Eilert Loevborg has meant more to you than you're willing to admit to yourself. Or am I wrong?

HEDDA. I'm not answering questions like that from you. I only know that Eilert Loevborg has had the courage to live according to his own principles. And now, at last, he's done something big! Something beautiful! To have the courage and the will to rise from the feast of life so early!

BRACK. It distresses me deeply, Mrs Hedda, but I'm afraid I must rob you of that charming illusion.

HEDDA. Illusion?

BRACK. You wouldn't have been allowed to keep it for long, anyway.

HEDDA. What do you mean?

BRACK. He didn't shoot himself on purpose.

HEDDA. Not on purpose?

BRACK. No. It didn't happen quite the way I told you.

HEDDA. Have you been hiding something? What is it?

BRACK. In order to spare poor Mrs Elvsted's feelings, I permitted myself one or two small – equivocations.

HEDDA. What?

BRACK. To begin with, he is already dead.

HEDDA. He died at the hospital?

BRACK. Yes. Without regaining consciousness.

HEDDA. What else haven't you told us?

BRACK. The incident didn't take place at his lodgings.

HEDDA. Well, that's utterly unimportant.

BRACK. Not utterly. The fact is, you see, that Eilert Loevborg was found shot in Mademoiselle Danielle's boudoir.

HEDDA (*almost jumps up, but instead sinks back in her chair*). That's impossible. He can't have been there today.

BRACK. He was there this afternoon. He went to ask for something he claimed they'd taken from him. Talked some crazy nonsense about a child which had got lost –

HEDDA. Oh! So that was the reason!

BRACK. I thought at first he might have been referring to his manuscript. But I hear he destroyed that himself. So he must have meant his pocket-book – I suppose.

HEDDA. Yes, I suppose so. So they found him there?

BRACK. Yes; there. With a discharged pistol in his breast pocket. The shot had wounded him mortally.

HEDDA. Yes. In the breast.

BRACK. No. In the – stomach. The – lower part –

HEDDA (*looks at him with an expression of repulsion*). That, too! Oh, why does everything I touch become mean and ludicrous? It's like a curse!

BRACK. There's something else, Mrs Hedda. It's rather disagreeable, too.

HEDDA. What?

BRACK. The pistol he had on him –

HEDDA. Yes? What about it?

BRACK. He must have stolen it.

HEDDA (*jumps up*). Stolen it! That isn't true! He didn't!

BRACK. It's the only explanation. He must have stolen it. Ssh!

TESMAN *and* MRS ELVSTED *have got up from the table in the rear room and come into the drawing-room.*

TESMAN (*his hands full of papers*). Hedda, I can't see properly under that lamp. Do you think – ?

HEDDA. I am thinking.

TESMAN. Do you think we could possibly use your writing-table for a little? What?

HEDDA. Yes, of course. (*Quickly.*) No, wait! Let me tidy it up first.

TESMAN. Oh, don't you trouble about that. There's plenty of room.

HEDDA. No, no, let me tidy it up first, I say. I'll take these in and put them on the piano. Here.

> *She pulls an object, covered with sheets of music, out from under the bookcase, puts some more sheets on top and carries it all into the rear room and away to the left.* TESMAN *puts his papers on the writing-table and moves the lamp over from the corner table. He and* MRS ELVSTED *sit down and begin working again.* HEDDA *comes back.*

(*Behind* MRS ELVSTED'S *chair, ruffles her hair gently.*) Well, my pretty Thea. And how is work progressing on Eilert Loevborg's memorial?

MRS ELVSTED (*looks up at her, dejectedly*). Oh, it's going to be terribly difficult to get these into any order.

TESMAN. We've got to do it. We must! After all, putting other people's papers into order is rather my speciality, what?

> HEDDA *goes over to the stove and sits on one of the footstools.* BRACK *stands over her, leaning against the armchair.*

HEDDA (*whispers*). What was that you were saying about the pistol?

BRACK (*softly*). I said he must have stolen it.

HEDDA. Why do you think that?

BRACK. Because any other explanation is unthinkable, Mrs Hedda. Or ought to be.

HEDDA. I see.

BRACK (*looks at her for a moment*). Eilert Loevborg was here this morning. Wasn't he?

HEDDA. Yes.

BRACK. Were you alone with him?

HEDDA. For a few moments.

BRACK. You didn't leave the room while he was here?

HEDDA. No.

BRACK. Think again. Are you sure you didn't go out for a
moment?

HEDDA. Oh – yes, I might have gone into the hall. Just for a
few seconds.

BRACK. And where was your pistol-case during this time?

HEDDA. I'd locked it in that –

BRACK. Er – Mrs Hedda?

HEDDA. It was lying over there on my writing-table.

BRACK. Have you looked to see if both the pistols are still there?

HEDDA. No.

BRACK. You needn't bother. I saw the pistol Loevborg had
when they found him. I recognized it at once. From yesterday. And other occasions.

HEDDA. Have you got it?

BRACK. No. The police have it.

HEDDA. What will the police do with this pistol?

BRACK. Try to trace the owner.

HEDDA. Do you think they'll succeed?

BRACK (*leans down and whispers*). No, Hedda Gabler. Not as
long as I hold my tongue.

HEDDA (*looks nervously at him*). And if you don't?

BRACK (*shrugs his shoulders*). You could always say he'd stolen
it.

HEDDA. I'd rather die!

BRACK (*smiles*). People say that. They never do it.

HEDDA (*not replying*). And suppose the pistol wasn't stolen?
And they trace the owner? What then?

BRACK. There'll be a scandal, Hedda.

HEDDA. A scandal!

BRACK. Yes, a scandal. The thing you're so frightened of.
You'll have to appear in court together with Mademoiseell

Danielle. She'll have to explain how it all happened. Was it an accident, or was it – homicide? Was he about to take the pistol from his pocket to threaten her? And did it go off? Or did she snatch the pistol from his hand, shoot him and then put it back in his pocket? She might quite easily have done it. She's a resourceful lady, is Mademoiselle Danielle.

HEDDA. But I have nothing to do with this repulsive business.

BRACK. No. But you'll have to answer one question. Why did you give Eilert Loevborg this pistol? And what conclusions will people draw when it is proved you did give it to him?

HEDDA (bow her head). That's true. I hadn't thought of that.

BRACK. Well, luckily there's no danger as long as I hold my tongue.

HEDDA. (looks up at him). In other words, I'm in your power, Judge. From now on, you've got your hold over me.

BRACK (whispers, more slowly). Hedda, my dearest – believe me – I will not abuse my position.

HEDDA. Nevertheless, I'm in your power. Dependent on your will, and your demands. Not free. Still not free! (Rises passionately.) No. I couldn't bear that. No.

BRACK (looks half-derisively at her). Most people resign themselves to the inevitable, sooner or later.

HEDDA (returns his gaze). Possibly they do.

She goes across to the writing-table.

(*Represses an involuntary smile and says in* TESMAN'S *voice.*) Well, George. Think you'll be able to manage? What?

TESMAN. Heaven knows, dear. This is going to take months and months.

HEDDA (in the same tone as before). Fancy that, by Jove! (Runs her hands gently through MRS ELVSTED'S hair.) Doesn't it feel strange, Thea? Here you are working away with Tesman just the way you used to work with Eilert Loevborg.

MRS ELVSTED. Oh – if only I can inspire your husband, too!

HEDDA. Oh, it'll come. In time.

TESMAN. Yes – do you know, Hedda, I really think I'm
beginning to feel a bit – well – that way. But you go back
and talk to Judge Brack.

HEDDA. Can't I be of use to you two in any way?

TESMAN. No, none at all. (*Turns his head.*) You'll have to keep
Hedda company from now on, Judge, and see she doesn't
get bored. If you don't mind.

BRACK (*glances at* HEDDA). It'll be a pleasure.

HEDDA. Thank you. But I'm tired this evening. I think I'll lie
down on the sofa in there for a little while.

TESMAN. Yes, dear – do. What?

> HEDDA *goes into the rear room and draws the curtains behind
> her. Short pause. Suddenly she begins to play a frenzied
> dance melody on the piano.*

MRS ELVSTED (*starts up from her chair*). Oh, what's that?

TESMAN (*runs to the doorway*). Hedda dear, please! Don't play
dance music tonight! Think of Auntie Rena. And Eilert.

HEDDA (*puts her head through the curtains*). And Auntie Juju.
And all the rest of them. From now on I'll be quiet.

> *She closes the curtains behind her.*

TESMAN (*at the writing-table*). It distresses her to watch us
doing this. I say, Mrs Elvsted, I've an idea. Why don't you
move in with Auntie Juju? I'll run over each evening, and
we can sit and work there. What?

MRS ELVSTED. Yes, that might be the best plan.

HEDDA (*from the rear room*). I can hear what you're saying,
Tesman. But how shall I spend the evenings out here?

TESMAN (*looking through his papers*). Oh, I'm sure Judge
Brack'll be kind enough to come over and keep you company. You won't mind my not being here, Judge?

BRACK (*in the armchair, calls gaily*). I'll be delighted, Mrs
Tesman. I'll be here every evening. We'll have great fun
together, you and I.

HEDDA (*loud and clear*). Yes, that'll suit you, won't it, Judge? The only cock on the dunghill –

A shot is heard from the rear room. TESMAN, MRS ELVSTED *and* JUDGE BRACK *start from their chairs.*

TESMAN. Oh, she's playing with those pistols again.

He pulls the curtains aside and runs in. MRS ELVSTED *follows him.* HEDDA *is lying dead on the sofa. Confusion and shouting.* BERTHA *enters in alarm from the right.*

TESMAN (*screams to* BRACK). She's shot herself! Shot herself in the head! Fancy that!

BRACK (*half paralysed in the armchair*). But, good God! People don't do such things!

Note on the Translation

The main problem in translating *Hedda Gabler* is to contrast the snobbish and consciously upper-class speech of Hedda and Judge Brack with the naïve and homely way of talking shared by Miss Tesman, Bertha and George Tesman. Hedda is a General's daughter and lets no one forget it. George Tesman has unconsciously acquired the nanny-like mode of speech of the old aunts who brought him up. He addresses Aunt Juliana as *Tante Julle*, a particularly irritating and baby-like abbreviation which drives Hedda mad every time he uses it. The last straw is when he asks her to address the old lady by it, too. To render this as Auntie Julie, as has usually been done, is completely to miss the point; it must be a ridiculous nickname such as Juju. When Brack tells Hedda where Loevborg has shot himself, he must make it clear to her that the bullet destroyed his sexual organs; otherwise Hedda's reactions make no sense. To translate this as 'belly' or 'bowels' is again to miss the point, yet Brack must not use the phrase 'sexual organs' directly; he is far too subtle a campaigner to speak so bluntly to a lady. What he says is: 'In the – stomach. The – lower part.' I have altered the name of the red-haired singer from Mademoiselle Diana, which is difficult to say in English and has an improbable ring about it, to Mademoiselle Danielle.

In the Norwegian, Hedda addresses her husband as Tesman except on the crucial occasions at the end of Act 1 and in Act 4, when she deliberately switches to his Christian name. Similarly, Brack calls Hedda Mrs Tesman when anyone else is present, but Mrs Hedda when they are alone together; only towards the very end of the play does he address her simply as Hedda. Although this usage is un-English, even for the period, it is, in fact, effective on the stage when one has the illusion of eavesdropping on a foreign nineteenth-century family, and I have let it stand. To allow Brack to call her Hedda the first time we see them alone together in Act 2 suggests an intimacy which they have not yet reached.

Methuen World Classics

Aeschylus (two volumes)
Jean Anouilh
John Arden (two volumes)
Arden & D'Arcy
Aristophanes (two volumes)
Aristophanes & Menander
Peter Barnes (two volumes)
Brendan Behan
Aphra Behn
Edward Bond (four volumes)
Bertolt Brecht
  (four volumes)
Howard Brenton
  (two volumes)
Büchner
Bulgakov
Calderón
Anton Chekhov
Caryl Churchill
  (two volumes)
Noël Coward (five volumes)
Sarah Daniels (two volumes)
Eduardo De Filippo
David Edgar
  (three volumes)
Euripides (three volumes)
Dario Fo (two volumes)
Michael Frayn
  (two volumes)
Max Frisch
Gorky
Harley Granville Barker
  (two volumes)

Henrik Ibsen (six volumes)
Lorca (three volumes)
David Mamet
Marivaux
Mustapha Matura
David Mercer
  (two volumes)
Arthur Miller
  (four volumes)
Anthony Minghella
Molière
Tom Murphy
  (three volumes)
Peter Nichols
  (two volumes)
Clifford Odets
Joe Orton
Louise Page
A. W. Pinero
Luigi Pirandello
Stephen Poliakoff
  (two volumes)
Terence Rattigan
Ntozake Shange
Sophocles (two volumes)
Wole Soyinka
David Storey (two volumes)
August Strindberg
  (three volumes)
J. M. Synge
Ramón del Valle-Inclán
Frank Wedekind
Oscar Wilde